You Are Not My Big Brother: Menticide Psychotronic Brainwashing

RENEE PITTMAN

You Are Not My Big Brother

No part of this publication may be reproduced, stored in a retrieval system or transmitted in any way by any means, electronic, mechanical, photocopy, recording or otherwise without the prior permission of the author except as provided by USA copyright law.

This book is not designed to provide authoritative information with regard to the subject matter covered. This information is given with the understanding that the author is not engaged in rendering legal or professional advice. Since the details of any situation are fact dependent, you should additionally seek the services of a competent professional.

Copyright © 2013 Renee Pittman

All rights reserved.

Mother's Love Publishing and Enterprises

ISBN-13: 978-1-7374060-1-3

DEDICATION

There is a time for war and a time for peace.

Choose your battle then STAND!

TABLE OF CONTENTS

Foreword vii
Author's Note ix
Synchronicity xix
Chapter One: Satellite Surveillance History 1
Chapter Two: Mind Invasive Psychotronic Technology 22
Chapter Three: Mind Reading Systems and Devices 45
Chapter Four: High-Tech Targeted 69
Chapter Five: Psychological Warfare 109
Chapter Six: Surprise Surprise 131
Chapter Seven: Victim of Circumstance 153
Chapter Eight: Eye-Opening Experiences 215
Chapter Nine: Psychiatry and Experimentation 243
Chapter Ten: Fall Down Then Stand Up 252
Chapter Eleven: DOD Voice of God Telepathy 269
Chapter Twelve: Satellite to Weaponized Drones 284
Conclusion 320
References 344
About The Author 370

FAITH

I will guide you.

I will turn darkness into light

before you and make the rough

places smooth.

Isaiah 42:16

And we know that all things

work together for good to them

who love God, to them who

are called according to his purpose.

Romans 8:28

FOREWORD

I grew up in the era of The Cold War, a time when every small town had an air raid siren and a civil defense plan, a time when any home that could afford it had an air raid shelter, a time when an Iron Curtain divided not just Berlin but the world in which I lived, a time when we feared powers we neither knew nor understood, a time when Joseph McCarthy and Joseph Stalin could be seen as two sides of the same coin. Novels and movies fed our paranoia about conspiracies by big business and government to override our democratic freedoms.

My generation grew up watching movies about spacemen visiting earth and newsreels about American Astronauts and Russian Cosmonauts and gigantic radio telescopes reaching out to touch outer space. At the same time, we began to hear about Area 51 and about government conspiracies to cover up the truth of real life alien visits to earth.

In those days, it was taboo to speak or write about government surveillance of ordinary citizens, massive cover-ups of wrongdoing by the military-industrial complex, secret wars in foreign lands, or the presence of aliens on earth. To do so invites being branded as weird or even crazy or even being 'targeted' and silenced. It was only safe to write of these things as fiction in novels and movies. Over the following decades, we have seen the predictions of George Orwell and others come true. In Great Britain, there is virtually nowhere to go without being caught on a government camera. Google has eyes on every street. Governments worldwide are imposing more and more restrictions on the rights of private citizens.

In recent years, a number of authors have dared to break the taboos and openly discuss the decline in our democratic freedoms, the processes and methods whereby this is happening, and the powerful forces of government and multinational corporations that are behind these changes. Pittman is one of these authors. Having had the opportunity to read her manuscript prior to publication, I find her documentation interesting and persuasive. This detailed and heavily researched book may prove heavy reading for some, but it is well worth the time and effort.

Many of Pittman's claims are precisely the sort that not that long ago would have had her branded insane, yet she cites proof after proof to support these claims. Drawing on official documents, internal correspondence, and websites of the United States government, developers of futuristic surveillance equipment now in use, other researchers, and other sources, Pittman demonstrates again the facts behind what she has written. Whether you choose to dismiss this author as a paranoid conspiracy theorist or to look with new eyes at the world around you and believe what she's written, you may be shocked at the degree to which your privacy has been violated.

Bob "The Equalizer" MacKenzie, B.A., M.A., B.Ed., has 40+ years, experience worldwide as a published author, poet, critic, editor, proofreader, teacher, mentor and Marketing professional, as advertised in Writer's Digest. Editor Dark Matter Press

AUTHOR'S NOTE

The effects of ionizing or nuclear radiation are well known as cancer causing. Nuclear weapons release a great deal of ionizing radiation in the high frequency range above visible light. The energy of the radiation is capable of breaking chemical bonds thus causing cancer. However, little publicized is that non-ionizing radiation used in direct energy weapons have proven historically to be equally as life threatening. The U.S. military has developed weapons using non-ionizing radiation below the visible range. Today microwave radio waves are used in mobile phones deliverable through communication towers. Any knowledge of health hazards from non-ionizing electromagnetic radiation has been strenuously denied. The only biological effect of non-ionizing radiation that the U.S. government has acknowledged for many years is heating, and accordingly, it characterizes Active Denial System technology as that which produces pain from sudden heating of the skin.

Today, it is a well-known fact that beginning in 1952, the Soviets invested years of time and resources in microwave (remote brain manipulation) technology. The United States discovered in 1962 the Moscow Signal after Soviet forces beamed invisible microwave radiation into the United States American Embassy in Moscow. The radar beam was deployed from a nearby hotel for over twenty years, triggering cancer, heart problems, cataracts, and emotional stress of employees. Later the radioactive waves would be attributed to the death of the American Ambassador, Walter J. Stoessel, whose office was in the signal's path. This was after his development of a mysterious illness resembling Adult Leukemia and he began bleeding from his eyes along with extreme nausea. Two of his predecessors also later died of cancer.

Not only were the Soviets using microwave to gather intelligence information, but they were also using U.S. State Department personnel as human guinea pigs for the low-level electromagnetic, extremely low frequency (ELF) testing. Later many of the approximate 1800 U.S. State Department personnel working at the embassy during this timeframe would be compensated by the United States Government for illnesses ranging from physical to psychological.

The resulting Ambassador's death was a wake-up call for the United States regarding the uses and effects of microwave technology and its capabilities as a powerful ELF weapon. This knowledge resulted in the first research program within the United States called Project Pandora. Project Pandora would later include a number of parallel projects, such as Project TUMS, MUTS, and BAZAR, involving the Central Intelligence Agency, Advanced Research Project Agency (ARPA) later DARPA, the State Department and all branches of the military.

By 2010 I was under a full attack by a group directing this powerful microwave weaponry into my home targeting me after they failed in a covert, intensely psychological effort to manipulate and influence me. They ended up empty handed in what appeared to be an unofficial investigation originating in Los Angeles, California using threats, acts of intimidation, bullying, covert physical torture, and degradation. This effort was combined with various advanced influence technologies little known to the public highly advanced in research, testing and development for decades. At the end of the day, they had no foundation for a valid legal case, never had, nor had gotten the egotistical gratification in which they apparently thrive or use to derive a sense of power and control. As a result, it appeared that they would stop at nothing to silence me as this book began to take shape.

Night after night, while I slept, and when waking the next morning it was obvious they were trying to implant fear and doubt technologically, via extremely low frequencies (ELF). When I woke, unaffected, it was they who appeared to be concerned. If it came down to me or them, I was expendable reflected in the escalation of the effort.

In the process of targeting me, they behaved shamelessly unethically, immorally, and horrifically by malicious prosecution. And due to eminent book exposure, it appeared that they were trying to make good on their promise that if I did not stop efforts to publicize, they would surely harm me saying first, "No one will believe you. You can't prove a thing," and "You don't even know who we really are."

One thing was certain due to the powerful microwave attacks I was now suffering I was definitely being systematically, intentionally crippled. This was by the focused microwave beam focused on knees, legs, balls of my feet and groin area nightly. These treatments left me barely able to walk each day. When I felt a sudden intense pain materialize appearing out of nowhere, I would immediately grab the layered heavy-duty aluminum foil I prepared for protection and cover the area where the pain originated and the pain would briefly stop. This was until those directing it turned the power level up. Or, they would direct the technology, wait for any reaction of fear via thought deciphering technology, if none, then say, "She's not scared" using this as justification to increase the intensity.

One night after apparently assessing my concern for the safety of my eyes they decided that my eyes would be the perfect target using the realistic possibility of blindness in hopes to really scare me. I detail the first of three stages of microwave toxicity in the image xisection of this book and the first stage is damage to the cataract and blurred vision. The attacks focused on my kidneys while I slept. With this and the crippling pain, it necessitated my getting up barely able to walk throughout the night to use the restroom which also contributes to sleep deprivation.

By March of 2011, it appeared that I was in the first stage of acute microwave poisoning. This group continually justified this vicious physical assault on me by calling me malicious names around the clock.

Part of the psychological operation Psy Ops is to emotionally cripple and terrorize the target. As the attacks grew more and more extreme, it was obvious that this group, sworn to uphold the law meant dirty, secretive business. Their effort to coerce me by technology confidently founded on the well-known and documented difficulty of numerous "Targeted Individuals" (TI) to prove that which is felt and heard, but unseen and undetectable.

Trying to get this book published also included tampering with everyone around me. Using the subliminal capability of the technology directed into an entire environment, it is subliminally, technologically easy to drive a wedge between loved one and others. With no one around me after complete destruction of relationships using everyone in my life, open season was officially declared on me.

While posting what I was enduring on my social network page, another target in Massachusetts, mentioned that in her case the microwave attacks had gotten so horrendous that she finally had to sleep in her bathtub hoping to escape the painful rays. I would remember this when things got tough for me. In my own attempt to protect myself I had no choice but to pad down my bathtub with blankets and pillows making it my temporary lodging, workstation, and refuge for a few days. This would be at least to get a galley proof of this book to order a final review.

Heavy duty aluminum as my protector could no longer fully withstand the influx of numerous portable microwave weapons now closer to me through the walls of neighboring apartments. The rays penetrated it immediately leaving numerous pin size holes rendering it ineffective unless tripled or quadrupled. Something in the material of the bathtub did provide temporary resistance from the radiation. This was until the pain beam was placed on top of a wall unit from the apartment below. A thick rubber mat I ordered which is used on gym floors also help to some degree. With the rubber mat folded under my bed blocking the waves from below, and Thermasheath-3, I was able to deflect 80% of the waves coming directly from next door upstairs also. R Max Thermasheath-3 is insulated foam building material with high grade aluminum on both sides. Two placed against the walls reduced a great deal of the burning attacks. And because they could no longer get to me this way effectively, the operation center took over using radar laser disseminated through microwave towers attacking me from overhead at times the entire front portion of my body which included my breast if I lay on my back. The only material documented to be 100% effective today is Thor Shield against Taser and microwave weaponry. However, Thor Shield is only available for law enforcement and military use.

Make no mistake about the toxicity of this type of technology. On a larger scale there is what is known as the 'electromagnetic soup effect,' of the space-based technology in which the World Health Organization writes:

'Electronic smog,' created by electromagnetic frequencies (EMF) is 'one of the most common and fastest growing environmental influences.' New evidence has linked 'electro pollution' with a rise in cancer, birth defects, fibromyalgia, Alzheimer's disease, Chronic Fatigue Syndrome, depression, learning disabilities and even Sudden Infant Syndrome.

Today, this technology comes handheld, portable, land, sea, and space-based. The harassment is so personally intrusive that close to home literally means close, within inches. In fact, the Forward Look Infrared Radar (FLIR) has an optical accuracy within five to ten inches of a target and can also act as an advanced delivery system in real time. It can literally feel as if a person or persons are in the same room with you torturing you. In reality, they can be miles away connected by computer terminals and satellites, and also today drones, connecting numerous towers both microwave and cellular prevalent everywhere today. Today "The Program" is fully operational and is spearheaded from state-of-the-art operation or fusion centers.

Portable so called non-lethal directed energy weapons are smaller versions of the larger military deployed Active Denial System patented for crown dispersal. One such portable weapon is the Mob Excess

Deterrent Using Silent Audio (MEDUSA.) The MEDUSA is also a portable documented telepathic ray gun. The ray gun sends a microwave signals into a person's head emitting sound only the person in the signal's path can hear. It is an effective tool from adjoining apartments.

The ability to watch my efforts toward publication motivated the severest of attacks on me. This capability presented the strongest hurdle and disadvantage overall.

Little known today, governments have their very own malware / spyware. An example is a version used by the Federal Bureau of Investigation (FBI) called the Computer and Internet Protocol Address Verifier (CIPAV.) It is a data gathering tool that the FBI uses to track and gather location data on those under Electronic Surveillance. The software operates on the target's computer much like spyware and is unknown to the computer operator that the software has even been installed or that it is monitoring and reporting on all of their activities. The CIPAV captures location related information, such as: IP addresses, MAC addresses, open ports, running programs, operating systems, and installed application registration and version information, default web browser, and last visited URL. Once the initial inventory is conducted, the CIPAV slips into the background and silently monitors all outbound communication, logging every Internet Provider address to which the computer connects, time and date stamping each action.

The technology made headlines in July 2007 when its use was exposed in open court during an investigation of a teen who had made bomb threats against his local high school. The FBI sought approval to use CIPAV from the Foreign Intelligence Surveillance Court in terrorism investigations or in covert spying investigations. It can be easily installed simply by clicking a random e-mail attachment or link on the web. The Patriot Act further legitimized its use. The spyware reports back everything that a computer does online. As a result, even editing became challenging for this book. Sometimes I would watch as an entire paragraph was highlighted and in the blink of an eye disappeared. Afterwards the undo button became my best friend.

The constant threat of, "Your manuscript will never see the light of day" and CIPAV, and PATRIOT ACT computer monitoring nudged me forward. Initially hoping for professional assistance with editing and formation of this book, I did sign on with a publishing company. However, when I received the manuscript back after professional editing and proofreading by three departments, with close to 1400 typographical errors, the Foreword missing, and a chapter out of place, I decided to cut ties and take full control of my personal story. One typo could change the entire meaning and cost me my life if misconstrued and the operation center knew this.

Having now completed this book, I hope that the reality of my truthful personal experiences will help someone in some way if but one. For those of you who still choose to disbelieve, know that what is done in the dark will eventually come into light. This has been proven to be an inevitable historical fact. Know also, and do not doubt or underestimate, that we are living in an age of brilliant scientific technological advancements. Please forgive any minor typographical errors in punctuation or grammar. I did the best I could under extreme duress in many ways.

This book is about a right to know whether believed or not. This book is about AWARENESS

Dear Journal,

September 6, 2010

My oldest daughter and I were returning from a sightseeing tour at the Grand Canyon today in Arizona when a typical mother-daughter disagreement erupted between us in the car. I can't remember exactly what we were arguing about initially. I was stunned by her revelation that my now ex-husband actually told her, two or three years ago, that the incident in the military, which gave me my rightful Veteran benefits, never happened. It was a devastating blow. As I tried to digest her words, I realized that essentially what my ex-husband told our daughter, after a 13-year marriage, and divorce which I initiated, was that after the traumatic incident he believed the person who assaulted me who neither of us knew well. This was even though he asked me to be his wife shortly afterwards. I was outraged that he actually vindictively told her this. He witnessed the after affect firsthand on my psyche during that timeframe. Ironically, with him also telling her how damaged I was afterwards, he inadvertently confirmed, without probably wanting to, that the incident left a definite psychological impact on me.

Dear Journal,

March 8, 2011

Today, I sent my ex-husband an e-mail. I asked him if he had any knowledge or involvement in the covert pursuit that has centered on me for a few years. Logically, I have to consider that if I am being investigated regarding the VA, that he has to be involved, whether he chooses to admit it or not. Why? If this is the actual foundation for this effort, there would not, nor could have ever been any investigation without him. If any investigator had spoken to him—and it appears that they may have, as they insinuate, and if he told them the truth, I would not have suffered the way I have senselessly and mercilessly. Instead of him replying to my e-mail, he called our oldest daughter, one of three from the marriage, over the phone who in turn called me. He told her that he did not even know what I was talking about nor did he have, amazingly, any recollection of, or knowledge of, any traumatic incident surrounding me before we were married. True, he learned about the incident a few weeks later. But, how could he forget the physical confrontation he had with the person?

After she phoned me with this information, I immediately e-mailed my ex again saying, "Let's see if you regain your memory under oath in a federal district court of law." He miraculously found his lost memory, remembering the incident, though not admitting involvement.

Is he motivated by a grudge? Is he holding me responsible for not getting promoted after the divorce on the police department? This too is something this same daughter would later tell me. Or, does he believe that I owed him something? Or, maybe, subconsciously he felt unfulfilled without the emotional vindictive release of destroying my life the way most plan during divorce procedures? Funny, after sixteen years of divorce, during an actual phone call, he made sure to tell me, "I am so over you!" If his involvement is factual, I only wish he had been "so over me" much sooner than this declaration. If so, I probably would not have had to suffer the victimization I have, by a sinister, ruthless group.

Oh well. It appears that God has other plans for my life, then and now. What choice do I have now but too… STAND!

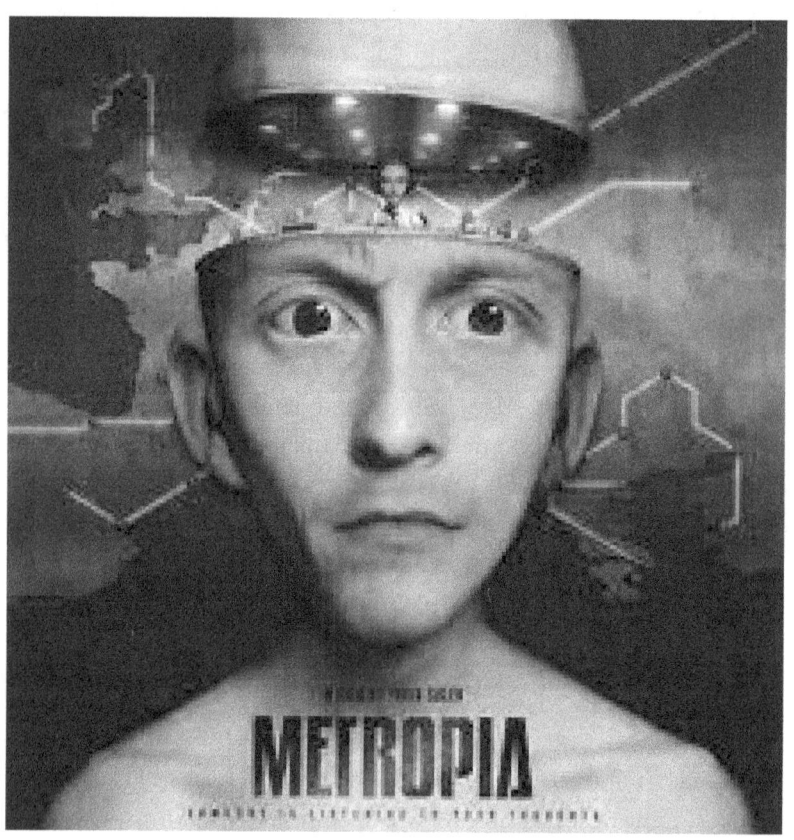

We are told of the factual patented, technological capabilitysuch as the technological "Hearing Voices Effect" beamed inside a person's brain from state-of-the-art operation centers, arrogantly, right before our eyes in Global Elite controlled media productions in mockery.

SYNCHRONICITY

On June 3, the day before the California Primary, Robert F. Kennedy began one of his most mentally and physically challenging efforts in one single day of campaigning unsurpassed by his entire campaign effort. He traveled more than twelve hundred miles, back and forth between Northern and Southern California strategically hitting each of the state's three media markets. He rode in motorcades through clogged streets of San Francisco for a tour through China Town and the neighboring environs, as well as San Diego, and the streets of Los Angeles, detouring briefly through a quiet residential neighborhood in Watts.

His determination had brought him to the brink of physical collapse after days and days of little to no sleep and relentless non-stop campaigning. However, he had unleashed a very tactile street politic that would serve him well by winning the California Primary. His hands were scabbed and bloodied from the thousands of handshakes over the past weeks. People felt they had to touch and connect with the warmth that radiated from this candidate. His obvious sincerity for a better America brought him the love and adulation of the hope within the poor black, white, and Hispanic communities similar to that of a rock star.

The detour in Los Angeles would connect Robert F. Kennedy with a little black girl who would later ride in the motorcade for the remainder of the trip. Rosey Grier would later confirm that during the brief detour there were no camera crews or photographer's following the motorcade until the progression again hit a major street.

June 4, 1968 Presidential hopeful Robert F. Kennedy spent the day before the primary relaxing with his family at the home of Director, John Frankenheimer, Manchurian Candidate (1962)

Excerpt - The Last Campaign: Robert F. Kennedy and 82 Days that Inspired America by Thurston Clarke:

"It took three men—Bill Barry, Rafer Johnson, and Rosey Grier—holding on to one another's waists in a chain, to prevent him being yanked into the street. An inebriated young man with a goatee leapt onto the hood and rode for blocks while screaming,

"Make way for Kennedy!"

Kennedy stopped frequently so he could ask the crowds,

"Are you going to vote for me tomorrow? ["Yes!"]

Are you just going to wave to Mr. Kennedy and then tomorrow, when I'm gone, forget about me?

["No!"]

Or are you going to vote? ["Yes!"]"

When he finally sat down his face was expressionless and his eyes unfocused.

A five-year-old black girl, whom he had earlier pulled into the car to keep her from falling under the wheels, sat in the backseat playing with a huge stuffed white rabbit. He placed her between his knees and began whispering into her ear. Finally, he stopped the motorcade. He and the girl got out and stood together at dusk in the middle of a wide boulevard, the girl clutching Kennedy with one hand and the stuffed rabbit with the other, waiting until a car could be found to return her to her parents.

***

Rosey Grier was one of Robert F. Kennedy's right-hand men. Roosevelt "Rosey" Grier is an American actor, singer, Christian minister, and former professional American football player. He was a notable college football player for The Pennsylvania State University who earned a retrospective place in the National Collegiate Athletic Association 100th anniversary list of 100 most influential student athletes. As a professional player, Grier was a member of the New York Giants and the original Fearsome Foursome of the Los Angeles Rams. He played in the Pro Bowl twice.

After Grier's professional sports career he worked as a bodyguard for Robert Kennedy during the 1968 presidential campaign and was guarding the senator's wife, Ethel Kennedy, during the Robert F. Kennedy assassination. Although unable to prevent that killing, Grier took control of the gun and subdued the shooter, Sirhan Sirhan.

***

FROM: Renee Pittman Mitchell

TO: Rosey Grier, July 14, 2015, at 2:00 PM

Dear Mr. and Mrs. Grier,

It was good speaking with you by phone, yesterday, July 13, 2015, and briefly again, July 14, 2015, as well as with Mrs. Grier.

I am glad that you actually recall the experience in question, that in 1968, specifically June 3, 1968, during Robert F. Kennedy's final campaign stops through South Central Los Angeles, the day before the Primary, Robert F. Kennedy's motorcade detoured through a residential neighbor of Los Angeles, California. During this detour, around 52nd Street and McKinley Avenue, a little Black girl was picked up. I completely understand that you did not have personal involvement with me but you do remember this fact.

I vividly recall that day. I was that little girl. I had made a sign out of a cardboard box, and using a broken broom handle taped to it, had written with crayons, "Vote for Mr. R. Kennedy, President, We Are to Young...."

***

You Are Not My Big Brother

FROM: Rosey Grier

TO: Renee Pittman Mitchell, June 14, 2015, at 3:24 PM

Dear Lady Renee Pittman Mitchell,

It was sure a surprise after all these years, to hear about that little girl that Senator Kennedy pulled into the car, as we were driving thru Watts, in 1968. This was near the end of the primary campaign for the Democratic nomination for president.

I was walking behind the car, trying to keep people from getting in the way of the car that Senator Kennedy was in.

A young man jumped on the hood of Senator Kennedy's car and no one could get him off. They called me and I ran up and asked him, "What are you doing on top of the car?" He looked around and saw me and said, "Hey Rosey" and jumped off the hood and gave me a big hug. I motioned for them to go ahead and Senator Kennedy said,

"No Rosey, get in the car!" And I did.

The next thing I knew, he was picking up a little girl and putting her in the car. The little girl stayed in the car for a while, and I was wondering how we were going to get her back to her family.

These are the details I remember.

> May the Lord bless you and keep you;
> The Lord make His face shine on you
> And be gracious to you;
> "The Lord turn his face toward you
> And give you peace." Numbers 6:24-26

Love, Rosey Grier

***

Many years after that fatal night, just after midnight, June 5, 1968, Sirhan Sirhan would claim that he did not remember shooting Robert F. Kennedy at the Ambassador Hotel and had never remembered exactly what happened.

Today he is now on the record, through his attorney, stating that the reason for his lapse in memory surrounding the murder is his now belief that he had been a mind-controlled Manchurian assassin, a victim of Project MK-ULTRA programming, held in a hypnotic trance, and set-up as the fall guy.

***

Regarding the little girl,

In the synchronicity of life, the little girl grew into a woman who, and through the hills and valleys of her life, would end up writing books about Mind Control technology and historical programs…

FACT OR FICTION?

CHAPTER ONE

"When I tell the truth, it is not for the sake of convincing those who do not know it, but for the sake of defending those that do."

— **William Blake**

In October of 1945, a gifted science fiction writer proposed the extraordinary idea of using stationary satellites to beam television and other communications signals around the world. Arthur C. Clarke (2001: A Space Odyssey, Rendezvous with Rama, The Hammer of God, etc.) reasoned that if a satellite were positioned high enough above the Earth's equator, its orbit could be matched by the rotation of the Earth. The satellite would then appear to be fixed in one particular spot in the sky. Because a satellite's orbital speed varies with its distance from the Earth, a "geostationary" orbit is only possible directly above the equator, in a narrow belt about 22,300 miles out. Although it took the technology a while to catch up with his simple but elegant concept, today there are hundreds of satellites taking advantage of his original thinking. In recognition of his pioneering vision, this band of outer space" real estate" is called the Clarke Orbit.

World of Satellite TV, Ninth Edition, Chapter1 (pp. 9-18), by Mark Long, The Book Publishing Company, Summertown, Tennessee, July, 1998). This was written in 1998 however today there are thousands of satellites orbiting the Earth.

An artificial satellite is a manmade object that continuously orbits Earth or some other body in space such as the moon; the sun; asteroids; or planets; Venus, Mars, and Jupiter, gathering information.

Today, there are about 3,000 useful satellites orbiting Earth from many different nations and for various reasons. Google Earth imagery, You Tube, reports 13,000 objects of which seven percent are fully operational.

Anti-satellite weapons are satellites armed with energy weapons having specific capabilities.

Navigational satellites use time signal transmitters to enable mobile receivers on the ground to determine their exact location. They have a relatively clear line of sight between the satellite and the receiver on the ground. This, combined with ever-improving electronics, allows satellite navigational systems to measure location to astounding accuracies in real time.

Spy satellites, now called reconnaissance or technical satellites, are Earth-observation satellites, or communication satellites. They are deployed for military intelligence. As a result, very little information is officially documented relating to their exact usage, although information has managed to seep through the cracks unofficially.

Under ideal conditions, the KH (keyhole) series of military and government spy satellites are able to produce image resolution within a range of five to six inches. The code name Kennan "Keyhole-class" (KH) satellites have been orbiting Earth for more than thirty years. Due to their presence and activity for intelligence purposes, their byproducts are relatively cost-free to a requesting agency, and the resolution is higher than what is otherwise available commercially.

The excerpt below from the Congressional Service Report (CSR) prepared for members of Congress dated February 1, 2010, gives a brief history of the artificial satellite initiative within the United States including analysis of the ethical use of satellite-derived imagery by law enforcement agencies, and the impact of this usage on the Fourth

Amendment Rights of American citizens. The report in its entirety, entitled Satellite Surveillance: Domestic Issues, can be found on the Internet. The excerpt reads as follows:

> Reconnaissance satellites first deployed in the early 1960s to peer into denied regions of The Soviet Union and other secretive enemy states have from time to time been used by civilian agencies of the federal government to assist with mapping, disaster relief, and environmental concerns. These uses have been coordinated by the Civil Applications Office at the United States Geological Survey, a component of the United States Interior Department. Post 9/11, the Bush Administration sought to encourage the use of satellite-derived data for homeland security and law enforcement purposes, in addition to the civil applications that have been supported for years. In 2007, it moved to transfer responsibility for coordinating civilian use of satellites to the Department of Homeland Security. The initiative was launched, however, apparently without notification of key congressional oversight committees. Members of Congress and outside groups raised concerns that using satellites for law enforcement purposes may infringe on the privacy and Fourth Amendment rights of US persons…
>
> In June of 2009, the Department of Homeland Security's Law Enforcement Spy Satellite "Pilot Program," which began in 2007, was terminated by the
>
> Obama Administration along with the National Applications Office of the previous Bush Administration. This program would have provided federal, state, and local officials extensive access to spy-satellite imagery—but no eavesdropping capabilities to assist with emergency response and other domestic security needs, such as identifying where ports or border areas are vulnerable. The PATRIOT ACT, however, did authorize the eavesdropping on computers, and any and all phones without judicial approval. Just before the midnight deadline on May 26, 2011, President Barack Obama signed a 4-year extension of three key provisions in the USA Patriot Act: roving wiretaps, searches of business records (the "library records provision"),

and conducting surveillance of "lone wolves" — individuals suspected of terrorist-related activities not linked to terrorist groups.

The Act was passed in the House by 357 to 66 (of 435) and in the Senate by 98 to 1 and was supported by members of both the Republican and Democratic parties.

Opponents of the law have criticized its authorization of indefinite detentions of immigrants; searches through which law enforcement officers search a home or business without the owner's or the occupant's permission or knowledge; the expanded use of National Security Letters, which allows the Federal Bureau of Investigation (FBI) to search telephone, e-mail, and financial records without a court order, and the expanded access of law enforcement agencies to business records, including library and financial records. Since its passage, several legal challenges have been brought against the act, and Federal courts have ruled that a number of provisions are unconstitutional. With the National Security Letter, no warrant is needed. The Department of Defense (DOD) directive below legally approved continued use of spy satellites within U.S. borders after the failure of the National Applications Office to materialize.

Signals Intelligence collection of targets within the United States is governed by the Foreign Intelligence Surveillance Act (FISA) and domestically by the Electronic Communication Privacy Act, (ECPA) and Executive Order 12333. Signal intelligence is intelligence gathering by interception of signals, whether between people, or whether involving electronic signals not directly used in communication, such as electronic intelligence or a combination of the two. The ability to intercept communication depends on the medium used. The medium can be radio, satellite, microwave, cellular or fiber optics. The role of satellites in point-to-point voice and data communications has largely been supplanted by fiber optics. Optical fibers are widely used in fiber-optic communications, which permits transmission over longer distances and at higher bandwidths (data rates) than other forms of communication.

Human beings can be tracked by computer generated biometric software which maps, DNA, gait, iris, and other physical features or also by Electroencephalography (EEG) computerized, and satellite radar. Electroencephalography is the recording of the prevalent electrical activity around the scalp.

It is difficult to determine the number of Americans being watched by satellites writes John Fleming, The Shocking Menace of Satellite Surveillance. For example, if there are 200 operational surveillance satellites, and if each satellite can monitor 20 human targets, then as many as 4000 Americans may be under satellite surveillance. The capability of a satellite's ability to monitor multiple targets is determined by the number of transponders on each satellite. The transponder is a key device in both receiving and transmitting information.

However, in my personal research, spy satellites can have dozens of transponders. There are five product categories that refer to transponders. These categories include earth stations of which there are 14 types, military products and systems, microwave equipment, video processors, spectrum analyzers and remote sensors used for targeting a person.

Inside the United States, as well as abroad, DOD support for law enforcement agencies is authorized in accordance with Chapter 18 of Title 10, U.S. Code. The legislation contains both explicit grants of authority and restrictions on the use of that authority for DOD assistance to law enforcement agencies-federal, state, and local particularly in the form of information and equipment. Section 371 specifically authorizes the Secretary of Defense to share information acquired during military operations and encourages the armed forces to plan their activities with an eye to the production of incidental civilian benefits. Under Sections 372 through 374, DOD equipment and facilities, including intelligence collection assets, may be made available to civilian authorities. U.S. Code, Title 50, Chapter 36, Subchapter 1, gives specific details on electronic surveillance laws. U.S. Code, Title 50, Chapter 32, Section 1520a, gives specific details surrounding lawful testing of technology, on human subjects, and the code documents that approval can be given for crowd control testing and use.

Although the Department of Homeland Security's plan for the National Applications Office was cancelled, based on the above directives, and Executive Order 12333, other avenues were taken which legally justified the continued use of real time and biometric signal intelligence capturing, collection, and tracking.

The National Geospatial-Intelligence Agency (NGA) was formed in 1996 as a separate entity of the imagery and mapping divisions of the Central Intelligence Agency (CIA), the Department of Defense, and the highly classified efforts of the National Reconnaissance Office (NRO) which builds and maintains our nation's fleet of spy satellites along with the Defense Intelligence Agency (DIA). The NGA, closely connected to the National Security Agency's (NSA) powers to spy domestically were expanded with legislation from Congress. However, it is believed and a high degree of probability that these efforts, including satellite surveillance, may have already been functioning in far more in-depth ways than just secretly listening in on phone calls, but also targeting and tracking individuals inside the United States many years back. In 2004, the NSA and NGA signed an agreement to share resources and staff and to link their "sources, data holding, information infrastructure," and "exploitation techniques." Although this agreement is classified, an NGA spokesperson explained in the article. The pact allowed "horizontal integration" between these two agencies defined as "working together from start to finish, using NGA's 'eyes' and NSA's 'ears.'" The NGA relies on information from the overhead photography captured by the National Reconnaissance Office. The government agency most heavily involved in satellite surveillance technology is the Defense Advanced Research Projects Agency (DARPA) connected to the Pentagon.

NASA is concerned with civilian satellites. However, there is no real distinction between the civilian and military satellites. All satellites are launched from either Cape Kennedy in Florida or Vandenberg Air

Force Base in California. It does not matter if they are military-operated, CIA-operated, corporate-operated or NASA's own. It is difficult to apply any real distinction between government and private satellites. The research by NASA involves all types of satellites. Neither the DARPA nor NASA makes satellites, as stated above; instead, they underwrite the technology while various corporations produce the hardware. The data collected by satellites is said to be in accordance with constitutional and federal law, and the executive policies of Executive Order 12333.

The Department of Homeland Security (DHS) hoped to create a wide network of centers that would be tied to the agency's day-to-day activities in the National Applications Office, according to the Electronic Privacy Information Center (EPIC.) The project, according to EPIC, "inculcates the Department of Homeland Security with enormous domestic surveillance powers and evokes comparisons with the publicly condemned domestic surveillance program of COINTELPRO." COINTELPRO is the 1960 program of the Federal Bureau of Investigation (FBI) aimed at destroying groups on the American political left, activist or whistleblowers.

After 9/11, the paradigm for domestic law enforcement shifted radically making it the duty of government to use its intelligence resources to help law enforcement agencies preempt attacks before they happened. This is beyond the traditional practices of gathering evidence to prove that a crime had already occurred. As a result, the interpretation of satellite use changed on United States citizens and took shape in a very different form and new agenda.

During the Bush administration, an agency called the Counter-Intelligence Field Activity (CIFA) became a weapon against anyone suspected of harboring ill-will against the Bush administration and its policies. After an investigation, CIFA was officially disbanded in 2008, and the Defense Intelligence Agency was given formal control of the Pentagon's main counter-intelligence vehicle incorporating intelligence and surveillance technology. Today, the DIA's Defense Counter-intelligence and HUMINT Center provides the same services that

CIFA does, albeit with one assumes more checks and balances. CIFA itself is not supposed to exist, but it still had a line item in the budget in late 2010. The point here is that offending the wrong person can result in your name given to be used as a human guinea pig and for many and varied reasons.

In the past, one method of intelligence gathering was through the use of a mobile unit connected to the NGA named the Office of Americas. It was called the Mobile Integrated Geospatial-Intelligence System, or MIGS that were loaded with equipment that allowed NGA analysts to download intelligence from U-2s and U.S. military satellites. However, today, the military, intelligence agencies, and police work have come together in numerous fused efforts around the country under a joint program spearheaded by the United States Department of Justice and the Department of Homeland Security. Fusion centers are actual physical structure where government, security, and public safety partners collaboratively work together sharing information, developing intelligence, maximizing resources, streamlining operations and analyzing data.

The Strategic Defense Initiative (SDI) became a reality by United States President Ronald Reagan on March 23, 1983. However, again, spy satellites quite possibly were already functioning and violating people's right to privacy when President Reagan proposed SDI, or "Star Wars." The Cuban Missile Crisis of 1962 demonstrated the military usefulness of satellites. The Strategic Defense Initiative at that time was for the use of ground and space-based systems to protect the United States from possible attacks by strategic nuclear ballistic missiles. The SDI laid official foundation for the use of satellite surveillance and most believe the classified, little known, satellite delivered technology which has trickled down to fusion center use on United States citizens today called "black bag" technology. Black bag technology is referred as patented psychological electronic "psychotronic" technology such as mind reading and infrared lasers that can assault someone even while that someone is indoors. Aviation Week & Space Technology mentioned in 1984 that "facets of the project (in the Star Wars program) that are being hurried along include the awarding of contracts to study…a surveillance satellite network."

This ideation was bound to be abused yet no group is fighting to cut back or subject to democratic control these programs or the terrifying new influence technology. As one diplomat to the United Nations remarked, "'Star Wars' was not a means of creating heaven on earth, but could result in hell on earth."

On December 30, 2008, a United States court in Kansas recognized electronic harassment by a ruling in the electronic harassment and gang stalking case of James Walbert of Wichita. Although this was a default ruling, the defendant a no show in court, Mr. Walbert had done a noteworthy job in successfully proving, using declassified government documents and radiation scans, the existence of and use of electromagnetic harassment technology and subliminal torture tactics directed at him of little known advanced technology. This ruling also combined his complaint of obscure microwave frequencies directed at him that Mr. Walbert was able to prove by forensic radiation scans used to detect extreme levels of radiation in his body. Also considered by the court was Mr. Walbert's claim of an intense, organized stalking effort also called Gang Stalking or Covert Harassment Groups surrounding him and his family which he stated began in 2004. A letter from the Missouri State Representative documenting 300 similar complaints to his office of harassment by energy weapon attacks was presented to the Court. The representative's office personally investigated many of the claims. The results were submitted as corroborating evidence for the Walbert case. Also lending credibility, Mr. Walbert had two policemen ready to testify on his behalf.

In the rudy2.wordpress.com, internet article on this case, the Missouri State Representative, after Walbert contacted him for assistance, convinced of the reality and usage of the technology himself later became active in efforts in Washington D.C. for the ethical use of what today is technological brilliance run amok. While there have been numerous legal cases from individuals seeking justice from identical situations, by technology described as undetectable weaponry, with secretive brain manipulation characteristics, or described as mind control, remote torture, electronic harassment, remote neural monitoring, or influence technology from other victims, Mr. Walbert is one of the few who has to date, successfully proven or won any type of official court ruling against these heinous covert activities.

I, for one, was thankful to the Representative for a statement in the Internet article acknowledging this very real dilemma of victims of this type of harassment. The representative is documented as saying:

"It's easier to discredit victims, because none of us wants to believe that this is happening in America. The weapons are undetectable, but the evidence, especially the United States patents I've seen and the victims I have spoken with, tells me this is for real."

The article also reports that one of his personal staff members, after she began investigating numerous complaints to the office, was covertly attacked by the weaponry in an effort to deter the investigation. The microwave technology literally boils the water of the human body, resulting in excruciating pain within a matter of seconds. Great lengths are being taken to keep what is happening today hidden from the public.

In my case, as with most, when I began to speak up, covert torture was escalated, and I was discredited through lack of knowledge or the ability to verify the existence of the technology and its use today by the average person. The overall disbelief of even the slightest possibility of it being directed at me was also outrageous to many. The public, overall, is completely unaware of what is happening today. There are also those who choose to stick their heads in the sand, and look the other way such as the three branches of government who passed the laws legalizing use of this powerful weapon system. Granted, most in the psychiatric community today have no real knowledge of these technologies and cannot check. The fact is, one of the most well-known original mind control studies, MKULTRA, was headed up by psychiatrist. Many were high level officials of the American Psychiatric Association and the Psychiatric Association of Canada who were willingly taking CIA funding to progress studies related to behavior modification while knowing these technologies emulate mental illnesses. The state representative's office, in the Walbert case, figured out that these cases do have merit, logically, why not others?

Although I am reasonably intelligent, articulate, and well groomed, the psychiatric manual doctrine that states, "Crazy people do not think they are crazy," also helped to discredit me as I tried in vain to convince people that my experiences are very, very real.

It was late November 2010, and I had just left the office of the Veteran Service Representative at the West Los Angeles, California, Veterans Administration (VA) facility after being denied assistance for temporary shelter now homeless. I had fled my new residence in Long Beach, California within 15 days after moving in due to portable energy weapon attacks coming from the apartment above me after returning from Arizona in early October 2010. The representative explained as I sat calmly in her office that morning that information documented in my medical records at VA hospitals in locations where I had lived between Arizona and California since 2006, which I intentionally had documented, while seeking therapeutic support to cope was the reason. She stated that the Salvation Army homeless shelter on the facility would not be able to accommodate my request for temporary lodging until I was first stabilized on anti-psychotic medication.

As a result of my determination to bravely speak up, the reality by experience was ever present that most, if not all, are first determined unstable. This was even more frustrating with Veteran Administration hospitals.

Artificial microwave voice-to-skull transmission, Neural Coding or Synthetic Telepathy, DOD Voice of God, Frey Effect, as officially called by the government today, was successfully demonstrated by researcher Dr. Joseph Sharp in 1973, announced at a seminar at the University of Utah in 1974, and documented in the journal American Psychologist in the March 1975 issue, entitled Microwaves and Behavior by Dr. Donald R. Justesen. Dr. Justesen, incidentally, worked for the Laboratories of Experimental Neuropsychology at the Veterans Administration Hospital in Kansas City, Missouri. If any doctor were really interested in truth, or even possible truth, I felt, and not a puppet for Big Brother or Big Pharma, with little effort could easily find a huge volume of case studies specifically associating the microwave energy weapon bio-effect with schizophrenia by similarity of symptoms. This is due to the documented capability of microwave technology's ability to carry voices through radio waves directly into the human brain.

(See: Microwave Bio Effect Congruence with Schizophrenia - Cog prints–same title on Internet by John J. McMurtrey online.)

I knew and understood the risk I was taking though the reality of homelessness and subsequent expertly crafted vulnerability created to destroy my life with homeless, emotional Psy Ops, and stalking stung a bit. Unfortunately, the non-stop terrorist effort around me had cost me several places to live and now sadly, I was homeless although I had the means to support myself.

I now lived with extremely degrading remarks, bullying, and acts of intimidation by electronic harassment of those manning the technology from the operation center. I knew firsthand that these situations are factual, exist, and are happening at alarming rates. They are happening not only in the Land of Oz, Kansas, which James Walbert lives, but across the United States and by reports all over the world.

I felt a wave of gratitude for the comments of the Missouri State Representative and his accurate assessment surrounding the discrediting of those courageously speaking up. He apparently is one of the few who recognizes the humane need for laws against these covert programs and the unjust, unethical efforts of individuals employed, who perceive lives as play toys heinously, and enjoy destroying them. The state representative joins other documented efforts by some in Congress who have gone on the record voicing moral concerns about what was once affectionately termed "Star Wars."

In October 2000, a congressman introduced in the House of Representatives a bill concerning these weapons. In this bill, the definition of a weapons system included:

any other unacknowledged or as yet undeveloped means inflicting death or injury on, or damaging or destroying, a person (or the biological life, bodily health, mental health, or physical and economic well-being of a person)...through the use of land-based, sea-based, or space-based systems using radiation, electromagnetic, psychotronic (psychological electronic), sonic, laser, or other energies directed at individual persons or targeted populations for the purpose of information war, mood management, or mind control of such persons or population. As in all legislative acts quoted in this article, the bill pertains to sound, light, or electromagnetic stimulation of the human brain.

A congresswoman introduced legislation that would prevent Homeland Security from using space-based satellite imagery for domestic surveillance. As chairwoman of the House Homeland Security Committee's Intelligence and Terrorism Risk Assessment Subcommittee at that time, she cited privacy issues saying:

"Imagine, for a moment, what it would be like if one of these satellites were directed on your neighborhood or home, a school or place of worship and without an adequate legal framework or operating procedures in place for regulating their use." She said in a statement when she introduced her bill. "I dare say the reaction might be that "Big Brother" has finally arrived, and the black helicopters can't be far behind."

My heartfelt gratitude for the efforts of honorable, patriotic, public servants and others who have morally taken a stand challenging the status quo and voicing their ethical concern regarding unchecked electronic surveillance laws, signal intelligence collection and satellite real time surveillances, and most importantly, the black bag, highly secretive influence psychological electronic technology's usage on unaware American citizens covertly and without official judicial involvement.

However, the efforts of those seeking the advancement of this massive program have prevailed, and the efforts of a few individuals have not been enough to curtail the efforts of powerful agencies seeking to use, and continue testing of remote neutral monitoring and remote influencing effectiveness of this weaponry. The objective is far too great by those seeking to control, individuals, groups and large populations. The massive testing seeks data related to whether, globally, humanity can be psychologically or physically controlled from outer space with little regard for the average individual or Constitutional, Civil and Human Rights.

Electronic Harassment is as a term referring to the use of electronic devices to harass, torture, and/or physically harm a person, not to be confused with cyber stalking. Currently two states have laws surrounding these technologies:

1. Michigan

Public act 257 of 2003 makes it a felony for a person to "manufacture, deliver, possess, transport, place, use, or release a harmful electronic or electromagnetic device for an unlawful purpose." Also made into a felony is the act of causing "an individual to falsely believe that the individual has been exposed to a... harmful electronic or electromagnetic device."

2. Maine

Public law 264, H.P. 868–L.D. 1271 criminalizes the knowing, intentional, and/or reckless use of an electronic weapon on another person, defining an electronic weapon as a portable device or weapon emitting an electrical current, impulse, beam, or wave with disabling effects on a human being.

In 2007, State Senator Joe Simitian (D-Palo Alto) announced that Governor Schwarzenegger signed his Senate Bill 362, which would prohibit employers and others from forcing anyone to have radio frequency identification (RFID) device implanted under their skin. The bill went into effect on January 1, 2008. Using radio waves, RFID can help identify and track objects, animals, or people. Devices known as "reader's access" hold the information on the tags. "RFID technology is not in and of itself the issue. RFID is a minor miracle, with all sorts of good uses," said Simitian. "But we cannot and should not condone forced 'tagging' of humans. It's the ultimate invasion of privacy."

Other states are not on the list of the extremely low number of states proactive against these unrestrained technology advancements. Noteworthy, Virginia has even documented concerns over privacy aligning a belief with the apocalyptic Biblical prophecy in a proposed Virginia law that limits the use of the coming microchip implant on humans because of a lawmaker's concern that the chips prove to be the Antichrist's "mark of the beast." James Walbert's resulting lawsuit centered specifically on the implantation of this device in his body without and it was done without his knowledge.

The Virginia's House of Delegates ultimately passed a bill that forbids companies from forcing their employees to be implanted with tracking devices, likely applauded by civil libertarians and for good reason. The Virginia state Delegate's reasons for proposing the law has as much to do with the Book of Revelation as with concerns over privacy in this digital age. The delegate said he is concerned that the implants will turn out to be the "mark of the beast" worn by Satan's minions. He further states:

"My understanding -- I'm not a theologian -- but there's a prophecy in the Bible that says you'll have to receive a mark, or you can neither buy nor sell things in end times," He said, as quoted at the Washington Post. "Some people think these computer chips might be that mark."

However, the microchip agenda marches on with even television commercials airing recommending chipping for various reasons, such as for healthcare.

Because of little public awareness of what is happening today, I now sat in the office of a West Los Angeles, California, Veteran Service Representative, denied temporary housing in a shelter due to my relentless quest to expose the truth, and the covert abuse and victimization surrounding my entire life.

I had long realized and accepted what I would be up against from previous experiences. It had been my experience, overall, that most would choose to believe me delusional before believing in the existence of these technologies or the factual uses and capabilities.

However, I made the conscious decision to continue to bravely speak up even after this saddening realization and insult. It is vitally important to not be silent or silenced. So, although I was consistently met with skepticism and disbelief, I continued my quest.

In Arizona, I was denied a much needed operation which would have helped with pain and gait, as the beam renewed intense focus on my hip area. Don't go to the VA, or any medical facility, and tell them that you are being targeted by a government agency beaming you with radio frequency technology thousands can guarantee you will get diagnosed as mentally ill, even if it is 100% true. This due to a doctor at the Arizona VA hospital, when consulted by the orthopedic surgeon reported that she felt me incapable of being restricted in the hospital for the surgery. After telling this woman what was happening to me, she pushed and pushed trying to convince me to use anti-psychotic medication which I continually declined. She believed she could not help me if I were effectively medicated. Admittedly, there had been a time when I initially questioned even myself, as do most initially would, understandably, when this type of personally intrusive Psy Ops surveillance begins. When someone is targeted in this manner, it is very, very hard to believe especially for the target at first. The reality that it is factually happening, along with the incredible capabilities of these advanced technologies is a bitter pill to swallow of hidden extreme evil. It is factually similar to science fiction but in reality, it is factually science nonfiction. This is especially true if a person is unaware of the many patented inventions or the laws deceptively approving their legal use.

After writing a Superior Court judge in 2006 after moving from Orange County, California to Scottsdale, Arizona, he confirmed that what I explained in my letter and my experiences those of as a federal spying program on steroids. I would later learn that it is not only a Federal program but today includes state and local levels of law enforcement and especially the military.

I thanked God for life, health, strength, and a sense of humor that morning. As I got up to leave the service rep's office, I felt a sharp pain briefly radiate up my leg as I stood. National Security Letters had provided knowledge of my medical history of which could be used for areas on my body to focus specific microwave attacks on to deceptively escalate. This resulted in "She can't walk" as apparent personal satisfaction of their handiwork.

Proudly I had again held my ground telling the representative of this hopeful book, what was happening in my life, and suggesting that if she were interested to check out my website, bigbrotherwatchingus.com, for further information. I also told her that I was in the fight of my life, saying as I left that my efforts were not only to help myself but also, if possible, to help many others with my experiences. Many are being unjustly abused and misdiagnosed and lives are turned upside down. I told her that I could not be swayed, moved or turned around no matter what. Sadly, there are people who have lost family, friends, homes, and employment as a direct result of these specific types of targeting in programs designed to first discredit strategically, then bank on the strategic determination of the target having a diminished mental state.

Admittedly, it was somewhat amusing to me when I thought of what people were probably thinking of me as I tried in vain to explain to them what was factually occurring in my life. I purposely had to try to keep the anxiety out of my voice, as most sat quietly watching me, emotionless. "I must appear to be an anomaly" I thought as I headed out to my car leaving the rep's office. Not only do I present myself intelligently, I'm told, but I also carry myself well. Thank God. For someone to look past all of this, including my intelligent conversation, and believe me schizophrenic was understandable, but amusing in a facetious way. Those targeting me were having the time of their lives watching their manipulative efforts played out in real time. However, what was not amusing was that if this group had their way, the use of a delusional diagnosis was exactly what they needed to discredit me and this book and continue the torture.

The fact still remained that while some may not believe that what I am professing is true, I felt that if I hung in there faithfully, the odds slowly could begin to change in my favor I learned. When this happened, it was a refreshing motivational lift. Some began to say, "Maybe there is truth to what she is saying after all" after researching the possibility for themselves. I had seen it happen as I became more involved and became acquaintances with others experiencing the same fate. In Arizona, those connected with law enforcement or having the ability to check or verify my claim, such as a judge, or legal system employees in various capacities knew of my accuracy.

As I unlocked my car door, I was glad that morning that I had told the Veteran Service Representative that I had petitioned the hospital director at the Long Beach, California, VA hospital for the hopeful removal of the misdiagnosis. It was worth a try. However, in actuality, it really did not matter. I could live with anything and knew that most doctors would not join forces with any patient's claims of a government conspiracy using advanced technology on them even if they knew it as possible truth. Some appeared to be too comfy in their world of psychological superiority over others and creating text book 'Disorders' to accept that they were possibly being used and duped in some cases to legitimize continued research, testing and development programs.

"If I can prove the technology exists" I told the representative that morning, "perhaps you can help me."

"If the VA cannot prove that the technology does not exist there may be a slight chance" I told her naive but hopeful.

"This is what I am requesting."

"I hope so," she replied, "Then I can help you."

Symptoms of schizophrenia, such as hearing voices, hallucinations and delusions usually start between the ages of sixteen and thirty. Most do not get schizophrenia after age of 30 something. And if so it is extremely rare and there are usually preexisting identifiers of some sort, I was told. It was in 2006 well past this age that I began complaining of odd incidents happening around me, inside and outside my residence. Prior to this, I had never, ever, anywhere, in my entire life, had any documentation of any diagnosis or of any symptoms even remotely resembling, or even similar to, any type of delusional disorder documented in my medical history, medical records, or more importantly observed or documented by those closest to me in my entire life.

It was also in 2006, as a result of unexplainable things happening around me, that I personally went to the VA hospital and told physicians specifically what I was experiencing. This was especially due to taunting coming from the background of both my cell phone and my land line house phone. I told them that it may possibly have something to do with a woman around me when I received my service connected compensation from the Veterans Administration who began acting unexplainably very strangely.

Lonely and isolated and in deep emotional turmoil, after returning home after my divorce without my children, I needed someone, a friend. I would later learn that this woman considered herself a recreational drug user. I had not seen her in well over 20 years. This woman had a good job, was a professional by appearance, and did not fit the modus operandi or stereotype.

It was by chance that I stumbled onto her secretly using drugs. This happened when I could not find her inside a social event she invited me to one night after a wedding and I went outside looking for her. I located her sitting in her vehicle with a strange man sitting on the driver's side. This person I would later learn was her connection. As I walked towards the vehicle, the expression on her face told me something was up but what, I was unsure. When she rolled the window down I could smell drugs and watched as she fidgeted trying to conceal something under my coat in her lap. I had a year and a half of sobriety under my belt when we first started hanging out, alcohol my drug of choice. The residuals of the failed marriage and emotional pain took its toll on my psyche for many reasons especially how I fled under the gun of a policeman ex-husband, forsaking the children, I felt briefly, and family home, just to get away from him.

However, being the vulnerable, emotional and psychological train wrecked I was and suffering from my poor decision during the divorce, as a no show in court, and the lowest of self-esteem, it was a matter of time before I myself, weakened. Anything to stop the intensity of the horrific pain would do. However, with me, where self-medication is concerned, my personality and consciousness fortunately, intelligently, would not allow me to cross over into complete loss of self into this lifestyle or for even an extended period of time.

When this hateful woman watched me trying to rebuild my life getting the therapy I needed, and assistance, she began laughing at me and calling me crazy, and later began asking me questions which I felt insinuated that I might be an expert on psychological diagnoses. I was diagnosed with trauma-related issues by the Department of Veterans Affairs. As I mentioned, I had not seen this woman in many years prior to her befriending me. She knew nothing about me or my personal life overall. However, I do vividly recall a conversation I had with her one night while we sat in her house talking. She told me that she regretted that in her life she had never gotten the opportunity to get to know her father. I told her I felt the same way. I said that sometimes, in God's plan for our lives, when our parents are unable to provide the care we need we are placed in a loving environment with those who can. I told her that my dad was incapable of raising me, and I never had any real bond with him and did not know him growing up. My mother died at an early age.

The poor soul, now 85 years old and living in a nursing home, whispered to me one day during a visit that a senior staff member who showed him a little extra kindness and attention wanted him and that she wanted him for sex too. He said this with a huge confident grin on his face, with his dentures moving around as he spoke, followed by a wink. I looked at him amused. There he sat in a wheelchair, a diaper necessary for incontinence, high blood pressure, and an enlarged heart. The amusement was in the fact that he was and had always been harmless.

However, one day in the background of my phone was an insinuation of an abnormal relationship with my father, saying "we think you had sex with you father." Yea right! It might be conceivable to an investigator if my dad had raised me as a child, and had influence over me, but he had not. I did not even know him until I was an adult. For the record, as far as any incestuous relationship with my father, as this woman, I would later learn told law enforcement, it simply was an outrageous, sick, disgusting, pathetic lie by a ruthless, jealous female mad at the world, secretly using drugs, and blaming any and every one that her life had not gone as expected. The sheer insanity was in the fact that she could do something of this magnitude which highlighted the fact that she is obviously screwed up. "there is also nothing honorable about the group targeting me, repeatedly accusing me, viciously, of something they know is not true relentlessly. How were these and other verbal accusations made? Believe it or not, by patented technology called synthetic telepathy, etc., from the location of the satellite's remote viewing entry point in my ceiling, and at times, and as stated in the background of my phones.

CHAPTER TWO

"All truth passes through three stages. First, it is ridiculed. Second, it is violently opposed. Third, it is accepted as being self-evident."

— **German philosopher, Arthur Schoenpenhauser**

Today, there are numerous U.S. patents proving the existence of various types of remote neural monitoring technology. Essentially a person, to person conversation verbalized audibly face to face is no longer necessary. Effective thought transmission resulting in conversations between two parties, without electrical devices can occur by voices beamed directly into the human brain carried through the nervous system from state-of-the-art operation centers. As shown below the ideation continues for official uses of the "technological telepathy":

Army Developing Synthetic Telepathy – Similar technology marked as a way to control video games, by thought, Eric Bland, Discovery News, and October 13, 2008

Pentagon Preps Soldier Telepathy Push, Katie Drummond and Noah Shachtman, May 14, 2009.

Both internet articles confirm the eventual use of, and existence of, technological telepathy and its application by the Department of Defense for use in the military and hope to create the "Super Soldier." Never has a statement made by Dr. José Manuel Rodriguez Delgado a now deceased professor of physiology at Yale University, famed for his research into mind control through electrical stimulation of regions in the brain had greater meaning.

Dr. Delgado is quoted, in a speech recorded in the February 24, 1974 edition of the Congressional Record No. 26, Vol. 118 saying:

"We need a program of psychosurgery for political control of our society. The purpose is physical control of the mind. Everyone who deviates from the given norm can be surgically mutilated. "The individual may think that the most important reality is his own existence, but this is only his personal point of view. This lacks historical perspective. "Man does not have the right to develop his own mind. This kind of liberal orientation has great appeal. We must electrically control the brain. Someday, armies and generals will be controlled by electric stimulation of the brain".

The website http://www.electronictorture.com/ except describes what the definition of electronic harassment is:

"Electronic harassment/electronic torture/electronic murder is about harassment, torture and possible covert murder using electronic weapons based on radio waves. These weapons have been refined in recent years and can cause effects comparable to many illnesses and/or injuries. These weapons are no longer imaginary but used today illegally on mostly random innocent victims not knowing what is happening to them…"

The first documented information on behavior modification technology, called the LIDA machine, was reported by American soldiers returning from the Korean War in 1950 to 1953. The purported purpose of the LIDA was for medical treatments; however, the North Koreans used it as a brainwashing device during the war. In 1984, Dr. Ross Adey, Chief of Research at the Pettis Memorial Veterans Hospital in Loma Linda, California, obtained from Soviet colleagues what is known as "a mini-Woodpecker transmitter," labeled the LIDA. The LIDA operated on a frequency of 40 MHz and bombarded the brain with low frequency radio waves. It was used experimentally by the Russians as "a replacement for tranquilizers and their unwanted side effects." The pulsed radio waves were said to "stimulate the brain's own electromagnetic current and produce a trance-like state." The manual describing the mini-Woodpecker said it was a "distant pulse treatment apparatus" for psychological problems, including sleeplessness, hypertension, and neurotic disturbances.

Interestingly, when the Associated Press reported on Adey's scoop, concluded that "the LIDA may have been the forerunner of a device that is presently bombarding Europe and the United States with very powerful waves. The Russian Woodpecker is the equivalent of America's High Frequency Active Auroral Research Project or HAARP. (Excerpt - Philip Coppens, Conspiracy Times – The Russian Woodpecker: experiments in global mind control)

Some targeted individuals when asked to pinpoint their first likely audible voice transmission into their heads report initially hearing someone call out their name as if originating from thin air. It was a man's voice for me one day then about a week later, a woman's voice called my name waking me from sleep. I as with most targets wrote both incidents off as my imagination or dreaming.

In reality, I would later learn this is likely a voice transmission test for effectiveness. The only imagination connected to this very effective, secretly deployed, patented technology is the brilliant imagination of the scientist who invented it.

Another capability of electromagnetic patented technology as shown on my website is technological sexual stimulation. This group would attempt to heinously use the technology to stimulate me sexually whenever around my dad as I drove him to and from church. They then would decipher my thoughts and my emotion for any relevancy or validity to any deviant sexual connection between my father and me. I can only imagine what was happening in my poor dad's head as we drove. At one point, every time I visited my father, it got so bad, that I was completely nauseated around him and had to stop going to see him for a while sick to my stomach.

They would underestimate me. Some might be reluctant; more concerned with what others would think of them and not reveal these types of heinous Psy Ops. This is especially true when related to these specific types of bizarre accusations but I obviously am not. The truth sometimes is not pretty and exposure of the psychopathic use of these capabilities is more important to me. Hear me when I say this again, and again. This technology is no laughing matter or a joke by far! You can bet these freaks in this and other operations are likely creating deviances with many people who have not a clue. This, and similar extreme psychotronic abuses were being done to me while they sat miles away pinpointing my location and tracking my every move biometrically, by satellite, watching, listening and remarkably holding court inside my head.

One of a number of patents used for sexual, excitation, stimulation and arousal is:

United States Patent # 6,017,302 - (January 25, 2000) Subliminal Acoustic Manipulation of Nervous Systems, invented by Hendricus Loos.

A brief excerpt of the abstract reads:

In human subjects, sensory resonances can be excited by subliminal atmospheric acoustic pulses that are tuned to the resonance frequency. The 1/2 Hz sensory resonance affects the autonomic nervous system and may cause relaxation, drowsiness, or sexual excitement, depending on the precise acoustic frequency near 1/2 Hz used...

I can report that the technology is quite effective in the hands of the unscrupulous masquerading as men of honor. What is lacking, when this specific technology is deployed against a target, is the normal stimulation of a healthy, mental and physical connection in willing sexual arousal between two people.

What amazed me also was that these men, using the Nine Step Reid Interrogative Technique, held an interrogation session literally inside my head. The first step of the Reid Technique is Positive

Confrontation. One would say, "We know what happen, but it only happened that one time" implying that there was inappropriateness on my part and also hoping to ingratiate themselves with me. The deeper psychological tactic was usually followed by extremely abusive names.

I often wondered if this was done possibly to change any interpretation of me as an intelligent, attractive, and genuinely good woman which too was verbalized by some of them at other times in the Psy Ops polar state. If they accepted this obvious truth, of me as honorable, it would mean that in monitoring me they would have to take responsibility for their actions and immoral acts and would no longer inhumanely seek to viciously destroy my life. One day, I was told by one saying I don't even feel good about calling you names. They needed to perceive me as a lowly human being in order to continue to justify their psychosis and horrendous victimization of not only myself but other human beings.

Factually, I discerned that it was they who were mind controlled and this reality was a mental block blurring the obvious truth for them. Those working in these programs are sicker than most would imagine though cleaned and polished on the outside for appearance. For me they remained on the first step unable to progress to the second technique. In light of failure, they attacked my sensitivities as soon as I opened my eyes each morning. The fact that they continued to maliciously say that there had been a non-existent sexual encounter with my dad revealed emotional cruelty which some just cannot take.

Again, I told them, there would also never be any person on the face of the Earth who knew the two of us, or observed us together, who would say they even suspected something so heinous. And, unbelievably, the woman who made this allegation had never in her entire life ever met my dad or laid eyes on him. For the most part, I would get irritated that he was always trying to impress me with the things he had done early in his life retelling the same stories over and over again.

However, I was grateful for him. When I was in a tremendous amount of pain, he tried to help as best he could after the divorce letting me stay with him. Contributing to the emotional technological crucifixion was the reality that I would have to stomach my policeman ex-husband's likely significant role, along with this woman. These two, it appeared, had a definite impact in the situation literally looming over my head connecting my life to faceless voices abusing me around the clock. They repeatedly implied my life useless, and on two occasions obviously hoped to plant a subtle suggestion that I should commit suicide. In fact, in late January 2012, an apparent LAPD officer visited my social network book page and boldly made a posting regarding suicide, specifically referencing one of my book projects. This book is the first in this series called Remote Brain Targeting. He posted regarding it:

"Dumb as f---, this demonstrates a fundamental lack of grasp on the concepts it discusses. Honestly, kill yourself."

This would mean nothing in most cases except there had been an attempt to implant suicidal suggestions in me. When I checked his social network page he brazenly listed himself as officially employed by the Los Angeles Police Department and also as a private investigator which indicates he knew full well of this technology first hand. Funny how I specifically said on the cover of the book that it is a compilation of research, testing and development programs historically. Compilation would indicate compiled information.

In these types of operations, it is known they never can come forth, if so exposing themselves, their operation and practices. However, subtle nudging of a person, apparently to take their own life is not out of the question if the target becomes a threat. Was my hopeful suicide, the ultimate goal and now the foundation of the vicious verbal assault by this group willing to say, or do anything to destroy me emotionally? While literally operating under the radar, there was an intense effort fully mobilized designed to push me over the edge? And if so, my ex-husband being a policeman had to have played a very significant role in the dogmatic effort though he probably felt that his vindictive secretive role would never be revealed.

The investigation started when I was numbed with pain, lost, confused, and in a psychologically weakened state. My brief substance abuse history was fortunately plagued by what I call "beneficial fear" along with the belief that in my heart of hearts that I am and always have been a better person and my life means something. Nobody said the road would be easy in life or that human beings will not make mistakes.

It was this belief that would motivate me to stop doing anything unhealthy after the short stint, and returned to my typical healthy lifestyle. I also had many more years of eating correctly and living right before the trials that devastated my life later on during that period of time. I was in total agreement with what a VA hospital physician had written in my hospital medical records after an assessment of me saying that substances were not recreational for me but were used for self-medication purposes only. It was true. This was based on my ability to put it down and walk away and never look back finally. In my case, I knew that I would never, ever look back on the nightmare of blinding emotional pain which a lot of people are still caught in and in some cases never make it out of darkness.

By March of 2012, I was nearing five years of sobriety in September yet efforts of my targeting continued without missing a beat. And for those questioning my sanity, after I spoke up about the technological targeting, I submit the fact that I am able to write about truthful events and experiences in full detail without anti-psychotic medication to stabilize a wondering, scattered or incoherent mind, or a mind unable to comprehend or out of touch with reality, and function on a day to day basis.

There is a bracket of weapons which were referred to by Leonid Ilyich Brezhnev, the general secretary of the Central Committee of the Communist Party of the Soviet Union, presiding over the country from 1964 until his death in 1982, when he told then United States President

Jimmy Carter that there should be a unilateral ban against certain secret weapons "more frightful than the mind of man ever conceived." And clearly there are many others that we are yet to learn about including advanced forms of infrasound weapons that can induce organ damage and illness from remote locations or by satellite radar laser.

Mr. Paul Baird on the website Satellite and Human Experimentation writes what he feels is desperately needed morally today:

1. A United Nation Satellite Committee and Non-Lethal Weapon inspectors.

2. An International Criminal Court prepared to handle class actions by victims.

3. A growth in public awareness surrounding any testing of experimental technology and I add: The need for responsible supervision of the use of certain technologies and those manning them.

Stated on Mr. Baird's website are also the comments of a senior investigator in the NASA Inspector General's office documented years ago. After having conceded to the existence of advanced influential technologies, then commenting on the evil uses for which they can and are put, he supposedly suggested, I advise we pray.

The psychiatric diagnostic manuals are partly written by and set up by government agency personnel Paul Baird also confirms. This is especially true in the United States to provide an easy means of discrediting people who complain about covert harassment. Psyche students are basically taught that if you cannot see it or it leaves no evidence existences, or did not happen, the complainant must be delusional. This I can personally testify to. Their position, therefore, is to protect government agencies and others allowing the following injustices:

1. All complaints about covert harassment can be dismissed as paranoia.

2. All complaints about, DOD Voice of God, voice-to-skull, Neurophone, Frey microwave, Neural Decoding, Synthetic or Artificial Telepathy technology, etc., can be dismissed as psychosis, delusions, or Schizophrenia.

3. All complaints about media feedback in surveillance can be dismissed as delusional.

4. All complaints about oppression, torture, abduction, etc., can be dismissed as fantasy.

"Most psychiatrists discredit complainants out of ignorance or self-interest, but others, including the spy agency psychiatrists who coined most of the numbered terms above, act with full knowledge," Baird says. "Some even work within the actual experimental programs that are designed to specifically study human responses to remote-control stimuli. Those behind these programs help to create assassins and vegetables, conflicts and conspiracies, attractions or aversions, successes or failures, and all as an experiment for political and economic advantage and control. Corruptible court and law enforcement officials, and others help to discredit those presenting the truth. It's all part of the conspiracies of silence which are run on certain important classified matters. For psych experts used in court proceedings, freeing the guilty and branding the innocent are well known practices.

What's not so well known, again, is that the psyche texts were prepared and vetted by agency psychiatrists to allow their colleagues to continue testing or use them to silence anyone speaking the harsher truths. Terms such as brainwashing and paranoid schizophrenia were, in fact, penned by spy agency psychiatrists principally to brand victims of covert harassment as being deranged and therefore not to be believed or trusted.

The delusional diagnoses are vital and as most learn is a highly effective benefit for those manning the technology in these programs. The patents do not lie.

Allan Frey found that if a microwave carrier was sliced and carried audio modulation, that audio could be heard by someone in the signal's path. The thin pulses of radio-carrier waves cause current to flow through the nervous system. The result is remote transmission; no wires or contact is needed. Two of today's numerous, subliminal message carrying patents are listed below:

1. U.S. Patent #4,877,027 - A hearing system, October 32, 1989, Wayne Brunker.

2. U.S. Patent #4,858,612 - A hearing device, August 22, 1989, Phillip L. Stocklin.

The latter involves microwaves aimed at the auditory cortex. A mike turns the sounds to electrical signal's which are treated so as to provide multi-frequency microwaves which are applied to the brain area today through microwave towers. Whatever sounds the mike picks up, such as voices are relayed to the target.

The Neurophone; U.S. Patent # 3,393,279, July 16, 1968 and U.S. Patent # 3,647,970, March 7, 1972 are both by Dr. Patrick Flanagan. Flanagan's method accomplishes voice to skull by satellite radar delivery, and has the same effect as microwave through towers.

Invented in the late 1958, this system can also transmit and mimic your voice or anyone's voice with automatic computer translations in many languages incorporated into the technology. This is helpful when those manning the technology are trying to convince the target that a suggested thought appearing as their own, for example is an admittance of wrong doing or guilt, in their own voice and own sounding words. There have been, over the years, numerous testing programs documenting the test results of technological telepathy in programs ran by the Air Force Laboratory for example. However, testing obviously must date back even further based on some of the official patent dates.

The Neurophone is a device that converts sound to electrical impulses allowing information to be transmitted to the brain by means of radio waves directed at any part of the body such as the skin. In other words, recorded or live verbal messages, noise, or music can be directed at an individual, and through the nerves, the signal then carried (involuntarily) to the brain, bypassing the inner ear, the cochlea, and the eighth cranial nerve. In its original form, electrodes were placed on the skin but with Defense Department development satellite deliverance is a capability.

Practically the Neurophone can be used to communicate with the deaf when used in a positive manner. Most advancement has great potential for benefit to humanity. Herein lies the first technologically induced "hearing voices" effect and in most cases a typical psychosis diagnosis. Those around do not hear a thing as the focused beam zeroes in only on the targeted individual.

A good example of this type of technology's rapid advancement into mainstream America can be seen in an actual ad campaign on cryptogon.com, December 7, 2007, entitled, Voice to Skull Technology in New York. The real, live, ad campaign is excerpted below. The ad campaign begins:

New Yorker Alison Wilson was walking down Prince Street in So Ho last week when she heard a woman's voice right in her ear asking, "Who's there? Who's there?" She looked around to find no one in her immediate surroundings. Then the voice said, "It's not your imagination." "Indeed, it isn't. It's an ad for "Paranormal State," a ghost-themed series premiering on A & E this week.

The billboard uses technology manufactured by Holosonic that transmits an audio spotlight from a rooftop speaker, so that the sound is contained within your cranium. The website Gawker posted an item about the billboard with the headline, Schizophrenia is the new ad gimmick, and asked, how soon will it be until, in addition to the do-not-call list, we'll have a do-not-beam-commercial messages-into-my-head list?

The modern term for brainwashing or mind control as stated earlier is psychological electronic. This term today can encompass a host of technologies, such as technological telepathy, mind-reading software using EEG Brainwave Monitoring Analyzers / Brainwave Scanner, and mood management technology designed to alter the consciousness. They allow remote neural monitoring and remote stimuli experiments as well as dream manipulation and thought studies. It allows people to be set-up, remote torment and torture, direct brain interrogation even while sleeping, murder, and much more. Some would also include scripted alien abductions for what are really clandestine scientific endeavors. This technology can activate behavior that would normally be suppressed or dormant within the human brain in subliminal suggestions or influences.

Below are a very small number of a large arsenal of patented technologies, patented officially at the United States Patent and Trademark Office. For a complete list check out the Patent and Inventor section of the website: bigbrotherwatchingus.com:

US Patent 5,455,589	Compact microwave and millimeter wave radar, Millitech Corporation
US Patent 5,489.818	High Power compact microwave source, Olin Corporation
US Patent 4,717,343	Method for Changing a Person's Behavior
US Patent 5,270,800	Subliminal Message Generators
US Patent 5,123,899	Method for Altering Consciousness
US Patent 4,877,027	Hearing System (technological telepathy)
US Patent-6,011,991	Communication System and Method Including Brain Wave Analysis and/or use of Brain Activity

US Patent 4,858,612	Hearing Device
US Patent 3,951,134	Apparatus and Method for Remotely Monitoring and Altering Brain Waves
US Patent–5,629,678	Implantable Transceiver (Radio Frequency Identification (RFID)
US Patent 5,878,155	Barcode Tattoo for humans
US Patent 5,539,705	Ultrasonic Speed Translator and Communications System
US Patent 5,629,678	Personal Tracking and Recovery System
US Patent 5,760,692	Intro–Oral Tracking Device
US Patent 5,868,100	Fenceless Animal Control System Using GPS Location Information
US Patent 5,905,461	Global Positioning Satellite Tracking Device
US Patent 5,935,034	Magnetic Excitation and Sensory Resonances (This patent is said capable of technological sexual stimulation from operation centers as a form of terrorism purposes.)
US Patent 5,952,600	Engine Disabling Weapon (Used numerous times to disable my car after being followed around town by Gang Stalkers/Covert Harassment Groups, etc., and also off duty policemen)
US Patent 6,006,188	Speech Signal Processing for Determining Psychological or Physiological Characteristics Using a Knowledge Base
US Patent 6,014,080	Body Worn Active and Passive Tracking Device
US Patent 6,017,302	Subliminal Acoustic Manipulation of the Nervous System.

US Patent 6,052,336 Apparatus and Method of Broadcasting Audible Sound Using Ultrasound as a Carrier

One day I asked those around me, "If during this entire period of their targeting of me, if they could show me any measure of success in the effort around me, I will not publish this book." I refused to be stopped no matter how great the sadness they hoped to create around me to include destruction of my family.

This was one of the very few times they were completely silent with no response from the 24-hour taunting. Sadly, they continued testing the heights of the technology believing I could not prove a thing. This, in the long run, would result in their stepping on their own genitalia because I would continue writing. Their only achievement around me was thereby my complete education of the operations of "The Program."

Truthfully, on some days I do not know how I survived myself or from where the inner strength came. Sadly, the possibility of me as a test subject was driven home by the fact that they appeared to be testing their newly provided advanced toys on someone with a diagnosis. This in my case meant Post Traumatic Stress Disorder.

Was I someone whom they felt could be easily used and abused and whom no one would care because of PTSD? The sheer coldness was in the fact that no matter what they said or did, this diagnosis would not change by trying to prove me a fraud in some way. Nor had I manipulated anything.

As mentioned, the delusional diagnosis came later as a result of the specific type of technological targeting I was subjected to. Any diagnosis does not mean ignorance they would learn a little too late. They used my valid startle-reflex reaction, typical of the trauma diagnosis as a sign of created fear and technological effectiveness. Each time I was startled, they credited themselves using these phenomena as proof, saying "She's scared" deeming the effort successful. I have never had any legal reason to fear them, their death threats meant nothing, and the repetitive games were getting old.

Although I do have trauma related issues, which had been unaddressed for many years after leaving the military, their abuse of me backfired on them. Once they learned that I would try and was capable of trying to protect my life, and standing alone, and that I even had the nerve to write about it, they were murderously angered.

How did they expect to compete with my right to publish what they were doing? In their minds, the only thing they knew was to keep trying to scare me, stalk me, and by portraying themselves as gangsters with threats while painfully torturing me. After they realized that I was not dumb, there was then their uneducated diagnosis of me. This new diagnosis suited their needs for the continued justification portraying me as a person misrepresenting myself in some way though none of them had a M.D. or Ph.D. behind their names and some just a high school diploma.

Today, in Hollywood movies and music, boldly, the puppet master is telling us what is officially happening as life continues to imitate art in film.

For example, in the film, The Adjustment Bureau (2011) there is a scene when Matt Daemon walks into a board room and sees people just standing there like statues. This clip demonstrates people controlled by suggestions but who realize they are. Thoughts pushed on another or influenced, are inserted in real time. A handler's ideas are inserted into the cerebral cortex of a targeted individual which manifest as a targeted individual's own and then acted out accordingly, the website Mind Tech Sweden explains. Sweden is one of the countries under technological assault for many years now. You simply do what you think you want to do, but the thought is not yours but those of the handler. Another example is a scene from this movie when the reporter knows she is on live national television, and acknowledges what has happened to her by saying I was in a trance. This movie is a good depiction of mind control and gang stalking and is very accurate, some believe, with the exception of walking through walls physically.

One day I sat thinking about this group of mucky mucks and the type of people they had to be behind the appearance of polished and ethical character and realized that mind control efforts had been completely effective and successful, not on me, thank God, but obviously on them. This was proven in the egotistical weakness of their inability to intelligently move on and determination to instead destroy life. They chose to linger, humiliate, degrade, threaten, and release the essence of what lurked inside them hidden from full public view under the mask of a uniform and Color of Law. Character truly is what a man, in this case men are in the dark.

After leaving the VA facility at West Los Angeles, I moved into a residential hotel while searching for a residence. From the operation center, I was zapped a few times with voltages of the spaced-based energy weapon confirming their watchful eye and the message that there was nowhere to hide though I was not hiding. One night I nearly fell off my bed from the power of the radar laser energy weapon's jolt.

The sentence below is an example of me, and many others, buying into initially, the deceptive phenomenon of mass organized stalking efforts. In reality, many situations are being micromanaged, from the operation center by a small group of operatives. They are holding the reigns of illusion management through the expansiveness of satellite real time surveillance and using this capability to tamper with any and every one around the target. This includes family, friends, and on a larger scale, the environment overall, for example an entire neighborhood.

Gang stalking is the deceptive name given to the technological assault motivated by a program in full use today and by appearance for many years. "The Program" operates from state-of-the-art operation centers or nearby military installations utilizing laws authorizing testing on the civilian population for crown control. In "The Program," they locate a target, for various reasons and began games of deception using mind control technology. Because it is done for various reasons, confusion is intentionally created. A person can be targeted about money (my compensation) resources (James Walbert's invention), or perceive as undesirables and used as human guinea pigs or simply by offending the wrong person and your name given to these covert efforts.

The website Mind Tech Sweden has an interesting take on The Program using what the author calls biological application or BioAPI below. From my personal experiences, in the United States, Bio API equates to human biometric signature tracking or signal intelligence collection. The website describes "The Program" aka gang stalking in the excerpt below. I have inserted my comments in parenthesis:

In the program, a target is repeatedly harassed. The people who are doing this have gone to great lengths to create ridiculous terms and reasons to cover up how the program or the technology in general actually works. Once one understands the nanotechnology base and BioAPI in general the entire operation becomes more of a running joke. (In my opinion, nanotechnology equates to miniscule microchip implants.)

There are countless terms on the Internet related to this ideal. (Note: organized stalking, gang stalking, covert harassment groups, Neighborhood Watch, Community Policing. If targeted by law enforcement, the latter two in a community are used.)

People think they're being microwaved, DEWs, voice to skull, etc. (Technology can and is being delivered by portable weapons also from neighboring locations, and again from operation centers or both. In my case while running errands the attacks were aerial and coming from the operation center, while home from adjoining apartments or both.)

This and the actual use of them is simply to create confusion for the public in an effort to help hide the BioAPI and how it's used against people such as yourself and your family. It's completely impossible to interface with the human body without some sort of middle-ware hence the requirement of a nanotechnology engineered

BioAPI. (The electromagnetic energy of the human body is used with patented inventions.)

The term gang stalking is a description of what a targeted individual, someone with phase 2 of the BioAPI, goes through when entered into "The Program" the website says. It involves countless random people all day long harassing them. A targeted individual will go to a restaurant and the food will intentionally be delivered cold, or they will get crank calls all day long. How can everyone instantly be out to harm and harass a targeted individual? (Noteworthy in programs connected to law enforcement people can be easily swayed by disinformation in definite community policing programs.)

What one needs to understand for example with a crank call, is the person accidentally calling the targeted individual really is accidentally calling them, the thought on what the caller wants to do or who to call is inserted in real time via the BioAPI and they act accordingly as if the thought was theirs. The most direct example of this in action is demonstrated in the, animated Swedish film Metropia (2009) clip (see MindTech Sweden website for the specific film clips.) This clip is 100% real. (Metropia is about a man hearing voices, knows they are not coming from him, and starts the road to discovery of a heinous plan to use him, thereby actually meeting with his controller. (This is an animated film. I think it was intentionally animated to desensitize people to the reality and harshness of technological telepathy.)

One of the false realities they (those working in The Program) try is to convince a targeted individual to believe is everyone suddenly is in on it. The targeted individual is typically too stupid (I prefer unaware) to ever figure out how everyone they know seems to know everything about them all of a sudden. (This reminds me when a relative was staying temporarily with me and she said, "I know how you hate smells" regarding how clean and fresh I like my house. I had not seen her in 20 years and wondered how she knew this about me. It is not something I have ever verbalized.)

This site (MindTech Sweden) demonstrates how it happens. An entire infrastructure of misdirection and disinformation has been created to construct a false possibility that gangs of people are actually out harassing someone. This is simply a cover to misdirect people away from how it really works – nanotechnology. (When I read this, had I not seen the patents for portable technology and experience pain beamed from neighboring apartments, I would say that the targeting was coming 100% from the operation center only.)

Speaking from my personal experience, biometric signature collection utilizing computerized software to influence works well when coexisting with the patented EEG thought deciphering capability of the Brainwave Analyzer. The handler knows your thoughts that are used combining with their technological telepathic ability. Everyone present can be toyed with and used as pawns and victimized without their knowledge. For example, my oldest daughter, saying called me a name, one day, out of the blue, while engrossed in her laptop as I walked into the kitchen frequently said by those monitoring me from the operation center. It was said to no one particular, and only she and I were present in the house. I asked her about it and she had not a clue.

The website, MindTech Sweden calls this Direct to Speech where thoughts of the handlers are inserted into person's mind by technological telepathy and the target thinks it is their thought.

The Purpose of Organized / Gang Stalking is defined by Mindtech Sweden.Com as:

The overall purpose of leveraging this technology directly against an unsuspecting, normal person such as yourself is to get you to act out in some way (In my case repeatedly being called malicious names followed up with electronic torture was designed to create a reaction and a highly agitated state of being whereas I would discredit myself by playing into the delusional diagnosis and as stated act out.) They want you to externalize the events they are creating in and around your life. (In my case where they went wrong with me is that I would externalize telling everyone within earshot and did not care if other's thought me insane once I knew I was right about what was happening.) For example, the handler is constantly controlling people around you such as family members to get them to suggest you have mental problems - the crazy theme comes up a lot. (They found a weakness in my oldest daughter especially and the middle daughter, when around me, and used especially the oldest nudging to try to have me committed right around book publication time.

When it failed, one of them became angry she failed, saying, "She done," referencing my daughter to me indicating that she was no longer of value and useful to them and they would harm her. They indicated that she would pay for her failure to get to me. However, later it would become questionable if she could be used for sexual exploitation, if I were not around. Based on my personal experiences, I would not put this past them as documented later.) It works (the strategic effort works) well against people who do not understand how everything is working Mind Tech Sweden says." "The people doing this are attempting to create a false reality around the targeted individual. The reality constructed is dependent on that TI's situation. For example, they attempt to find something that the targeted person does not like (i.e., dogs?) and then everywhere a targeted individual goes there will be dog's there. (They know what your likes and dislikes are by use of mind reading software and listening to your thoughts all day. In my case, whenever around strange women, "She thinks she's cute," was directed at me by strangers who likely did not even know why they said this. Using Direct-to-Speech for example, standing in a checkout line at the store, the fat lady behind me would say this or it appeared someone said, "The police are after her" when I entered a room such as the coffee shop appearing that it was said by those already there.)

I know it sounds skeptical, but as I, and many others have learned, they bank on the fact that people will think these situations too far out to mention or outrageous as they easily use the technology to broadcast drama into an entire environment. This is all done by sitting at a highly advanced mega computer system. All I have to say is BRILLIANT! They thought I had a weakness with people saying that I thought I was cute believing this hurt me. It actually did bother me when I was in grade school!

In the end, no matter how many people appear to be harassing or gang stalking a targeted individual, in reality, writes MindTech Sweden, it's only just one guy (or in my case several, again working in shifts around the clock, who do use neighbors.) in a data center controlling everyone and everything about and around a targeted individual in real time. Reality is always the opposite.

They try to portray everyone as harassing a targeted individual; in the end mostly, it's just the BioAPI (Biometric signature/ real time surveillance operation center radar delivered influence technology which again, includes portable versions deployed effectively from nearby locations.)

Mind Tech Sweden website also mentions a specific nanotechnology called Ocular implants which allows the "Handler(s)" to see through the eyes of a Target Individual.

Your eyes as lenses via technology was reported by BBC News in 1999 when a team of U.S. scientists, from University of California Berkley, wired a computer to a cat's brain and created videos of what the animal was seeing. Computer fiber optic radar laser can likely create this same effect via satellites. For more information on this phenomenon, check out:

British Broadcasting Company (BBC) Online: Sic/Tech. Monday, October 11, 1999 - Looking Through Cats' Eyes, by BBC News Online Science Editor, and Dr. David Whitehouse.)

After waking in the morning, if I thought, you look a mess while surveying myself, lovingly, in the mirror the person watching me would reply "She's not that cute" or "She's fat" reinforcing negativity. Or as I fixed my hair, she's cute was said next, in their games of emotional see-saw using negative and positive comments as a variation of typical good cop/bad cop tactics. And to show how sick these puppies really are, they constantly wanted to see up close if I were attractive as they scanned others to find out and at times sent an operative who came out in person to see if I were then commenting "She is cute" said over and over again afterwards. I don't need these deviants to like me! And the opinion of fools means nothing to me. They developed a sick fascination with me. I believe, largely because most are unable to withstand the horrific psychological and physical abuse and fight effectively as God had strengthened me too. A person not having a clue is their powerful, controlling edge. In my opinion, their showing up validated the mentality of a pack of wolves looking for eye candy and appearing to be more motivated by sexual stimulation. In order to fear them I would have to respect them.

This satellite optical eye leaves a woman, completely, fully exposed in what should be even the privacy of her bathroom by undisciplined men having front row real time seats and a private showing designed for humiliation.

Herein lays another example of the beginning foundation for a delusional diagnosis. While visiting a friend in the hospital, using the brainwave analyzer, they deciphered my thought that her boyfriend was handsome as he and I sat around her bed laughing and joking. It was just an innocent thought. I did not think that I wanted to take him home and bed him down, just that he was handsome. This resulted in during the visit as I sat there talking to them both, drama being played out verbally inside my head by those sitting at their computer terminal watching us. I was actually being accused that I did factually want my friend's boyfriend. Imagine for a moment someone trying to explain this scenario to you without the ability to produce any physical evidence or proof.

The human brain emits weak radio frequencies in the sub-1000Hz range. The principles of radio tell us anything that can produce a radio signal, can also accept one. This results in the establishment of a physical transport layer. A physical transport layer allows for two-way communications. The voices are beamed directly into the brain the same way that cellular towers beam voices into your cellular phone.

Sadly, for many, if a person is trying to convince you of the reality of this type of scenario, you naturally could surely, deemed him or her off if you did not understand that it is completely possible today.

CHAPTER THREE

It has become appallingly obvious that our technology has exceeded our humanity.

— **Albert Einstein**

In 1959, Saul B. Sells, a professor of social psychology at a minor U.S. university submitted a proposal to the Central Intelligence Agency (CIA)to build for them the most sophisticated electroencephalography machine that would have an integral computational capacity to analyze and, hopefully, make sense of the brain waves it recorded.

In other words, the professor proposed to make a machine that could tell the CIA what a person is thinking. The CIA approved the project in 1960, adding library research with five objectives. The fifth objective of the research was, "Techniques for Activating the Human Organism by Remote Electronic Means." The entire assignment was thereafter known as MKULTRA subproject 119, MKULTRA being the CIA's notorious mind control program. It was based on the erroneous notion that the Soviets already possessed the means to control minds and the U.S. had to catch up as rapidly as possible.

The Montauk Project was alleged to be a series of testing to develop psychological warfare techniques that included time travel. This project was conducted at Montauk Air Force Station on Montauk, Long Island, New York. The Montauk Project is said to be the offspring of The Philadelphia Experiment. This experiment allegedly aimed at using "electromagnetic shielding" to make the USS Eldridge invisible to radar detection. The goal was the manipulation of military applications of the magnetic fields.

Using highly advanced computer generated Electroencephalogram (EEG) technology the brain waves around an individual's head can be monitored by satellite writes Paul Baird, Satellite and Human Experimentation. The transmitter is therefore the brain itself. This works similar to how body heat is used for iris satellite tracking (infrared) or mobile phones as tracking devices and even how planted electrical bugs can be tracked as transmitters.

In the case of the brainwave monitoring, the results are fed back to powerful computers that have a vocabulary of thousands of words and phrases in many different languages.

Lawrence Pinneo, a neurophysiologist and electronic engineer working for Stanford Research Institute, a military contractor, is the first known pioneer in this field officially. In 1974 he developed a computer system that correlated brain waves on an Electroencephalograph with specific commands. In the early 1990s, Dr. Edward Taub reported that words could be communicated onto a screen using the thought-activated movements of the computer cursor.

The brainwave scanner's first program was developed in 1994 by Dr. Donald York and Dr. Thomas Jensen. In 1994, the brainwave patterns of forty subjects were officially correlated with both spoken words and silent thought. This was achieved by neurophysiologist Dr. Donald York and speech pathologist Dr. Thomas Jensen from the University of Missouri. They clearly identified twenty-seven words and syllables in specific brainwave patterns and produced a computer program with a brainwave vocabulary.

Today, using radar delivered by satellites and high-powered computers, there is an ability to decipher human thoughts instantaneously and from a considerable distance. Monitors then use the information to conduct conversation after the audible Neurophone input is applied to the target or victim.

A good example and more recent advancement in this area is Brain Gate. Brain Gate is a system, currently under development and in actual clinical trials, designed to help those who have lost control of bodily functions or limbs. The sensor is implanted into the brain and then monitors brain activity by converting the intentions of the person into computer commands. Brain Gate essentially is mind reading software also.

The Malech Remote Brainwave-Altering Machine, United States Patent #3951134 April 1976 by Robert G. Malech is technology that allows remote interrogation from an operation center. Although recent articles or televised reports on this subject give the impression that mind reading technology is a new phenomenon:

> Mind Reading: Technology Turns Thought into Action - Jon Hamilton (May 12, 2011)
>
> Mind-Reading Experiment Reconstructs Movies in Our Mind - Associated Press (Published September 22, 2011)
>
> We're closer to mind reading than you may think - Emi Kolawole (October 31, 2011)
>
> Can A Satellite Read Your Thoughts? - Physics Revealed, July 13, 2010, by Deep Thoughts

CBS television news program's documentary on mind reading technology shown on June 28, 2009 by Leslie Stahl which can be accessed online is an example.

Today, many people are targeted and homeless which is the end result of strategic financial ruin. Shelter facilities are prime testing grounds for human guinea technology testing. During my brief stay, as mentioned earlier, on the VA facility, it appears that a woman was 100% targeted also. What made me suspect the woman in the shelter? While talking with her one night about this manuscript, shortly after I had arrived, her eyes grew big, and her face lit up in surprise after reading my blog on my website on the targeting and this forthcoming book. She then told me that she had complained to the VA hospital in the emergency room one night about exact incidences occurring in her life. She said that after emergency room personnel heard her story, the VA police were called as a personal escort to escort her directly to the psyche ward. She confided that after the incident she never said another word about what was happening to her or to anyone else.

This I learned is typical of a lot of targets and to the great advantage of those doing the victimizing. Of greater interest to me was her telling me that during that time frame, her boyfriend was employed by Northrup Grumman. Northrup Grumman, a defense contractor, in Los Angeles, California, is one of many corporations on the record in the Washington Post expose' Top Secret America website, documented as doing top secret intelligence work for our government.

Although her boyfriend was eventually fired from the company, she told me, similar things were happening to him right before he was fired and he had become so paranoid that it frightened her thereby taking herself to the emergency room that night. He too complained of identical harassment by technology, tracking, and what appeared to be organized gang stalking and told her that it is, very, very real.

One of the roles of Northrup Grumman listed on the Top-Secret America website is in the area of psychological operations. A brief description of the term "psychological operations" by Top Secret America is defined as:

Traditional psychological operations, including the creation and delivery of messages via leaflet, loudspeaker, radio, or television; the newer "influence operations" associated with the creation of Web sites and the use of social media to extend United States influence, both overtly and covertly; and the separate clandestine and covert activities associated with influence, deception and perception management.

Hmmm, influence, deception, and perception management. The investigative report divides top secret work for our government into 23 different categories. Companies working for our government provide services in the following areas:

Air and Satellite Operations, Border Control, Building and Personal Security, Counter-Drug Operations, Counter-IED Explosives Operations, Counterintelligence, Cyber Operations, Disaster Preparedness, Facilities, Ground Force Operations, Human Intelligence, Intelligence Analysis, Law Enforcement, Management and Administration, Naval Operations, Nuclear Operations, Psychological Operations, Special Operations, Staffing and Personnel, Technical Intelligence, Training, Weapons Technology.

A surveillance satellite exploits the fact that the human body emits infra-red radiation, or radiant heat. According to William E. Burrows, author of Deep Black, "the infrared imagery would pass through the scanner and register on the charged-couple device array to form a moving infrared picture. This picture would then be amplified, digitalized, encrypted and transmitted up to one of the satellite data system space craft for downlink to earth."

With the advent of programs such as Analysis, Dissemination, Visualization, Insight, and Semantic Enhancement (ADVISE) in research and development within the Department of Homeland Security, and Threat and the Vulnerability Testing and Assessment (TVTA) portfolio, the ADVISE, technologies coexist with high-speed surveillance computers with biometrics software, and laws such as the Communications Assistance for Law Enforcement Act, many governments today now possess an unprecedented ability to monitor the activities of their subjects.

The Defense Advanced Research Projects Area (DARPA) of the United States, mentioned as first named ARPA, is responsible for the development of new technology for use by the government and the military. DARPA is heavily involved in satellite surveillance technology as an arm of the Pentagon. DARPA set up the Total Information Awareness Program in 2002 which promised to provide "total information awareness" through "large, distributed repositories" including "biometric signatures of humans" and "human network analysis and behavior modeling" now used in "The Program."

Biometric satellite surveillance or signatures (vital statistics) of humans refers to technologies that measure and analyze human physical and / or other behavioral characteristics for authentication, identification, and screening purposes. Examples of mostly behavioral or physical characteristics also include gait or voice.

When comments were made during any of my conversations with others from the ceiling, to my trained ear, I could hear them. I watched as people not having a clue of the full capability of these technologies, or their existence in unethical hands, then make abrupt changes in their feelings or opinion of me and for no apparent reason and negatively.

Today many of these types of tactics can be verified, not only by my firsthand experiences and observations, but also by the firsthand personal experiences and observations documented by many, many other intelligent Targeted Individuals. There are numerous websites such as: targeteindividualscanada.com, mindjustice.org, raven1.net, peacepink.ning.com, and peoplezapper.com, to name only a few of literally thousands raising their voices in the unified effort of exposure. There are also volumes of documented information in newspaper articles, magazines, videos, to include scientific studies and testing of technology over the years.

In early 2006, when the targeting escalated to the next level for me, my oldest girl was around me and probably placed under surveillance also. After I moved to Arizona, in March, she phoned me one day extremely frightened from Los Angeles. I had been in Scottsdale, Arizona, about six months at that time. While watching television, a strange message appeared on the television saying, "We are watching you and can see you," at the top of her television screen. On another occasion, a similar message appeared but this time the television was off though still plugged in. She told me it frightened her to the point that she ran out of her apartment scared to death. When researching later, I found the patent below that is one of many technologies capable of doing this from operation center mind games:

US Patent # 5,270,800 (December 14, 1993) Subliminal Message Generator, Sweet. Robert L. Abstract

A combined subliminal and supraliminal message generator for use with a television receiver permits complete control of subliminal messages and their manner of presentation. A video synchronization detector enables a video display generator to generate a video message signal corresponding to a received alphanumeric text message in synchronism with a received television signal...

Even more important, during that time, someone tried to enter her apartment while she slept just before daybreak one morning. The person or persons were actually able to unlock one of the locks to her front door but were unable to unlock the deadbolt which woke her up as they tried. I immediately had her locks changed. Those in the operation center had repeatedly threatened sexual assaults of both me and her. In fact, another author on this same topic, satellite terrorism, documents that he became proactive after a family friend, targeted, was repeatedly drugged and sexually assaulted by men tracking and monitoring her then entering her home.

After returning home from Arizona in June of 2007, while using her computer, I noticed she had been doing extensive research also on websites defining schizophrenia or hearing voices. I did not say anything to her about my observation nor asked her why. I noticed her search finally zeroed in on a singer named Nina Simone. Nina Simone, who birth name was Eunice Kathleen Waymon. She was an African American singer, pianist, arranger, songwriter, and a civil rights activist associated with jazz music that was later diagnosed with Schizophrenia. One of the primary goals of this program as far back as the 60's was testing on activist and efforts at discrediting people as mentally has always played a role in this regard.

Nina Simone was born in 1933 and died in France in 2003. Her music was highly influential in the Civil Rights Movement in the United States. My daughter is a budding artist. Later during a general conversation, I told her that one of the first signs of an effective technological telepathic voice transmission to someone after entered into "The Program" is the target's name being called out as a test. She told me that she had heard someone calling out her name several times with no one around her. I will never forget the look of great relief on her face for this information which helped her connect the dots of her sanity.

The technology can be used for good or ill and based on my experiences it holds far too much power for human being with imperfections, weaknesses and megalomania deviances.

In fact, I had been staying with the middle daughter, right before the shelter incident. I slept under protective covering I purchased and of which I had taken to carrying with me wherever I went. Early one morning I was woken by loud scratching noises coming directly from the wall next to her head and the ceiling above her as she slept soundly. Realizing what might possibly be happening to her from similar experiences throughout the night, with me, with operation center personnel implanting some type of requests echoing in my head upon waking, I got up and took the covering off me and draped it where the scratching noise was coming from around her head. The noise immediately stopped.

When she woke, after the both of us going to bed in joyous laugher and her saying how happy she was that I was there with her temporarily; to my great surprise an argument erupted between us minutes later. I was shocked. The argument was so heated that I was forced to move immediately. This is how I ended up homeless at the West Los Angeles, California, Veteran's facility.

The website below is a good source of information and has an extensive, credible, and well documented timeline of official testing programs within the United States entitled Unwitting Victims Targeted Individuals = TI Support site:

LINK:
http://www.unwittingvictim.com/TimeLine2.html

Today testing continues and it has flourished. Post 9/11, intelligence operations, analysts and data imagery, was outsourced and today also involves a large number of contractors and private corporations as well who are playing various roles.

The two-year journalist investigative report by Top Secret America, mentioned earlier, from the Washington Post resulted in substantial information verifying contractor involvement as a fact saying:

Before September 11 about 3000 state and local government organization were involve in counterterrorism. After the attacks, intelligence reports indicated threats were everywhere. Local police stepped up to help. Emergency Management agencies set up to respond to natural disasters were ordered to be prepared for chemical, biological and nuclear attacks. Many new Homeland Security offices opened. For most of the country's history these were located on borders now they have expanded into middle class America. To coordinate all this, the FBI set up Joint Terrorism Task Forces across the country.

Local and state police, the CIA and a dozen military departments participated. Then States created fusion centers to analyze the increasing flood of information. The Department of Homeland Security gave states billions of dollars. By 2010 there were hundreds more government organization working on counterterrorism at the state and local level. Federal agencies grew by a third. 41 new federal offices were opened in Texas alone where official worried about threats from al Qaeda and drug cartels. State run organizations doubled. City and country organizations flourished with federal grant money. Nearly 10 years after 9/11, about 4000 government agencies worked on counterterrorism. Many of them helped to collect and store and analyze information on thousands of U.S. Citizens and residents.

The website begins to unravel the huge maze and connects the dots of numerous agencies: government; military; civilian; federal; state; and local law enforcement working out of fusion centers. These centers operate often at undisclosed locations listing only post office boxes as physical addresses at times.

As of July 2009, approximately 72 fusion centers exist nationwide. However today it is reported well over 100. These entities work under the auspices of local law enforcement, often integrating with the state's police force, Department of Justice, or Office of Emergency Management.

In April 2008, the Wall Street Journal and the Los Angeles Times both reported on a new Los Angeles Police Department (LAPD) directive which compels LAPD officers to begin reporting "suspicious behavior." "LAPD Special Order #11 dated March 5, 2008, states that it is the policy of the LAPD to 'gather, record, and analyze information of a criminal or non-criminal nature, that could indicate activity or intentions related to either foreign or domestic terrorism,' and includes a list of 65 behaviors LAPD officers 'shall' report."

Some of the suspicious behaviors include taking notes, drawing diagrams and using binoculars. This means that normal, day to day activities, deemed suspicious by police, are now open to scrutiny, and misconception far too easily. Suspicion can then be used as a foundation for satellite surveillance of a person or persons without a warrant or valid or confirmed justification. Officers in addition to their other duties today are creating a stream of intelligence data about a host of everyday activities involving patriotic Americans. According to the newspaper article, this information is then fed to local fusion centers across the country part of the dense intelligence maze.

The Los Angeles Police Department's (LAPD) Counter-Terrorism and Special Operations Bureau (CTSOB) or Intelligence Division is responsible for planning, response and intelligence and also fits the definition of a technologically advanced center and is an example of nationwide local police department capabilities today. The LAPDs Real Time Response and Critical Command Division (RACR) is the department's state-of-the-art satellite surveillance division.

NSM Surveillance is one of private company located in Spring Valley, California, not far from the San Diego Airport that provides state of the art surveillance solutions to law enforcement, federal agencies and also military communities. NSM's solutions incorporate both owned IP and third-party technology, including secure communications (microwave, satellite), mobile surveillance systems, command and control software and covert camera systems. Their clients include FEMA, Department of Defense, Department of Justice, Baltimore Police Department and the Los Angeles Police Department and the Super Bowl.

(**Source:** online PDF - SSG Solutions Centers Brochure 8 – NSM Surveillance - Quick View).

I could not deny the role of the Los Angeles Police Department or the role of a fused (Fusion Center) effort around me which snowballed as a challenge to take me down in my defiance. It seems that once these programs get their hooks into a target it is for life and they don't leave in lieu of any validity unless the target is totally neutralized by even death. This again is due to the nature of these types of targeting which again are designed to test technology and Psy Ops effectiveness part the main goal. Why should they leave? They can sit comfortably at a computer terminal victimizing and abusing many by employment. And it appears that moral consciousness does not direct them humanely in the group dynamic of these operation centers.

The Associated Press reported that new Attorney General Guidelines for the Federal Bureau of Investigation (FBI) authorized opening investigations without evidence of wrongdoing around 2008. Did this mean that investigations could be opened based on suspicious or terrorist profiles using race, religion, or ethnicity as risk factors or more commonly racial profiling? It appears so.

With little effort, and as a result of Top-Secret America, I was able to trace four civilian contractors specifically involved in intelligence analysis in Los Angeles, California. Northrup Grumman kept popping up as one of the key players as well as Lockheed Martin.

In fact, operational control of the primary cyber-security contracts to the federal government involves numerous defense contractors such as Lockheed Martin Information Systems and Global Solutions. Lockheed's mission and combat support solutions Central Command is located in Norristown, Montgomery County, Pennsylvania. The system is called the Lockheed Martin Government Electronic System (GES) United States Airspace Management – Radar and Satellite Surveillance Automation.

Many corporations doing Top Secret work in the civilian sector are working hand in hand with our government. The Veterans Administration (VA) has or had a contract with the Harris Corporation which has the capability to provide satellite communications services also. It is unclear on the Harris Corporation website if they are actually providing this specific service to the Department of Veterans Affairs or publicized.

What was happening to me is legal by laws approving testing on American citizens in one sense, and illegal, unethical, immoral, and inhumane in another sense due to physical torture, destroying my body, and attempted radio frequency brainwashing. Could the Department of Veterans Affairs all along been playing a significant role in the unethical treatment of me although they vehemently denied their involvement on the two occasions? I know of a few other Vets pointing the finger at the VA. I went in to talk to them personally. Seeking answers, I had also gone to police stations and other agencies in my search for the truth and even to the FBI headquarters personally and alone. The first time to the VA was in 2008 and again while living on the West Los Angeles, California VA facility at the end of 2010, as I mentioned now homeless. Admittedly, logically, no one is going to tell you they are investigating you especially if as a test subject and by a psychophysical technology.

One thing was absolutely clear while I sat talking with the Special Agent, in the OIG, detailing my experiences, and this hopeful book is that if he could have escorted me directly over to Building 500, the large hospital on the facility and personally had me committed at that very moment he would have undoubtedly done so and brazenly hinted at doing just that. It was not until I heard a faint voice, a man's voice, which he heard also, emanate from the ceiling just over our heads say "This girl is no joke" did his playful, arrogant, sarcastic, demeanor quickly change and his expression immediately become serious as if looking at me with new eyes. I was not a threat or danger to myself or others and nothing I said was threatening, however when I left the factually they did try to contact VA hospital personnel attempting to have me picked up from the shelter on the facility. The only threat I became was by exposing the technological effort destroying lives and their trying to silence me. I had nothing to hide and was on a mission to find out just who this motivating force was.

In 1928 in Los Angeles, California, single mother Christine Collins in a movie played by Angelina Jolie returns home to discover her nine-year old son Walter is missing. Her plight is publicized, and the Los Angeles Police Department is deemed incompetent, corrupted by the Chief. Several months after Walter's disappearance, the LAPD tells Christine that her son has been found alive. Believing the positive publicity will change recent criticism of the department, as incompetent, the LAPD organizes a public reunion. Although "Walter" claims he is Christine's son, she says he is not. Captain J. J. Jones, the head of the LAPD's Juvenile Division, insists the boy is Walter and pressures Christine into taking him home "on a trial basis." Christine persists saying it is not her son. Later, armed with proof from others, a school teacher, etc., she tells her story to the press. As a result, Jones sends her to Los Angeles County Hospital's "psychopathic ward." She befriends inmate Carol Dexter who tells Christine she is one of several women who were sent there for challenging police authority in the movie. Dr. Steele deems Christine delusional and forces her to take mood-regulating pills. Steele then says he will release Christine if she admits she was mistaken about "Walter;" she refuses.

As told by this true story, these tactics by law enforcement are nothing new and definitely not unheard of historically to discredit anyone exposing corruption and efforts to discredit and commit the whistleblower to a mental institution.

Eldon Byrd was a military scientist who worked for the Naval Surface Weapons, Office of Non-Lethal Weapons. From 1980 to 1983 Byrd ran the Marine Corps Non-Lethal Electromagnetic Weapons project. He conducted most of his research at the Armed Forces Radiobiology Research Institute in Bethesda, Maryland. "We were looking at electrical activity in the brain and how to influence it," he once confirmed.

He was commissioned in 1981 to develop electromagnetic devices for various purposes including "riot control" clandestine operations and hostage removal resulting in extremely low frequency (ELF) weaponry. The result is the Active Denial System (ADS) and various versions of it in many sizes.

In the context of controversy over reproductive hazards to "Video Display Terminal operators," and ELF, Byrd wrote of alterations in the brain function of animals exposed to low intensity fields such as emitted by energy weapons. He noted that the offspring of exposed animals "exhibited a drastic degradation of intelligence later in life and couldn't learn easy tasks indicating a very definite and irreversible damage to the central nervous system of the fetus." Using the Video Display Terminal, as an example, and operators exposed to weak fields, there have been clusters of miscarriages and birth defects with evidence of central nervous system damage to the fetus. Byrd also wrote of experiments where the behavior of animals was controlled by exposure to weak electromagnetic fields.

At a certain frequency and power intensity, they could make the animal purr, lie down and roll over. When Eldon Byrd died of cancer, some suggested it was under suspicious circumstances. Realizing the nature of his electromagnetic frequency (EMF) weaponry research before his death Byrd became somewhat of an advocate for mind control victims, trying to help them measure the signals they are harassed with. Having worked with such technologies he knew claims could be legitimate and he validated that such claims were seriously worth investigating. It was Eldon Byrd who initially funded Dr. Adey's LIDA machine testing for its therapeutic effects.

The Radar Flashlight (see image section), military grade, see-through-walls technology is a portable seven-pound, battery powered device that is intended to cost law enforcement agencies less than $1500 per unit. It is a relatively low-powered device that can be stored in the trunk of a police vehicle for use on an as needed basis.

The Silent Guardian by Raytheon is a portable, heavy duty microwave pain beam available for use by law enforcement today and also appears to be the portable device provided to neighboring stalking operations.

Keep in mind that the capability of millimeter wave x-ray technology is a critical component in campaigns of through-the-wall torture and harassment also.

This relatively new surveillance technology, for law enforcement, has been available for the past 10 years. This technology has the following specific capabilities:

- The ability to see through walls, and most common construction materials. The ability to generate detailed, through-the-clothing images of individuals in the room or homes under surveillance.
- The units can be operated remotely from a nearby home or apartment.
- The units can track movement, and monitor speech, heartbeat, pulse, and other bodily functions remotely.
- The units can provide precise distance measurements for targeting individuals under surveillance with weapons.
- The units are portable, silent, and can be disguised or hidden in a typical residential home or apartment.

A remotely targeted infrasound weapons showers victims with silent, focused sound waves in their homes. When exposure to infrasound is prolonged, it can become a slow kill murder weapon. Indeed, an untraceable murder weapon, as it leaves no evidence of its use on the victim. Infrasound becomes particularly deadly if it is used during the victim's early morning sleep hours. Why? This is the period of time when the body normally produces the lowest levels of Cortisol. Artificially stimulating Cortisol production during this time disrupts the body's' normal Cortisol production in the worst possible way. In effect, the sleeping body perceives infrasound as a threat and elevates Cortisol production to cope. Since the victim is asleep, the Cortisol is not used, and remains in the body, damaging life-essential body functions. If a weapon producing silent infrasound is targeted at a victim for months, or even years, how long will it take for it to cause the victims' death through deadly health complications?

This appears to be a key question currently being researched regarding testing of the through-the-wall infrasound weapons involuntarily on individuals.

Acoustic weapons see through-the-wall surveillance technology, migrated from military applications to civilian law enforcement by intent.

The Synetics Corporation was awarded Department of Defense contract #DAAE30-99-C-1003 on November 18, 1998 to develop the Difference Acoustic Wave Generation System. This weapon generates a tightly focused sound or ultrasound beam that may be remotely directed towards the target. They are described as sonic bullets, sonic grenades, sonic mines or sonic cannons. With sufficient energy, the resulting infrasonic waves of very low frequency sound can be disabling or lethal. They can kill under certain conditions. Extremely high-power sound waves can destroy the eardrums and cause severe pain and disorientation thereby incapacitating a person. Less powerful sound waves can cause humans to experience discomfort and nausea. According to the contract, they are geared "...for police and personal use." These units are also designed specifically to be portable. Later, I would be targeted on a nightly basis via infrasound through drones over my home.

During the Republican National Convention (RNC) held in New York in 2004, there were numerous news reports on the presence of the Long-Range Acoustical Device or LRAD. This unit, purchased by the New York Police Department, was part of the crowd control arsenal during the convention. ABC News, in their article "RNC to Feature Unusual Forms of Sound" made the following statement regarding the capabilities of LRAD:

"When in weapon mode, LRAD blasts a tightly controlled stream of caustic sound that can be turned up to high enough levels to trigger nausea or possibly fainting. Unlike microwave technology, the operators themselves remain unaffected since the noise is contained in its focused beam." In commenting on how the weapon is operated, it further stated,

"The sound beam is even equipped with a viewfinder so the operator can precisely target the audio by finding a person in cross hairs."

The weapon is tunable so that it can deliver audio messages or painful acoustic beams. And, that acoustic beam will only be heard or felt by the person it targets alias in the same style as other technological subliminal voice transmission technology. A similar acoustic device is named the Low Dispersion Acoustic Projector or LDAP.

The smaller versions were designed to target, a single individual remotely, with a focused acoustic beam through the walls. The designer's intent was to make these weapons light and portable to be carried by one man. Law enforcement was among the intended users of this weaponry officially. Today portable acoustic weapons are easily controlled by a user and done effectively entirely from a Panasonic "Tough Book" laptop computer. The Panasonic Tough Book laptop system includes all of the necessary system control software for the different levels of intensity of pain dissemination from adjoining apartments or from vehicles parked into front of the target's home.

These smaller versions also act as portable real time viewing and a live video display with a joystick to direct the acoustic beams.

(Excerpt Gang Stalking and Directed Energy Weapons Torture, by badexperiment, August 8, 2009)

The Community Policing Prevention Program Initiative was largely a development of protocol with a strong component of community organization and mobilization founded on principles of community-oriented policing. Today numerous programs are funded also under Neighborhood Watch. A list of Congressional authorized purpose areas for the Byrne formula grant funding program, for these endeavors presently includes 29 enumerated specific purpose areas. In recent years, Congress amended the list to include such areas as homeland security projects and the Neighborhood "Watch-like" projects.

What is not publicized is the resulting covert technology being provided to these groups of communities and civilians and their training and sworn to secrecy. As a result, of using neighbors, law enforcement takes harassment to a whole new personal level. These groups can get away with things that law enforcement could not and are thereby allowed to operate freely from any legal ramifications due to this backing. Law enforcement is not going to arrest or stop those they motivate and can easily look the other way in combined technological stalking campaigns

Even while visiting family in Northern California and staying in a motel one night alone, one of my daughters visiting my ex-husband's family in the area, the room next door to me was immediately rented by those connected to these efficient networks across America which coexists with the inescapable satellite tracking and at times of off duty officers or other operatives. In the nearly vacant motel, on a weeknight, two men showed up specifically requesting the empty room next door to mine on the top floor. I was in the building corner room with only one connecting wall. Their request specifically of the room next to mine was confirmed by the management office when I inquired who had rented the room after hearing the door slam shut loudly for my benefit announcing "We're here" and the subsequent noise of the focusing of the see-through-the-wall technology and microwave energy now deployed into the room and under full attack. I got up immediately and went out to purchase aluminum foil as the light humming noise of the microwave technology began.

Gauging a person's emotions is a vital part and plays a major role in The Program's technological effort. It can be accomplished using patented technology such as the patent below:

United States Patent # 6,292,688 - September 18, 2001 - Method and Apparatus for Analyzing Neurological Response to Emotion Inducing Stimuli.

Future inventions such as facial thermographs are currently in development for law enforcement. This will allow machines to identify certain emotions in people such as fear or stress, by measuring the temperature generated by blood flow to different parts of their face if stopped by police for example. The problem here is that technology, being technology is wrought with inconsistencies and assessments. Technology cannot determine human feelings and is subject to calculations and guided by the beliefs, or prejudices, of those applying it and their agenda which is not always honorable. Law enforcement officers believe that thermographs have potential for them to identify when a suspect is nervous which might indicate that they are hiding something, lying, or worried about something. However, these emotional reactions are not limited to these factors alone. This is where the problem surfaces through inaccuracy and wrongful victimization can occur.

When the dust settled over my situation two operation centers, the Joint Regional Intelligence Center (JRIC) a fusion center in, Norwalk, California in Los Angeles County and the Los Angeles Police Department's Counter-Terrorism and Special Operations Bureau (CTSOB) or Intelligence Division along with the LAPDs Real Time Response and Critical Command Division (RACR) satellite surveillance division as likely locations stood among the tallest trees in my mind's eye. However, the military would later play a vital and major role also. All of these locations are definitely state of the art operation centers. Could one of these locations also be the location of the infamous law enforcement "War Room" documented later as likely housing the brilliant influence technology being used today along with the deployment capability of the debilitating painful electronic weaponry invading my life?

The JRIC in Norwalk is one of the numerous major urban area fusion centers nationwide that together with the FBI, Joint Terrorism Task Force, are at the heart of the information intelligence sharing initiative as stated on the website:

The high degree of intelligence information sharing and agencies working in close proximity to each other involve not only federal, state, and local but also fire and public safety organizations like the United States Coast Guard, the Transportation Security Administration, the Department of Homeland Security – Office of Intelligence and Analysis, to include the Sheriff's Department.

The question of the hour, after learning of the reasons that this type of surveillance could be bogusly approved on an American citizen was, had someone intentionally used a false, trumped up charge of drug trafficking for the high-tech surveillance around me? It began to appear so. If so, in my case this was an utterly false and ridiculous allegation typical of the relentless effort surrounding me. And for it to linger, by 2012 with me sober nearing five years was even more outrageous with the appearance of using me 100% as test subject. If my personal targeting succeeded in scaring up a legal case, it would be all the better for the effort's justification of existence. I had never in my life been a person who consumed or purchased large amounts of drugs, nor would they ever find anyone to say that I had.

What a wonderful concept, I thought to myself as I looked over the JRIC website absorbing everything detail. What a wonderful concept in a perfect world, I thought. However, in the imperfect, electronically harassed, attempted mind manipulation advanced technology, satellite tracked world of degradation and insults, I lived, the reality of the unmonitored, blatant abuse of my rights stood illuminated as horribly wrong. The overall devaluing of and dehumanizing of my God-given life spoke volumes of those privy to this technology. And, they were, undoubtedly, one hundred percent interrogating me, and making suggestions while I slept at night, using the vulnerability to manipulate me. At times my waking during the process to use the restroom was immediately followed up by being calls names and their hoping to convince me that I had admitted the truth a lie in a deep near comatose state.

Thanksgiving morning, 2009, I woke in excruciating pain in the lung area in the right side of my back. I could not even move an inch due to the intensity. That morning when I opened my eyes and laid in bed relaxed, I heard the man asking the woman, "Does she say where it hurts yet? The women then replied no. When I attempted to rolled over to go to the restroom a sharp penetrating pain radiated through my body and I was then paralyzed in horrific pain. In disbelief, I tried several times to hoist myself out of bed unsuccessfully. I finally was able to roll off the bed onto the floor and reached for my cellular phone dialing 911 then crawl to the toilet and hoist myself up before crawling back to the room and waited for the ambulance.

When the ambulance arrived, I had managed to then crawl to the door and unlock it for the paramedics but was unable to stand up. At the hospital, I was diagnosed with pneumonia that erupted out of the blue with no symptoms beforehand whatsoever. Admittedly, this is another type of incident that is very, very difficult to prove as what I believe as microwave symptoms mimicking something else, believe it or not. I remain convinced of the likelihood of a radar laser attack to my back throughout the night as I slept which may have been the culprit based on the conversation I distinctly heard from the two in the operation center.

As the nightly attacks both physical and psychological continued, I finally understood yet another reason why they found it necessary to watch me sleeping. I was grateful to the superior court judge who in 2006 surprisingly responded to one of my first letters which helped me to confirm the possibility of advanced procedures and gave me an understanding of what was possibly happening to me, and around me, after an extremely rough adjustment to the reality of the slightest possibility admittedly even for myself. Knowing what was available after my research ultimately helped me recognize various subliminal ploys and also became a coping mechanism for me through awareness.

Inevitably, and undoubtedly, these technological abuses will continue to permeate the very fabric of our Constitution, Civil and Human Rights if left unaddressed and not exposes. They are quietly doing just that today. My rights were stripped away as if I did not matter at all. I should have been afforded the opportunity to address any allegations against me and not be subjected to attempts to coerce through physical tortured by those ruthlessly literally operating under the radar.

I am also within what was once a First Amendment right to tell this story which they tried to prevent up the last letter. In the Congressional Service Report, Satellite Surveillance: Domestic Issues, documented earlier, dated February 1, 2010, the authors summarize, for Congress the satellite surveillance issue within the United States specifically regarding satellite surveillance into the privacy of a person's private residence:

If a particular type of satellite surveillance is deemed to be a search within the meaning of the Fourth Amendment, it is permissible only if its conduct is reasonable. The "reasonableness" of a search is through a balancing test that weighs the degree to which the search intrudes upon an individual's legitimate expectation of privacy and the degree to which it is necessary for the promotion of legitimate government interests.

After nearing eight years, they had searched everywhere, to include private parts of my body including my breast, and between my legs. They had found and gained nothing worthwhile yet lingered.

It is absolutely outrageous to have those working in these programs intentionally watching and violating a person inside their home and saying, "Ugh," when the person pulls down their underwear attempting to humiliate them when using the toilet or reporting if they are clean while a woman is on her period for example. Fortunately for me I am a very clean woman in all facets of my life. I can only imagine how some must suffer if they do not meet the standards of those watching as they seek anything to break a person down.

The continuous tracking of an individual crosses many boundaries along with GPS devices attached to a person's vehicle. The report below further states:

***

Surreptitious GPS data collection by law enforcement, without judicial oversight, imperils fundamental associational rights that have long been recognized, in particular privacy in one's associations. An individual's locational data can be easily used to create databanks of networks among people and institutions, associations that are personal, private, and should be beyond the reach of the government absent good cause. To be clear, the devices are useful for tracking a vehicle or person in real-time, but the data also can be permanently stored and subjected to pattern analysis.

The data can reveal not just a person's whereabouts, but also habits such as where he shops, banks, worships, and seeks treatment. If a police officer has decided to follow an individual's every move by secretly installing one of these devices in a vehicle, that individual may never know about it. If what the government discovers about the individual and his comings and goings, twenty-four hours a day, does not lead to the inception of a criminal proceeding (or he does not have the ability to look at the undercarriage of a vehicle and ascertain whether or not such a device has been implanted), he may never discover the fact that the government has collected this sort of data about him. Moreover, since law enforcement is not presently required to seek court approval before installing such a device on a vehicle, it is impossible to know the pervasiveness of this practice. Therefore, it is all the more important that the law make every effort to keep up with technology in order to safeguard the constitutionally protected rights of the people...

Because of the undetectable unseen characteristics of covert advanced technological targeting these operations obviously feel in most cases they will ultimately win by even the capability to drive a person, mad, and either to suicide, push them over the edge, to going postal, or use a technological energy weapon slow kill by organ damage.

In these programs, these attacks can, as stated can continue for years by the same individuals employed by The Program. If a person fight's, resentment can also foster a desire by capability to torment a person mercilessly. Today, make no mistake about it, there are destructive manipulative groups using mind control technology.

However, I and many other activists, stand illuminated in and by the light of god, called to a moral purpose, I believed wholeheartedly, and will not be stopped or silenced!

CHAPTER FOUR

"If God sends us on strong paths, we are provided strong shoes."

— **Corrie Ten Boom**

I hurriedly showered and dressed one morning under the normal watchful eye of the satellite heading to the local library not far from the hotel where I now lived in Phoenix, Arizona. My lease expired in Glendale in July of 2010 and I moved into the hotel my life in limbo. By 2010, I had become somewhat knowledgeable, though far from expert on remote neural monitoring. For me this meant acceptance of the eagle eye of a satellite with my name on it. The surveillance meant every aspect of my life was an open book even when seeking legal assistance about what I was enduring, to include viewing during medical appointments.

For example, those targeting me made sure their presence was known during an appointment to my gynecologist one day in Arizona hoping to personally humiliate me from the operation center viewing. As I talked with the OB/GYN doctor then prepared for a pap smear the men and what later sounded like a woman watched and listened in real time. As I positioned myself lying on my back my feet in the stirrups, the bottom portion of my body nude but covered by a sheet. I then heard "Dang, I would hate to be down there." This was said by one of the two women who were around me at that time in Arizona. I then heard laughter erupt from her male counterparts sitting obviously near her watching the scene. She apparently had made a funny. She probably felt good about it and maybe she even felt more like one of the boys as a result.

As I prepared to leave that morning, a man moaned sensually as he watched me fix my bra into place, and I was briefly disgusted. I felt my blood pressure rise, however using positive self-talk, I was able to regain composure. What real choice did I have but to live with the unwanted attention directed at me by sexual comments and overtures in the invasion of my life and self?

It was shocking in the early stages of the targeting when I first I began to literally hear someone speaking inside my head. At first, I thought that there must be was a tiny microphone planted somewhere around me or even inside my car. But as I went from place to place outside of my residence and vehicle, I could still hear comments being made that sounded like thoughts originating inside my head but in a man's voice or a woman's voice or at times as the two exchanged comments about me amongst themselves. As I drove around listening to music in my car, while running errands or appointments, something was undoubtedly surreal.

Whenever my ears felt as if I were descending from or ascending into high altitude such as in an airplane, I began to recognize that they were zeroing in on my head by satellite radar, because at that point, I would hear them literally commenting on what I was thinking or where I was going at that moment. I also began waking confused about documented events in my past first in late 2009. However, I would regain clarity quickly as the brain fog lifted.

I tried to recall where I had stumbled upon information specifically detailing the subliminal interrogative capability of the mind manipulation technology. I remembered that while researching, I learned that this type of technology, when used positively, can actually reprogram the psyche by positive affirmations, similar to reprogramming by hypnotic suggestions. It can be used for positive subliminal reinforcement in many areas such as assisting in stopping smoking by suggestions using subliminal influences, overeating, and even self-esteem building for example. Some very impressive, successful results are today being achieved with the Inner Talk® technology commercially. Inner Talk® actually re-programs the subconscious mind which in turn dictates our realities.

In a report to Congress, it mentions that due to the techniques involved in extracting questionable information by the "black bag" mind control technologies and more importantly the powerful influence capabilities of these technologies that those highly placed in the intelligence community shy away from willingly reporting these methods publicly. This impairs the discovery process in court proceedings because they don't want what they are doing known.

For example, if patents such as, Methods and Systems for Altering Consciousness are described by patent below are used to alter the target' reality:

U.S. Patent, #5,123,899. June 23, 1992

Description: A system for stimulating the brain to exhibit specific brain wave rhythms and thereby altering the subjects' state of consciousness.

U.S. Patent, #5,289,438. February 22, 1994

Description: A system for the simultaneous application of multiple stimuli (usually aural) with different frequencies and waveforms. Electro Magnetic Field (EMF) monitoring / interference is one of the most insidious and secretive of all methods used by the agencies. Similarly, EEG cloning feeds back the results of EMF monitoring in an attempt to induce emotional responses (e.g. fear, anger, even sleep, etc.)

There are numerous documented cases where during actual face to face interrogations with a person in the physical presence and custody of law enforcement that a person is badgered and manipulated into the results sought through the purposeful expert confusion and verbal bullying, and repetitive assault of the interrogation process. Even more upsetting is learning afterwards, that law enforcement had been gravely wrong, destroyed an innocent life for years with no apology forthcoming for the man or woman who spent years in prison wrongly.

True also is the realization that the science of biometrics relies primarily, not on human science, but on putting faith and trust in computers in many cases to correctly identify individual components. It does not take into account that computers are machines that cannot make emotionless judgments. Reliance on computers can and has cause wrong diagnosis and led to innocent individuals being profiled and placed under surveillance. The decisions to not allow information on methods to be exposed thus tilts the scale of justice for all concerned. In other words, there is conflict of interests due a desire to avoid scrutiny of unscrupulous practices. There is also the debate centering on the technology as a preventative tool versus it being used to gain information through influencing the target.

Gradually, almost in steps of a standard operating procedure it became apparent that they were seeding thoughts to support their goal with me hoping it would stick subconsciously. They tried everything in the book. They classified me as a person holding racial prejudices. When I thought about the racial prejudices, I was also amused and wondered how they would attempt to explain the fact that I routinely attended a church which was ninety percent non-African American in Scottsdale, Arizona, and fifty percent non-African American in Los Angeles, California.

So heinous and destructive are these programs that whenever I was out shopping and a child came into my environment they would immediately begin to maliciously taunt me saying that I was interested in the child sexually and then say this interest originated from me. No, it didn't. I have never had any sexual deviancies surrounding children or anyone else. What they were doing was playing on random thoughts running across a human mind as the mind acts as filter. They were playing on a specific thought which crossed my mind one day when I remembered playing house as a kid with another little boy at about seven years old. This materialized into me being a pedophile and resulting ongoing ridiculous taunting in this ever- present agenda to insult and torment me. The same thing happened when they observed me watching other women innocently in the 24-hour surveillance. I would be later taunted as being gay. News flash women size other women up all the time. It's a girl thing. But with technology in hand those working in these typical groups, look for anything they can stretch into being abnormal and into something filthy used to exploit and attack a target psychologically. Again, this is part of the Psy Op's manual of an emotional attempt to breakdown the TI.

I was grateful that morning as I approached the library steps. I thanked God for their ongoing failures with me. They were unsuccessful in planting thoughts in me that were out of character for me and untrue because it is not who I am. They were unsuccessful due to certain beliefs not being a part of who I ever have been or would be. As a result of this, I could not be programmed to create my own demise as they hoped. What if they could have nudged me into pedophilia?

I began to easily recognize any deviant thought, contrary to my normal feelings and beliefs with awareness. I trained myself to recognize the source, and remember the motives of the source. If they could prove I was a racist, then they could prove that I was anti-government, anti-American, and felt that I, as an African American, felt I was owed something from slavery. I had even been accused of this one day. If they could prove me materialistic, that would be for obvious reasons. If they could prove me a sexual deviant, then they could probably say that I was promiscuous, incestuous, and that I was faking my distaste for the constant sexual harassment and sexual exploitation by them and the incident in the military. However, proving I was crazy seemed to be what they felt would benefit the effort the most as stated previously. Slowly they began to recognize that this book could be a worthy adversary to their agenda in manifesting a large degree of credibility for me as evidence of my ability to formulate clear thoughts and a clear-thinking process revealed in my writing.

It had been the unwanted personal attention from the males tracking me, which laid the foundation for this book, and anger in the very beginning.

Each time a thought did not sit well with my soul, I would immediately self-correct. I would do this using prayer and affirmations. I also was alert to thoughts that were not initiated by me consciously as best I could be. If a person is unaware of Direct to speech, this can be very challenging. If something out of the ordinary or grotesque popped into my head while picking fruit at the supermarket, I suspected that it was a subliminal effort; though again, the extreme subsequent pressure feeling materializing subsequently around my head was also a clue at a given moment by the beam. What they were doing could and was being done to me between two states, California and Arizona effortlessly. There are thousands various types of crafts orbiting our planet today and one tracking me with my name on it. It takes just three satellites to blanket the entire Earth with detection capability.

There was also a definite physical reaction of increased physical anxiety as a sign in my body and alert to my mind when they arrived by radar laser focus. During these times, I could only imagine what they must have been trying to spoon feed me using the inaudible Voice to Skull. Fortunately, the physical and psychological reaction of anxiety and agitation, and the alerting high- altitude feeling were immediate giveaways as my mind rejected whatever they were saying subliminally. When I felt my body react physically, this was a clue for me to stop whatever I was doing and focus.

I had to learn to be ever mindful at all times as best I could. This was literally for my sanity's sake. Whenever I felt the aberrant sensations of random anxiety even while driving around, I immediately pulled off the road, turn off the music and just listen to what popped into my mind. I then would breathe deeply to relax myself from the technological panic that also erupted out of the blue. This would help me tremendously. Or if at home, I would turn off the television, stop what I was doing at that very moment, and just listen to my thoughts again and again for any evidence of deviance from the norm. Fortunately for me, I had known me for quite some time. As a result of me knowing me I could distinguish, immediately, between anything different from the 'me' I had known all my life.

The sexual comments were relentless that morning just prior to leaving. It was the fact that they were watching me in the bathroom that sickened me the most. However, I had to learn to tolerate, endure, and cope with this as best I could. What choice did I really have?

One night while trying to cover myself with protective material as I lay in bed watching television, in the hotel in Arizona, I could feel the sexual stimulation beginning by one of the men. I then listened, horrified, to him say to me using Synthetic Telepathy, "You know you like it." I was highly insulted. I cannot think of any normal human being who would enjoy being sexually stimulated by strange men operating remotely, who in doing so, believe that the woman actually enjoyed being abused in this manner while being called horrifically degrading names on top of it. Why would they even believe this? Could it be that because of their personal issues that they felt others were having as much fun as they were?

They had technologically moved into my life unwanted and uninvited around the clock. This covert ability obviously, seemed to blur their line of reality and ethics. I still to this day don't understand why they would enjoy doing this to someone if they are the images of integrity of which they portray themselves to be in uniform.

They were nothing more than a bunch of cowardly bullies wanting to keep these activities silent. It was apparent that some had egos that were so misguided that they, lacking self-control and discipline, would watch me studying or reading things I enjoy to better myself and then say that I was their type of woman they would date and definitely have sex with. Newsflash women want honorable men they can respect.

This reality especially troubled me in cases of women more vulnerable than me.

One would hope that a person or persons would be of strong moral fiber in these positions. But they were not appearing to be totally the opposite. Those working these programs should be held to an even higher standard of integrity and discipline than most.

One of them, it seemed, did developed an unnatural attraction and fixation on me more so than the others. He did so as a result of an apparent inability to separate himself from his genitalia. Some were angry that they had not convinced me to fear them. And, admittedly, I was doing my very best to give them Hell at every turn.

As they followed me around, if a woman they felt attractive entered my environment, I then would have to listen to them turning their attention and debate on her. And if a woman was not up to their standards, such as too much makeup for example, they surely voiced their opinion in the operation housing a unified overabundance of testosterone or pack of wolves. I felt strongly that it would not be above some them to attach themselves to some unsuspecting woman and follow her home without her knowledge and toy with her. Thoughts like this angered me. Unfortunately, if a woman had no idea what was happening she unfortunately could be very easily preyed upon. She would be first sexually stimulated, and then one of these characters would show up and direct her attention via radio frequencies at her as suddenly having interest in the operative. Some even believe themselves so clever that they were not above showing up, undercover, in my environment this way.

Due to them not seeing a man around me, I felt that they believed that I was lunch and single women are prime targets for this type of targeting it is reported. What woman in her right mind would involve herself with men who constantly mentioned a goal of sex with her or even with a member of her family, in this case one of my beautiful daughters?

I did not know these men personally, although I had seen quite a few of those involved in some manner on occasions as they tried to follow me around town or tried to sneak in and out of residences close to me. When they began to involve my daughter in the targeting, I knew that there was nothing on the entire planet that would stop me from doing everything in my power to bring this situation to the light. There had always been the question with me whether they immorally were remotely viewing her as eye candy, or as an official target, or both?

I learned that if I gave them any indication that I liked them, it could result in one literally knocking on my door for more games believing they had an edge. I learned that if I did not clarify how I really felt about them, their egos would definitely tell them that I, and probably other women, could be used. Some believe themselves unaccountable to anyone in these secret operations and it appears they aren't monitored at all. In Arizona right before I left, one of these men who leaned on me heavily with the sexual arousal technology thinking he had me brainwashed showed up, as he said he would in hopes of intimacy.

Fortunately, I had not allowed myself any vain ideation that their effort around me was anything more than conceited investigative tactics and a hope to use anyone they could. When I entered the hotel building one day, as soon as I exited the elevator, he walked out into the hall at the other end from a room and gestured to me to come and talk to him. "Yea right, partner!" This is an example of the mentality of these men. If anyone is delusional, it is unmistakably them. When the right person comes along, or when I am ready, he will materialize and he will also be able to stand through anything also and incapable of manipulation from this group. Having a relationship is impossible when targeted. I was also told "We are not going to allow anyone around you" saying basically they would sabotage any relationship. I was even told by one that he would marry me one day after listening to my thoughts of a love interest. It would be a cold day in Hell before I looked in their backyard. In close to five years I had not been in a relationship due to their tampering in my life. A young woman on my social network page being targeted wrote me one day saying that in fifteen years of interference in her life as a target, she had been prevented from establishing a close relationship and it saddened her and she was lonely.

I just can't say this enough; the inability to come officially, ethically and morally to my door was an ever-present reminder of the illegitimacy of these targeting. This technology in the hands of mere mortals has apparently created monsters. Intelligence in its own right, over physical beauty can be an aphrodisiac for some more evolved humans. However, all this group cared about was how a woman looked in real time. Arrogance seems especially true in the realm of the mentality and character of men of law and their spirit of entitlement.

My rightful fight and their inability to conquer me nudged them on and resulted in their curiosity and focus to win at all cost to my chagrin. However, after the rough start, I began to fight tooth and nail. In my view, they undoubtedly held the positions of deviant stalkers, nurtured by this powerful intrusive technology. And apparently, in my case, they were willing to stretch the covert limits trying of 'officially' harm me. The bone in my left leg suffered the most as a result. It began to slip out of the joint socket with each step when I walked from the around the clock treatments. My knees were next.

Today billions are being poured into DOD Homeland fusion centers who organize local police, and neighborhood watch groups for other programs which result in the targeting of innocent civilians called, the 'See Something – Say Something' program. This effort is placing millions of U.S. citizens into what are defined as 'unwitting target' watch lists which also includes family members. The subject then can become victims of non-consensual human testing of war weapons per Department of Defense (DOD) Directive 5240.1-R.

This DOD regulation sets forth procedures governing the activities of DOD intelligence components that affect United States persons. It implements DOD Directive 5240.1, and replaces the November 30,

1979 version of DOD Regulation 5240.1-R. It is applicable to all DOD intelligence components. Executive Order 12333, "United States intelligence activities" stipulates that certain activities of intelligence components that affect U.S. persons be governed by procedures issued by the agency head and approved by the Attorney General. Specifically, Procedures 1 through 10, as well as Appendix A, herein, requiring approval by the Attorney General, contains further guidance to DOD components in implementing Executive Order 12333 as well as Executive Order 12334, "President's Intelligence Oversight Board."

Accordingly, by this Memorandum, these procedures are approved for use within the Department of Defense. Heads of DOD components shall issue such implementing instructions as may be necessary for the conduct of authorized functions in a manner consistent with the procedures set forth herein.

This regulation is effective immediately and the Procedures as stated below:

Procedure 1	General Provisions
Procedure 2	Collection of Information about United States Persons
Procedure 3	Retention of Information about United States Persons
Procedure 4	Dissemination of Information about United States Persons
Procedure 5	Electronic Surveillance in the United States for Intelligence Purposes
Procedure 6	Concealed Monitoring
Procedure 7	Physical Searches
Procedure 8	Searches and Examination of Mail
Procedure 9	Physical Surveillance
Procedure 10	undisclosed Participation in Organizations
Procedure 11	Contracting for Goods and Services

Procedure 12	Provisions for Assistance to Law Enforcement Authorities
Procedure 13	Experimentation on Human Subjects for Intelligence Purposes
Procedure 14	Employee Conduct
Procedure 15	Identifying, Investigating, and Reporting Questionable

Appendix A
Activities

The Milgram Experiment proved delusional patriotic obedience to authority figures. It was a series of experiments conducted by Yale University psychologist Stanley Milgram. Milgram set out to measure the willingness of participants to obey authority figures who instructs them to perform acts that even conflicted with their personal conscience or beliefs. The requests could be to fulfill acts which cause others pain or even death. The results proved that people obey either out of fear or out of a desire to appear cooperative with authority.

The study proved that many people will obey and even act against their own will, better judgment, beliefs and desires. Milgram also observed the reluctance to most to even confront those who abused their power in the study. Many war criminals claimed they were merely following orders and could not be held responsible for their actions, in the trials following World War II. Were the Germans in fact evil and cold-hearted, or is this a group dynamic which could happen to anyone, given the right conditions and requests by authority?

The justice system is designed as a forum to ethically address allegations. Law enforcement is not, nor should be, a haven for those who confuse their roles secretively and who use extreme covert physical pain or malicious psychological coercion to elicit the manufactured response they want. There is absolutely no excuse or justification for this. I highly doubt if they would be able to get away with what they were doing had their efforts, actions, and tactics been monitored and open to the public view and scrutiny. And, why was there a continuous debate on my appearance anyway? I slowly began to feel that in some way this group felt that they were in a position to play God. And why should they not? I remember one day praying and one of them pretending that he was God's voice responding to my prayers.

Sadly, if anything, detailed later, I served as shallow entertainment after they locked the fiber optical eye on me around the clock. They watched my and daughters and I as a group and made comments which indicated that not one person, but several could be watching us at a given moment in the show. Regarding how a person looks, I take offense to this knowing that some of the best people on the planet are not beauty queens although someone loves them dearly anyway and believes they are. To further substantiate my belief of appearances, one of them factually told me one day saying, "The only reason you are still alive is because we think you are cute." How dare them! This is not a compliment nor do I need to be complimented by this group of freaks!

One night, after one of them continually tried to ingratiate his self with me by continuous flattery my patience ran out with his nonsense. It is not necessary to tell me I am cute all day and every day by obvious motive. I look the same each day and I am okay looking. After his continuous attempts, I made it clear that I was not available to him and definitely not interested telling him off by insults. He then appeared to become angry, and I listened as he used the technology to make extremely loud thumping noises on the ceiling of my bedroom while in Arizona by the satellite radar laser arm. I asked him, hoping he would get it, "How could you even think I would be interested in you after how you all have treated me?" I said, "My daughter is visiting soon, and I have no doubt that you people will again be right in the bathroom with her as she showers inside my home." When I told him this, he then replied, "Yep."

The characteristics of shallowness, pettiness, and maliciousness, had never been a part of my character but a fighting spirit would be later in life. Yes, I also had to take a good long look at my reactions to their constant taunting, and realized that my reactions were playing a key role in fueling the situation admittedly and buying into the strategic agitation. I had to acknowledge that my sometimes anger and responses, though rightful, did contribute to feelings of success on their part and their hope to keep me off centered. As a result, they probably felt that they were getting to me and getting somewhere. I justified my emotional outbursts, telling myself that to fight; I needed to get down into the trenches with and at their level. However, that changed as I grew and realized that my ongoing anger could and would spill over into other areas of my life and innocently to others if I were not careful. I had to do my best to not take my anger out, though I'm human, on other individuals randomly and unintentionally. In awareness, I was not going to allow them to change me from the loving person I had always been and known to be by others.

"Character cannot be developed in ease and quiet. Only through experience of trial and suffering can the soul be strengthened, ambition inspired, and success achieved."

Helen Keller

In March of 2009, while driving through Arizona, I was pulled over and learned to my great surprise learned that I had, not one, not two, but three felony DUI warrants.

On October 4, 2010, all charges, including a property damage charge of $100,000 were dropped. The situation had run its course by my court compliance for just over 18 months later. It would become obvious that those targeting me had an active role in the effort to entrap me as the effort began unfolding in my life as a take down. A fraudulent accusation had been submitted by an agency that I falsely hit an imaginary six-foot brick wall during the car accident in 2007 thus resulting in the $100,000 damage of property allegation. In reality, it was documented that this was not true at all. I was going 30 miles an hour or less and hit a small brick medium in an unmarked construction site without lighting.

I pulled out of Oakland, California, a warm spring day in March of 2009, with a stopover in Arizona for furniture left there in storage. Most of belongings were left in Arizona after a car accident incapacitated me in 2007 in Scottsdale directly related to ongoing technological terrorism. As I packed for the trip, I was repeatedly forewarned that I would not make it to my destination of Albuquerque, New Mexico. This was done by taunting coming from the background of my cell phone while locating a new residence by phoning apartment rental complexes and submitting applications. I ignored the warnings believing that I had absolutely no legal issues. This was until I was pulled over in Arizona, jailed, and had no choice but to make Arizona my residence for a year and a half to satisfy court requirements. Arizona would at that time become my home a second time in 2009.

As mentioned, in early October 2010, I was greatly relieved of this tremendous burden with dismissal of the charges. I prepared to return home to Los Angeles, California to the security of a familiar environment where I had been born and raised. I knew I had been blessed and was grateful.

Despite my honest determination to prove the covert harassment's role in the accident in 2007 and its continuance to this day, I was unsuccessful and this resulted ironically in dismissal of the charges due to overall disbelief of my plight. The court could not accept the legitimacy of the advanced technology allegation or the factual satellite surveillance role around me as true without opening up an entire can of worms.

However, the situation was far from over I learned when I returned to California now mildly handicapped yet again hopeful that once again relief was on the horizon. Sadly, it was not and I again wondered when it would be.

One thing I knew for certain, as long as they persisted I would fight. I was not playing nor was my life a toy. This was in spite of their accusations that I thought they were playing with me.

Using this perception, they justified stepping up the games. They refused to accept that they held no advantage of power or control the objective of this type of targeting. They foolishly would not even shut their mouths and watched as I continued to document every single word said to me for publication.

After six or seven years, depending if they started in late 2005 or early 2006, they were fruitless. They were, however, expert at looking for someone to blame for a good and rightful fight on my part. When they saw that I would still publish this book, in late spring of 2012, "We better not lose our jobs" was said as if I held this type of power over the situation. On the contrary, I did not. They had signed up for, and signed their own ticket. If anything resulted from this employment wise, it would be by their actions and their decision to continue a now counterproductive intimidation effort. Factually, I had heard a man, sounding as if a supervisor, white, nudging the blacks into actions one day. "We would be lucky to get out of this one just keeping our jobs," I heard him say one morning as I listened. I weighed in on the psychological impact a statement could have on those working under him as a threat of loss of employment and livelihood as the torture escalated.

Later, I recognized one of the same groups of three older white men who followed me around in the 99 Cents Only Store, in 2006 when the DEA were around me, discussed later, when he also showed up in April of 2012 while I had breakfast with my daughter and her visiting best friend near the airport waiting on my daughter friend's return flight back to Denver, Colorado.

When I was forced to move in November of 2010 from my residence, becoming homeless, it was a young white man operating from the apartment above me at that time. This individual appeared to be the technological guru, from what I could gather, and it appeared so by the comments that he was the person they went to for training on the technology and was likely military. In the beginning stages, I would hear an older African American possibly a supervisor also, asking him questions on the technology's specific uses or should I say abuses.

This younger white man, in his 30's also seemed to take special pride in calling me a "F—king this or that" bright and early each morning from the operation center setting the pace for the flock each day and later seemed to be the most offended when others in the group said I was intelligent and very clean. The race of the individual stalking effort is dependent on the environment you live due to the need to blend into the environment.

In 2008, I began documenting everything happening in my life and happening around me officially. I did so initially hoping only to pull this group officially into the open through the mere thought of book exposure naively. I was also motivated after one of the blacks attempted yet another, blatant, undercover sexual encounter with me. As time progressed I eventually came to suspect that the targeting was being directed was likely by a task force albeit fused. After I finished documenting every word they said to me and did two years later, in 2010, I had well over 300,000 words and over 1,000 pages and enough for three good sized books of random notes.

Surprise, Surprise! With me, physical pain, threats, insults, degradation, and humiliation served as a spring board for me to take action through great difficulty. This is why I could not understand why they would not comprehend that their group actions were unproductive. I am a very sensitive person, though life has toughened me to a vital degree. As they said and did things to hurt me repeatedly, pain gave way to anger which slowly began to build and build and I transferred it to paper positively. At first the notes were so full with rage that they would have to be heavily censored if published. To my amazement and theirs, the potential for a real book began to materialize on its own. They watched my renewed determination and one of them had the gall to tell me one day, "We made you." And, he sounded like he ridiculously really meant and believed it. They had not made anything. They had given me lemons; I made lemonade. The only thing they gave me were very few choices to protect myself from the abusive covert encroachment and victimization.

One of the neighbors, as part of the motivated harassment group network now living next door to me, I suspected entered my apartment in Arizona in 2009 and took one of the discs I had saved the manuscript on. I guess it was safe for me to assume at that point the reality had finally settled in that publication could occur even if I was not entirely sure it was possible initially. I knew it had to be someone connected to the effort. I purposely had gone into my walk-in closet, knowingly, under the usual watchful eye of surveillance and placed three copies of the manuscript in a specific area in my closet. Do not negate the power of any harassment efforts set up in nearby locations using laptop computer real time energy weapons technology along with stalker having accessibility inside your home. When I walked around at home, if in the kitchen, I could feel the sting of the weapon, if I then moved to the bathroom, I could feel the sting and pain there too. I could also hear the weapon noise as it shifted positions following me in the walls from the likely laptop computer weapon system next door.

On the day that I placed the disks under my folded sweaters on the very top shelf, I had just sent three copies of this manuscript out by emails for consideration for publishing to three publishing companies earlier that morning. I then left home to attend to business and run errands.

When I returned home a few hours later the sweaters were tussled and two of the disks now lay plainly in sight with one missing. After that incident, I went out and purchased a small safe to lock anything of value in whenever I left home. And, the way they left the once neatly folded sweaters was obvious proof and also a sign that they had been there and it appeared they wanted me to know it again to incite fear. If they felt that something in my story could be used against me or used to help them, by all means use it. I wanted the situation in the open.

Anyone can be investigated; I had no problem here. After someone mentioned the VA as an investigative entity in its own right to me one day, I went straight to the Phoenix, Arizona, Regional Department of Veterans Affairs headquarters. I explained what I was experiencing. The VA staff member I met with then told me that they routinely receive a large amount of phone calls from people telling them that a Veteran is a fraud and faking the documented information which granted service connection. However, "We have your records" the Veterans Service Representative told me. Realistically, as a VA doctor had also told me, did someone really think they were going to take the PTSD diagnosis away? It was unheard of he said and ridiculous.

As the incredible veracity of a factual effort hit home by 2009, I realized that I had a choice to either allow myself to continue to be a victimized, scared to speak out in fear of ridicule, or I could stand. I was numbed from the personal abuse especially inside my home that occurred day in and day out.

It was after two near breakdowns, both in 2007, after the near fatal car accident that I made the subsequent decision to become proactive and to take my life back. I had to accept that what was happening to me was very real and not allow myself to be hurt any longer by disbelief.

There are twenty-six million veterans in the United States today ninety-two percent are male and eight percent female. I had gone to the VA facility in 1999 seeking nothing. I have never misrepresented myself at any time in my life to gain the benefit that I was ultimately rightfully awarded. For anyone to say that the Department of Veterans Affairs staff can be deceived, or are unable to do their jobs, competently, or can be easily fooled, or have little awareness as intelligent professionals seemed to be only the attitude of self-serving law enforcement. They typically believe themselves expert on everything under the sun and again without having the educational background to back up their assessments as highly educated physicians. And the ones around me definitely operated from a typical "in the hood mentality" later while briefly living in a predominantly

African American neighborhood in Los Angeles, thus the typical name calling and degrading of African American women by black men involved.

In my case, it is documented that I was resentful at the probing and prying into my personal life, when I first arrived at the VA facility and nearly did not make it through recovery because of it in Long Beach, California in December of 1999. And it was not me but the Department of Veterans Affairs experts who tied my behavior with a greater cause and ultimately the incident in the military. Something was undoubtedly going on with me which experienced individuals apparently recognized. I would later learn that alcoholism and substance abuse also called 'disorders' are typical results of other issues as foundation.

The fact that I had also told someone after the incident in the military, who later asked me to marry him, meant nothing to this group which by itself defined a non-existent court case for them. Someone believed that the influence technology would get them different results other than the truthful account of what factually happened to me, and they tried and tried, and tried. They could not erase the documented after effect during that timeframe documented in my military personnel file. However, they were willing to go to great lengths to control my mind, and the situation part of non-consensual human guinea pig technology testing efforts. Plainly stated, the situation had backfired on them. And, it appeared that they did not have the ability to accept this, "Man up" and move on.

My angry reactions to any implication, by staff on the facility of me having any issues while on the VA facility in any manner, are officially documented officially as unhappiness. This however, meant nothing to this group hoping to use me and make their reputations on me it seemed as a conquered technologically manipulated victory. And their perception of me as reasonably intelligent seemed to stimulate this group more so.

My truth would stand even if they managed to subliminally manipulate and influence me that the incident did not happen. I could see myself standing in court saying, with no attorney because none will touch these cases, "Your Honor, I told someone about the situation many years ago. This person then asked me to be his wife." The judge, "Was this person in the room at the time of the incident?" My reply would be, "No." This was revealing also as being move of a vindictive motivation by my ex.

I had no agenda when I told him what happened to me weeks later. Nor could I predict future events. This fact made their efforts around me a ruthless, inhumane waste of time, energy and resources but apparently not a waste technologically due to egotism. These things they knew already. They had too typical of an investigation. I still had resentments of them believing that a person with any type of issues had to be ignorant. I was not ignorant. The VA had approved me taking classes at a trade school where I had maintained close to 4.0, grade point average seeking to get a job which would have significantly changed my VA service connected status. I ultimately did not complete the job reentry program because of extreme stress in 2008 resulting from tactics of using people around me and in any environment in this case the trade school I was attending and spreading disinformation there and also to the on the job training program I was assigned.

After moving into the apartment in 2008, in Signal Hill, California one year after arriving home after the first intentional yearlong stay in Scottsdale Arizona, 2006 to 2007 after the debilitating car accident, night after night, law enforcement was held up in the vacant storage apartment next door to me, using and also supplying neighbors, in this case the manager's family, with the X-ray Vision techno to view me inside my apartment.

Yes, I had come a long way from when I first made it to the Department of Veterans Affairs facility in 1999 more dead than alive, dysfunctional for many years, severely and critically depressed, and close to the edge. The Department of Veterans Affairs VA hospital staff literally stepped in, took control, though I fought them, and literally saved my life. Now years later, I was unintentionally pushed into writing about the experiences, as a protective measure by a group seeking to use and abuse me. Who knew? It appeared they gotten in too deep, thinking me an easy target and were blind sighted? One told me, "We did not know you were intelligent" one day. Intelligence has nothing to do with it at all!

During the last months of 2011, I was repeatedly told we are around you now only due to "that book" and that they wished I would not publish. And it began to appear that they were willing to stop me anyway they could which began to take on the appearance of covert attempted murder and I realized they were directing one night the microwave Direct Energy Weapon at my heart. In reality, by the time I became ill from the massive doses of radiation, this book would be long published and my kids as beneficiaries and hopefully anyone else I had managed to somehow help with my painful story I reasoned.

One night, to insure my motive's pure, I asked myself, "Why should I proceed" with the book? I did not want to operate from a place of vengefulness in my life. My answer was numerous, the personal verbal degradation, the manipulative psychological and physical painful attacks, the violation of my most basic right of all - my human rights, the constant sexual exploitation and stimulation and arousal, the attention and zeroing on one of my daughters and yours, and most poignant of all, I had done nothing wrong! And, if satellites are to be deployed domestically, it is vital that the most rigorous checks and balances and oversight mechanisms are in place.

The only way these covert operations can be brought to worldly attention and hopefully impact change is to continually reveal these operations, bravely, as some of the most inhumane violations in the history of man. Targeted Individuals must do anything they can by taking a stand. I had my mission and I chose to accept it.

I heard it said, "If a lot of people are saying the same thing, there is a good chance that it is true." A lot of people, all over the world, are doing and saying just that about global surveillance, electronic weaponry and psychological electronic mind control technology.

Today, it appears that the novel, "1984" by George Orwell has become a covert technological reality.

On days when the constant taunting was exceptionally ruthless, as ridiculous as it may sound, or look, putting wet tissue balls in my ears helped to drown out substantially some of the continuous, nonstop verbal chatter to a dull roar. The wet tissue balls also helped the ringing in the ears, associated with the tinnitus effect documented as being associated with the Neurophone satellite message delivery system. The tissue balls only worked when the radar laser was directed at the back of my neck carrying their verbal insults. I was willing to try anything to stop the incessant chatter even if it looked ridiculous. However, when operation center personnel figured out that I could not hear them after a few days of no emotional registered response from me on their computer monitor to their remarks, they then switch to direct communication to the brain alternating between the two, reaffirming evident use of many methods of technological telepathy.

When I crossed the state line into Arizona, heading for Scottsdale, in March of 2006 for the first time, I had no idea of the magnitude of the intense surveillance effort and technological pursuit that followed me. I also continuously underestimated the disbelief from others I would encounter when telling people what was happening to me. Most people, after telling them, naturally thought no one was so important for this to happen to them and least of all an average person like myself and on such a large scale that contributes to disbelief and discrediting also. Perhaps historically this may have been true but not today.

There are numerous books: A Nation Betrayed, Carol Rutz; Project Bluebird, Dr. Colin Ross; Controlling the Human Mind, Dr. Nick Begich; Excalibur Briefing, Lt. Col. Thomas E. Bearden; My Life Changed Forever, Elizabeth Sullivan; Remote Stalking, Sheryll Thompson; Remote Viewing, Tim Rifat; A New Breed–Satellite Terrorism in America, Dr. John Hall. Dr. John Hall is associated with the website Freedom from Covert Harassment and Surveillance and a doctor, along with Tim Shorrock's, Spies for Hire –The Secret World of Intelligence Outsourcing, to name only a few. Obviously, I am not the first to write on this subject.

These books, as their defining titles reveal are written about, satellite surveillance, electronic surveillance, mind control, brain manipulation technology, and the phenomena of covert harassment / gang stalking essentially founded on another historical termed called Mobbing. Mobbing is defined below as:

A tried-and-true method of elimination known as mobbing has been with us for a long time. It is simple, efficient and scalable. It is insidious and pernicious as it hides behind a veil of lies and justifications. It is designed to be difficult to detect or prove. Those that do see it are terrified and are too intimidated to speak out. This silence emboldens the bullies and the mobbing process continues and escalates to its predictable, stereotypical and inevitable result the elimination of the targeted individual, group or race. (Editorial excerpt Mobbing – A Familiar Pattern)

Stalking embodying this dynamic extends to Neighborhood Watch and community policing groups and are motivated by and originating from a single source of leadership. This form of targeting usually involves law enforcement as instigators who meet routinely with these groups. (See gangstalkingworld.com)

In my case, regarding another person's experiences and books on the subject, I made it a point not to read their stories. There are many speaking up today in one form of expression or another. I realized that these situations, by design mirror each other very closely. Although a person can be targeted for varied and different reasons, I could not allow myself to be influenced by the similarities of experiences of another targeted individual and myself as an author.

There have been many newspaper articles written on the subject. In the Washington Post article, Mind Games, January 14, 2007, reporter, Sharon Weinberger writes that she "obtained records that note that the official patents were based on actual human experimentation, for the technological telepathy. In October 1994 at the Air Force Laboratory, scientists were able to transmit phrases into the heads of human subjects, albeit with marginal intelligibility. One must bear in mind that the first Voice to Skull patent was in 1958, by Patrick Flanagan and his Neurophone. It was confiscated by the government and returned ten years later resulting in the first official patent in 1968 by Flanagan.

As recent as 2006, researchers at the University of Washington were working on an electronic chip (implant) that could control nerve connections in the area of the brain that controls movement similar to Brain Gate. In 2008, the Army gave the University of California, Irvine, scientist in California a 4-million dollar grant to study Synthetic Telepathy. Synthetic Telepathy is defined on synthetictelepathy.com as "the art of electronically transferring thought directly to and from a brain." The primary objective of the University of California, Irvine's scientific grant is stated below:

The brain-computer interface would use a noninvasive brain imaging technology like electroencephalography (EEG) to let people communicate thoughts to each other. For example, a soldier would "think" a message to be transmitted and a computer-based speech recognition system would decode the EEG signals. The decoded thoughts, in essence translated brain waves, are transmitted using a system that points in the direction of the intended target.

In a magazine article in the Washington Post Magazine, January 16, 2007, entitled, Thought Wars, "One thing is certain about the emerging sub-culture of self-described mind control victims: The agony is real," writes reporter Sharon Weinberger.

Two women, among others who are very informative in publications disseminating information through research of mind control technology, or weapon warfare, are one, Sharon Weinberger, also author of Imaginary Weapons: A Journey through the Pentagon's Scientific Underworld, Aerial Mind Control. Judy Wall, The Threat to Civil Liberties. Ms. Wall is the Editor/Publisher of Resonance

Newsletter of MENSA Bio-electromagnetics, Special Interest Group, Nexus Magazine. This specific article appeared in the October – November 1999 edition of the magazine. Many thanks for their efforts.

In November of 1992, a Wall Street Journal (WSJ) article mentions a mind-control operation performed jointly between the United States and Canada beginning in 1955.

Financed by the Central Intelligence Agency through a phony front organization called the Investigation of Human Ecology, about $60-75,000 went to Dr. Ewen Cameron at McGill University in Montreal, Canada. The Canadians allegedly picked up the rest of the tab, of about $200,000. Even though this is 1950s dollars, considering the nature of covert funding there is no real way to know exactly how much was spent on this project the article states.

However, we can look even further back to inventions documented as laying the foundation for what would later become advanced technology used to decipher human thought through brainwave pattern analysis.

In 1920, Hans Berger, a psychiatrist, developed the Human Electroencephalograph (EEG – brainwaves). It's important application from the 1930s onwards initially in the field of Epilepsy set the stage. The EEG revealed the presence of electrical discharges in the brain. It also showed different patterns of brainwave discharges associated with different seizure types. The EEG helped to locate the site of seizure discharges and expanded the possibilities for neurosurgical treatments, which became much more widely available from the 1950s onwards in London, Montreal and Paris. The development of the electroencephalograph as an apparatus for detecting and recording brain waves, offered brain physiologists later the key to unlock the mysteries of the body's pivotal organ of thought, intellect and personality and set the stage for psychological electronic technology, which would enable man to eventually read human thought by combining electromagnetic energy and microwave radio wave with various other technical applications.

A chapter of the biography of Alfred Loomis (November 4, 1887 – August 11, 1975) details Loomis's experiments with reading brain waves that began in the 1930s. Loomis was an American attorney, investment banker, physicist, philanthropist, and dedicated patron of scientific research. He established his secret Loomis Laboratory in Tuxedo Park, New York, and his role in the development of radar is considered instrumental in the Allied Victory in World War II along with Nikola Tesla's work. He became a major player in defense research and development during World War II.

The book written about his fascinating life is called, Tuxedo Park: A Wall Street Tycoon and the Secret Palace of Science-That Changed the Course of World War II by Jennet Conant. In WW I, Loomis worked for the U.S. Army Ordnance and is credited with the inventions of the Aberdeen Chronometer, a microscope centrifuge, and a pressurized fire extinguisher. Loomis and his staff in laboratory studies conducted experiments in sound waves, spectrometry, and the precise measurement of time in the early 1920s.

In the late 1930s he worked on a small microwave set in his spare time, which was mounted on a truck. The military Active Denial System, a large version of a directed energy weapon today is mounted on the Humvee military vehicle.

Nikola Tesla's inventions dates back even further to the late 1800s and what Tesla called "Radiant Energy" is the dynamic of electromagnetic energy.

President Franklin Delano Roosevelt's Science Advisor advised the President that he thought all civilian and military projects should be brought together under one roof. As a result, the National Defense Research Committee (NDRC) was created. This agency would eventually play a major role in brain manipulation technology research beginnings.

The NDRC was part of the Council of National Defense that had been created during 1916 to coordinate industry and resources for national security purposes by an order of President Roosevelt on June

27, 1940. Vannevar Bush (no relationship to the Bush presidential clan it appears) then director of the Carnegie Institution pressed for the creation of the NDRC. His motivation was based on experiencing the lack of cooperation between civilian scientists and the military during World War I. Bush managed to get a meeting with the President on June 12, 1940, and took a single sheet of paper describing the proposed agency. Roosevelt approved it in ten minutes. Government officials then complained that Bush was attempting to increase his authority and to bypass them—which Bush later admitted as factual saying:

There were those who protested that the action of setting up NDRC was an end run, a grab by which a small company of scientists and engineers, acting outside established channels, got hold of the authority and money for the program of developing new weapons. That, in fact, is exactly what it was. (Bush 1970, p.31–32)

In the June fifteenth letter which appointed Vannevar Bush to the head of the committee, Roosevelt outlined that the NDRC was not meant to replace the research work done by the Army and Navy in their laboratories or through industry contracts, but rather to supplement this activity, by extending the research base and enlisting the aid of the scientists who could effectively contribute to a more rapid improvement of important devices, and by study determine where new effort on new instrumentalities may be usefully employed. (This is quoted in Stewart 1948, p. 8) Bush would later go on to become one of the founders of Raytheon, one of the largest government contractors in history.

On March 16, 1955, the United States Air Force ordered the development of an advanced reconnaissance (spy) satellite to provide continuous surveillance of preselected areas of the earth in order to determine the status of a potential enemy's war-making capability. In October of 1957, the Russians launched Sputnik 1. It was the first man-made object to be put into the Earth's orbit.

Since the deployment of the first artificial satellite, Sputnik, artificial satellite capabilities have grown and expanded. Satellites have detection abilities that are so accurate that they can zoom in on a letter held in someone's hand and read easily. The spy satellites are essentially space-based telescopes pointed at the earth instead of the stars.

They can be controlled to probe deep within the interiors of a building, outside, deeply underground and in any type of weather. The information is then relayed to a computer terminal where a person or persons sit monitoring the information gathered.

What most do not know is that the satellite radar laser directed energy weapon can enter through the ceiling, travel down the wall, and position itself to target any area on a human body. And it appears that computer software desensitizes its user to the technology's deadly results creating the appearance of playing a harmless computer game complete though the effects can be lethal.

Many technologies are now highly advanced since their first patenting and testing in the early 1900s such as the radar, laser, coils, or what Tesla called, Radiant Energy – electromagnetic energy, laying the foundation for HAARP for example. They now stand as testimony of what the brilliance of the human mind can achieve. But true also, these advancements can also menacingly stand as examples of how in the wrong hands, with wrong intent, the advancements can be used for a self-serving ideology and used to possibly psychologically enslave and influence populations and simultaneously. And, today, it is said this goal can be achieved not only through the High Frequency Active Auroral Research Program (HAARP), later reported to have closed down, originating from Tesla Coils, but also the Ground Wave Energy Network, (GWEN) towers.

GWEN was once said to be the operation center controlling microchip implanted individuals long before micro chipping slowly appears to be becoming fashionable through television commercial advertisement today. Today Radio Frequency Identification tracking is digitized.

The radar laser beam directed at a target allows the computer to read a person's mind or thoughts by EEG brain wave patterns, listen to conversations, and to harass and physically torment as discussed. The technology can also manipulate electronic instruments in the person's environment. Again, in The Shocking Menace of Satellite Surveillance, John Fleming, an example I have used in the other books also, he writes:

Unknown to most of the world, satellites can perform astonishing and often menacing feats. This should come as no surprise when one reflects on the massive effort poured into satellite technology since the Soviet Satellite Sputnik, launched in 1957, and caused panic in the U.S. A spy satellite can monitor a person's every movement, even when the "target" is indoors or deep in the interior of a building or traveling rapidly down the highway in a car, in any kind of weather (cloudy, rainy, stormy). There is no place to hide on the face of the earth. It takes just three satellites to blanket the world with detection capacity. Besides tracking a person's every action and relaying the data to a computer screen on earth, amazing powers of satellites include reading a person's mind, monitoring conversations, manipulating electronic instruments and physically assaulting someone with a laser beam...

The feature of sounds recorded for playback at a later time is a noted feature of the patented satellite delivered Neurophone. In my case, for example, the sound of my garage door opening which I shared with other tenants where I lived. This sound was followed by the sound of what appeared to be someone then opening the apartment door downstairs and entering the residence below. A short while later I would feel the intense ray of the microwave pain beam assaulting my body. In reality, however, everything was coming from the operation center and when I checked the apartment was empty and dark. This was verified when I heard the door sounding as if opening one day and went downstairs again to investigate. Everything was again quiet and I saw no one. Had I fallen for this, I could be easily deemed unstable, having played right into the game plan. The technology's use in this manner also became a reality for me during the summer months in Arizona.

This time during my unplanned layover as mentioned in 2009, for the DUI hearings. In the unbearable Arizona heat of the day of over 100 degrees temperature with my air conditioner running on full blast and the house cool and comfortable, my smoke detectors would sound first in the bedroom where I was working on this manuscript. After I silenced it there, the one in the kitchen would suddenly sound, and so it went back and forth until I finally had to remove the batteries from both detectors. I had to replace no less than five adapter power cords for my laptop computer that kept mysteriously burning out. When the cord blew on the brand-new laptop of less than six months old, I began to suspect radar laser as the likely cause.

Of the most insidious of the technological capabilities delivered by satellite is subliminal consciousness altering capabilities. In his book Confrontation in Space (1981), the author G. Harry Stine writes that computers can read human minds by deciphering the outputs of electroencephalographs (EEGs) or brain waves. The fact that they were tampering with, manipulating, and misconstruing my thoughts as they continually repeated, you're this or that, initially was a source of great pain and anguish for me. It was also painfully disappointing that this was being done by people holding public trust and sworn to act ethically. This was a bitter pill to swallow because essentially, you have nowhere to turn for help officially if the victimization is perpetrated or motivated by law enforcement and covered up.

By the end of summer 2010 in Arizona, I was sitting on my couch in my apartment in Glendale, Arizona after the unplanned stay beginning in March of 2009. I sat quietly listening to anything I could hear coming from the newly rented apartment above me and a new tenant of about two weeks. A day before, I listened to a somewhat muffled but a distinct man's voice say, "Got her" shortly after the new tenants moved in as I sat on my couch. This was the beginning of my first encounter with the portable technology's capability to make a person sick. A young redhead now lived upstairs. Another young woman, there before I moved in, moved out shortly after I moved in.

The manager mentioned her sadness at her abrupt move stating she had been a faithful tenant for many years and was sorry to see her go. Later I would begin to see a pattern of neighbor's immediately moving out and people connected with covert harassment groups moving in. And many targeted reports this happening, also, unbelievably. There is a large funding for these efforts that must be used for something.

It appeared that I was someone's employment opportunity or at least free rent. With a new tenant above, me after the seven-month vacancy upstairs, I sat and listened to a now very familiar pattern. It was the sound of something, sounding quite heavy, being moved around in sync with my every move below.

When this started with the first tenant shortly after I moved in, after confirming to myself that I was accurate, seven months earlier, I immediately went into reverse harassment mode angry at the terrorism that started typically within days. I wanted to make them just as uncomfortable as they were making me. I began banging on the ceiling with the broom handle. I did this whenever it appeared that the person was factually following me from room to room told by them stopping precisely wherever and whenever I stopped above. In most cases, I had learned that instead of calling the cops as most neighbors logically would if someone below banged the ceiling, those involved in these groups would not. In this case, regarding the previous tenant a young Hispanic woman person apparently decided to move probably not wanting to be involved anyway. Her involvement was the result of having the misfortune to be connected to my apartment and recruited in the effort. There was a brief respite from above during the time the apartment above me was vacant as stated for the seven-month period. This was before this recent female and the familiar looking man unloading his truck with her meager belongings, of which there appeared to be no real furniture moved in. I immediately recognized the man, from somewhere, though I could not place him at first. The dark blue pick-up truck he drove was also familiar to me though I could not place it either.

I had to ask, why was the apartment specifically above me requested with several other much nicer apartments available around me? I made a mental note of this. Another new resident on the bottom floor soon followed. It appeared that I had a knack for clearing a building when I moved in. Even before I saw the cleaning crew go in next door to clean, the apartment was immediately rented by a group of young men in their early 20s.

One thing that struck me as odd was the pronounced overly friendly manner of one of the young men on the lease. He seemed to go out of his way trying to ingratiate himself with me or buttering me up for the kill. It was not long after the young men settled in that I was in my bedroom watching a movie when I heard someone outside my window say exactly what was being verbalized to me inside my apartment projected from the area in my ceiling. I thought it was my imagination when I first heard,

"She's gone."

When I got up to see who was out front, there were two young men standing in front of my apartment door smoking cigarettes.

This was the beginning of my first real experiences with covert street theatrics in the form of inconspicuous threats from complete strangers. I did not at first believe that I had heard correctly what was said. To make sure I got up, muted my television and crept to the front door standing quietly listening to see if it would be repeated. I was rather annoyed by these young people. It seemed that they actually preferred to hang out just outside my front door lately rather than inside their apartment or their front door. On this particular day, "She's gone," was not repeated. I went back to my bedroom brushing it off as my imagination and continued my movie. A few nights later I heard my neighbor and friend's congregate outside again. This time I distinctly heard one of the now three young men standing out front say,

"They say she's gone."

Another standing with now three men then said, "Yep, she's gone."

Now convinced, I got up and went into the living room and peeked out through the blinds to see who actually was standing there. It was the same young man, the overly nice one who lived there with two of his unidentified friends. After the remark, the conversation instantly changed to something about their automobiles. I then tippy-toed back to my bedroom but decided to open the patio door in the bedroom in case something else was said. If so, I would confront them. I needed to be completely sure before making any accusations. When they heard my patio door open, I then heard the door of the neighbor's apartment open then shut with them going back inside and everything becoming quiet outside once again.

I was shocked. I could not believe my ears at first. However, this soon became a familiar pattern and a regular occurrence albeit it sporadically. It was always when one my neighbors, one of two on the lease, and some of their numerous friends, who came and went all day, stood outside smoking cigarettes or marijuana. So many people were going and coming in and out that I at first thought that they were selling marijuana as the pungent odor escaped the opened door once or twice when I was coming home. The next morning the area around my front door would be littered with cigarette butts.

However, at that moment I now sat listening, after the lengthy vacancy upstairs to someone moving around, and yet again, following me from room to room with was the portable Direct Energy Weapon. Shortly afterward this, within a matter of weeks, I would begin catching hell from all sides, top and below on both sides of me from neighboring apartments. In this case, I did what I always do. At first, I needed to be sure that I was being followed by portable technology. From past experience, I remembered another neighbor in Oakland right before I left had called it an X-ray Vision machine though she denied having one. To see if I was actually being followed, I would move from my bedroom to the couch in the living room, sit, wait, and listen, then to the kitchen, then to the bathroom. Each and every time I would hear the floor boards creaking as someone above me followed me around from the apartment above me. The walls were so thin that on some nights, I could hear a person snoring in the apartment on my east side which housed an older couple. At first, from their side I would hear scratching noises typical of someone trying to position something against the wall. This stopped shortly afterwards when I pounded on the wall adjoining our bedrooms one day and then called the police.

One day, after moving from place to place toying with the newest neighbor upstairs, I did not move when I heard something obviously placed over my head. My experiences prior to this, had not been the distinct physical sensation or reaction I felt on this particular day as some type of fluid appeared to entered my body. The sensation that day was followed by a man's voice saying, "Got her." He sounded triumphant as if his objective was a success. It was my understanding prior to this, that I was only being watched. I did not know that through the radioactive waves toxic chemicals could be passed. Even though I would move around, I really had no idea why, health wise, that I needed to continue to do so until that day.

I was sitting on the living room couch, glued to my seat, trying to build my website. I had been frustrated for days as I tried and tried to input important information and it would not fit where I wanted it to on the site. I finally, now had the website domain manager customer service representative on the line. I could not afford for the call to be dropped if I moved due to blind spots in my apartment so I sat on the couch with my cellular phone glued to my ear and my hands firmly placed on my laptop keyboard while the representative walked me through a procedure.

Instinctually, I knew that I should be covered in the protective material I had recently ordered but I did not move never believing that someone really wanted to hurt me at first. On a popular radio talk, the show host had recently interviewed a security expert in electronic surveillance, technology, and harassment. On the show, the guest mentioned protective covering which I immediately ordered. Mylar was mentioned also and fabric embedded with copper thread. I knew I would need something to hopefully protect me so I ordered it immediately. However, at that moment, I did not move believing it was more important for me to get the website up and running. I believed that it would help to substantiate my claims by providing a long list of United States Patents and Trademark Office information and other substantiating information for hopeful credibility. I noticed increased activity around me as the situation continued to escalate especially as those monitoring me watched me fast at work either editing this book or working on the website.

When ta man's voice said, "Got her," that day, I could not deny that I felt a sensation seemingly of some type of vapor from the crown of my head, and slowly, fluid like, creeping down my neck, shoulders, and back. It appeared to stop in my abdomen as I sat. I listened just prior to this to what sounded, like a large version of some type of equipment which landed with a marked thud overhead. Later I remembered something I had read while doing research on energy weapons. The website said:

The Directed Energy Weapon (DEW) range, even from handheld lasers can stun, shock, or impair vision or even permanently damage eyesight. These non-ionizing particle beam weapons, range in size from hand held to portable, such as the Xavier 800, which is tripod mounted, to the six-foot diameter mobile mounted dishes and satellite delivered impulses on military vehicles. The radiation beams can effectively target and temporarily paralyze a single person or a brigade of soldiers. In the case of prolonged or direct exposure to powerful military-grade devices that can shoot potent, concentrated beams of microwaves, x-rays, gamma rays, and even sonic wave frequencies. This high-tech weaponry is said to be capable of inflicting very serious damage and even behavioral changes upon its human targets. According to some reports on declassified government research projects, some DEW can even alter human behavior by projecting frequencies, even embedded messages-directly into the brain, bypassing the auditory organs using microwaves raising the once fantastic notion of externally administered mind control as a reality...

I had foolishly taken myself from under the numerous protective shielding I usually wrapped myself in, in exchange briefly for completing the website. My protective gear included various items which reportedly deflect the rays such as even mirrors, a bathroom rubber mat I purchased, and I even slept under a wet towel over plastic hoping to reduce the microwave heating pain which first boils the water molecules. I hoped the waves would first absorb the moisture from the wet towel before getting to my body. Each night I slept under what felt like a ton of bricks which restricted my movement and was extremely uncomfortable but at least I could walk the next morning.

The question that now plagued me, as I sat listening to the customer service representative's direction, was how could I prove that what they were doing to me was factual or that the extreme physical discomfort I felt was real? I continually asked myself this question and was repeatedly asked this by others.

My repeated plea of come into the open with any allegations or leave me alone went answered. I had written numerous letters at that point, well over 100 to anyone whom I felt could help me or just put a bug in an ear of some official. Several highly placed government offices said that there was nothing they could do, for legal reasons in the tortuous effort. Again, this is albeit inhumane, it is legal. What bothered me was that they did not find it necessary to consider laws governing moral use of these advancements obviously here to stay. Was this an oversight?

The technology now ran amok in the hands of those who appeared to be uncivilized and who also possessed a self-preserving, cowardly, sadistic streak. They watched me writing letter after letter and read the responses along with me when I received responses back and laughed at my efforts. It appeared that I was their helpless prey and they had me just where they wanted me. In the Superior Court judge response, back to me in 2006, he suggested contacting my Congressman. I contacted the Congressman in the area where I now resided in Glendale, Arizona. After I explained what was happening, his office responded that the situation was out of his hands and of which he could not get involved also. This reply further substantiated the effort around me, which appeared more covertly illegal, than legal as slow death.

After hearing the man's voice say, "Got her," that day, I woke up earlier than usual the next morning. I did this at times in my life when there was something pressing or nagging at my super conscious urgently needed acknowledgement or some issue needing my full attention. My mind would habitually, persistently set off a silent alarm saying, "May Day, May Day, you needed to address this immediately" which prevented a full night restful sleep. "Got her," rang in my ears all night from the day before when I foolishly did not move.

I crawled out of bed and went directly to my laptop to find out if I could possibly be physically poisoned from the technology through laser, radar or by the smaller versions of Directed Energy Weapons. I typed just this into a search engine Can a person be poisoned by the Directed-Energy Weapons? I was immediately inundated with several websites. However, the two below caught my eye related to a factual chemical laser:

MIRACL, or Mid-Infrared Advanced Chemical Laser, is a directed energy weapon developed by the US Navy. It is a deuterium fluoride laser, a type of chemical laser.

The MIRACL laser first became operational in 1980. It can produce over a megawatt of output for up to 70 seconds, making it the most powerful continuous wave (CW) laser in the US. Its original goal was to be able to track and destroy anti-ship cruise missiles, but in later years it was used to test phenomenologies associated with national anti-ballistic and anti-satellite laser weapons. Originally tested at a contractor facility in California, as of the later 1990s and early 2000s, it was located at a facility (32.632°N 106.332°W) in the White Sands Missile Range in New Mexico. It is noted that today, these weapons are advanced and come in various sizes.

I also stumbled onto information defining Chemtrails:

What Chemtrails Really Are-The Short Scoop

Various sizes of gas plasma orbs are associated with this technology. The satellites can be programmed to track and monitor various frequencies on different parts of your body. These crossed-energies can be used to cause a person to become a sort of physical electromagnetic soup, from the poisonous, toxic Chemtrails...

I was grateful for the accurate information and even more grateful to learn that chelating products were effective for cleansing and combating even toxins in every organ of the body. I later would also use Triple Leap detox and laxative tea, and also Moringa Powder to detoxify.

For the pain left after the burning rays, Kool and Fit sprayed to my legs three times a day provided some relief. During this timeframe, I also noticed that upon waking, my hands, arms, and feet were freezing cold and numb. They even had begun to feel numb at times and tingled from lack of circulation to these areas. When I then keyed information on chelating products into the search engine, I learned that one of the main symptoms of heavy metal poisoning includes pain in the legs after walking only short distances, numbness and tingling.

Although these new discomforts were unnatural, I initially attributed them to normal escalation of the body's aches and pains. However, after reading from the website, I began to believe that a toxic effect quite possibly could be what the male voice upstairs meant when he said, "Got her," the night before. Whether I was right or wrong that morning, I got dressed and headed to the health food store to purchase the chelating product. I would be there as soon as the doors opened.

Today it is a fact that MKULTRA that sponsored mind control zombification until exposed in the 70s simply went underground and experiments continues especially related to drugs both legal and illegal and psychophysical technology development.

Today the laws approving testing on united states citizens are written so that anything can be justified in the name of crowd and riot control, for prevent civil unrest to include testing of biological warfare. Logically, it goes without saying that untested technology, with no data to back it up as successful or final results means nothing and is valueless. It just does not make sense to legalize something when test results of the abilities are not known. Does it? And if you read the laws, see bigbrotherwatchingus.com, this time the technology approval tab, it clearly states that U.S. citizens do not have to be informed of non-consensual human guinea testing by many methods specifically also biological

CHAPTER FIVE

"Character is what a man is in the dark."
— Dwight L. Moody

These psychological operations are designed to do whatever is believed will have the greatest impact on the target emotionally. They are also well versed in the psychology of using, repetition as a highly effective method of mind control in the form of repeated threats, degradation, insults, etc., etc., etc.

One of the technologies capable of gaging emotional responses abstract is below:

US Patent # 5,507,291 (April 16, 1996) Method & Apparatus for Remotely Determining Information as to Person's Emotional State

Stirbl, et al. Abstract - In a method for remotely determining information relating to a person's emotional state, a waveform energy having a predetermined frequency and a predetermined intensity is generated and wirelessly transmitted towards a remotely located subject. Waveform energy emitted from the subject is detected and automatically analyzed to derive information relating to the individual's emotional state. Physiological or physical parameters of blood pressure, pulse rate, pupil size, and respiration rate and perspiration level are measured and compared with reference values to provide information utilizable in evaluating interviewee's responses...

No time, place or space was sacred for me. It was horrific in the beginning until I adjusted. During my menstruation, when I pulled down my underwear to change pads, I heard someone say, "Ugh" about a very natural feminine occurrence common to all women which includes their wives, sisters, mothers, daughters and girlfriends.

One night I heard a click at my front door in Arizona. I thought someone had hit the door with something. I got up and peeked out the window. There was no one in sight. The next morning when I opened the door the lock to the metal screen door was unlocked and surprisingly the door swung wide open. Could the sound of the lock being turned be the click I heard the night before? I had without a doubt, undeniably locked both doors when I came in and checking before bed.

One night, just as I left to return a video before the video store closed around midnight, a strange car pulled into one of the parking stalls right before I walked by. I watched to see who would exit the vehicle but the driver just sat there never even turning around. Through the slightly tinted windows, I saw a man who then turned off the car engine. I got into my car pulled out slowly still waiting for an exit. When I returned there was no one in the car, however, a strange man sprung out of nowhere cutting off my path just as I neared my front door. He came from around the corner of the building near the bushes. Because of the bushes, he was concealed and I could not see him. There was nothing on the side of the building from where he came except more parking stalls and the apparent continuous hope by those monitoring me to create fear that I would be murdered by some unknown assailant.

The continuous effort to position the electronic torture technology over my head was nonstop from the apartment above me from that point on but now was curtailed by my continuous moving around especially after the first experience and my becoming physically ill or getting out of the house more and working at the library. After the first successful attack, and inability to catch me in one spot again, I heard the door open and close one day upstairs and my new neighbor leave with a new face with her other than the person who had moved her in. I watched them through the partially closed blinds as they got into her little red Pontiac Sun Fire and pulled out of the parking lot. I breathed a sigh of relief. However, it would be short lived when to my surprise, I heard someone, trying to be extremely quiet tippy toeing across the floor upstairs again. Apparently a third person had stayed behind determined to outsmart me in their game of toxic electromagnetic extremely low frequency cat and mouse.

As I watched the man and woman leave, it finally dawned on me where I had seen the other man in the blue pickup truck that helped her move in. I had seen him while leaving Pretrial Services, in the Phoenix Justice Center after the twice weekly court required check in and while heading home related to the DUI issue. On this day, I observed the same truck darting in and out of traffic. When the driver finally pulled directly behind me he slowed obviously reaching his destination of effort following me. I looked at the man in my rear-view mirror that day and looked at the pickup now parked in one of the stalls outside my apartment building. I realized the person tailing me was the exact same man and that he now was connected to the new tenant upstairs and probably the one left behind and creeping around.

This person would take a step, stop briefly hoping to prevent me deciphering his location, then take another step then stop again. This went on until he had slowly etched his way directly above me overhead. However, as soon as I heard him stop I quickly changed locations. Tired of playing, I decided to get out of the house for a while on this particular day. I passed on taking the broom handle and pounding the ceiling. I left quietly and peacefully. It would do me good to get into the fresh air and sun.

I was thankful for the goodness that had nudged me to get out of bed about a week prior after the very first successful positioning of the energy weapon. I was also thankful to be led to what I had learned would cleanse my body of the toxins and was now using the chelating products. If this was what was accurately happening, and it appeared so, detoxifying immediately became mandatory to hopefully prevent cancer.

As mentioned earlier, we are dealing with "Star Wars" aka connecting technology related to the Strategic Defense Initiative, connecting communication tower deploying space-based weaponry. "Star Wars" also involves the resulting combination of Chemtrails necessary for creating an atmosphere that will support electromagnetic waves, ground-based electromagnetic field oscillators called gyrotrons and ionospheric heaters. Poisonous Chemtrails are being released into the environment and into the very air we breathe as a result of the electromagnetic waves necessary to sustain these technologies miles above the earth. Contrails are playing a role also via military air craft deployment for weather modification testing for effectiveness for political control of populations.

Gaging emotions and terrorism are necessity in fear-oriented campaigns by law enforcement. I was watching a movie one day when an intense love making scene began playing in the movie. I then listened as a man said "She's getting turned on," using this patented technology. Factually, I had begun to actually get a little flustered about the scene in reality but this was technologically coming from the operation center.

I was self-admitted to the veteran's hospital in Phoenix, Arizona, voluntarily twice as a direct result of the targeting in summer 2007. After the car accident, annihilating my right ankle, specifically, a great sadness engulfed me that was emotionally devastating. The first time I heard someone say "Ugh" with an exaggerated tone of disgust was actually from one of the women of two in the group around me in Arizona during the second layover in Arizona, one white, the other black.

It was shortly afterwards that the men began to center their verbal abuse on how unclean I was supposed to be motivated by these two. The overweight African American female, who I saw coming from what I thought was a vacant apartment a few doors over from my apartment one day followed up her comments with, "She thinks she's cute" which was again, a flashback and reminder of young immature, insecure girls on the playground in grade school disliking those who seemed to have confidence.

Traditionally, the people who were the most heinous with the covert psychological and physical assaults were the weekend shifts and also the shift which came in around 10:00 p.m. at night until early the morning hours. These hours appeared to be their bewitching hour.

When the first neighbor moved from the apartment on the ground floor, next door shortly after I moved in and right before the young men moved in to this apartment, a few pests ran temporarily into my apartment. I have never had a problem with pest before and they were immediately exterminated, however, not soon enough. I listened as the critters became proof of how unclean I was supposed to be from the tall thin white female.

I had seen her before. She and another man showed up in Arizona, and followed me into the Boston Market restaurant one day as I ordered side orders. I overheard her while I stood in line to order trying to convince the man with her that I was factually scared as they both eyeballed me with intimidating stares. I ordered my food walked past them, got into my vehicle, drove home, ate, watched television then fell asleep.

This woman looked exactly like the tall thin female in California, although different hair color who popped up at my church in 2008 sitting in the vacant seat next to me one day. I was not sure if she was the same woman because I did not think that I important enough for someone to travel to Arizona after me although it was only a few hour's drive and even less by plane and inexpensive. That day when the pastor spoke of the abundance in the universe, and I and everyone else in the church cosigned his statement with a nod or verbal acknowledgement, this woman made a sound indicating that she was disgusted by my agreement.

Later when I returned home in Signal Hill, after realizing who she possibly was, as one the voice coming from the wall during that timeframe, I called her a name then joked that she held my hand a little too tight when church was over when the entire congregation stood holding hands during closing prayer as a matter of routine. She had obviously made it back to her workstation and was now watching and listening to me along with others in the center gaging any fearful reaction. She was pissed that I suspected who she was, told her so, and that I insulted her. She and the black female, after I also called her a stereotypical name both became my nemesis.

The extra attention I was getting from some of the men was unwanted and apparently did not sit well with the women especially when the men started proclaiming how smart I was supposed to be. These women after all worked closely with the men and it probably angered them knowing they acted like typical men looking for visual stimulation.

In 2008, when I first noticed the likelihood of targeting by satellite surveillance, I initially heard one of these very same women, in Signal Hill, California say that I was cute too. At that time, I believe I was being targeted by the DEA after my six-month bout. Because of this belief, I began calling the DEA headquarters in Los Angeles, California every day when I heard the satellite energy my residence in the ceiling. One day when I did, the person on the line, identifying himself as a Special Agent, appeared to be more concerned with how I knew it was satellite surveillance and the DEA.

When the men continued to show up in my bathroom at shower time every day, I called them each day complaining. Finally, an angry woman answered the phone after someone abruptly hung up on me after my first call. She angrily told me, before I could speak, "That case has been transferred to the FBI." Surprised by this or any acknowledge at all, I asked, "What case, mine?" She then said harshly "Yes," then "Call them." She then hung up in my face. Now sober the case had been passed on.

Ongoing petty insults ran the full gamut even to comments that I never washed my hair. They had learned from watching me that African American women do not have to wash our hair daily with each shower. This is due to excessive dryness and very little natural oil production. It takes sometimes up to two weeks for oil to build up in our hair even more so with kinkier types. If we washed it every day the hair will become dry, brittle, and even break using oil stripping shampoo daily. Their observance of this fact resulted in daily comments of, "She never washes her hair" also said as a sign of my uncleanliness.

If you have to wash your hair regularly due to oil production, that is okay. However, do not try to insult me, or call me nasty names, about something you do not understand. These pathetic efforts are by what essentially are petty, shallow minded individuals working these operations playing childish games. However, these relentless attacks effectively get to some intensely due to, ongoing around the clock, verbal insults, relentlessly. When they made ridiculous comments, I responded in kind. Finally, the women declared venomously, "I just can't stand her."

In the heat of Arizona summer nights, I could not even put on a night gown in the privacy of my residence which I had worn often over the years without being accused by the black female of wearing it for the benefit of the men watching me inside what should have been the privacy of my residence. The gown was pretty but not sexy in any way. Eventually these women got some of the weaker minded men on their band wagon surrounding my supposed uncleanliness and unattractiveness. The unclean tactic then initiated a full and thorough investigation of my underwear when I washed my clothes. After this official investigation, the men, then declared me as having their final seal of approval saying, "She's very, very clean."

This investigative knowledge soon became the new repetitive comment of choice whenever I used the restroom as they watched insuring I knew they were observing me. One day the men watched me knowing that I was on my period. I needed pads from the store and had to go out while having painful cramps. I threw on some clothes and headed out the door with the men in tow saying, "Ugh. She did not even take a shower".

What balanced the situation for me was that as I went about my normal day to day activities outside of my home, people from all walks of life and races, responded positively and kindly to me for no reasons at all. As those watching observed this, I was then called a phony or they said that people liked me because they did not know me. This was meant by my harshness replies back to their harassment. On the contrary, it was they who did not know me. Their personal interpretations of me were based on the barrage of insults I had become effective at hurling back at them. My motto, "Two can play that game."

Mostly everyone connected or involved with me knew of the investigation around me and a few apparently were playing along whether they wanted to or not. I knew that it was imperative that I navigate through the harsh storm circling overhead or perish from the propensity of it all. The greatest worthwhile lesson for me would be the ability to stand fiercely, fighting for my life, faithfully, trusting, and most importantly alone in the physical sense.

First, and far most, after the car accident, I urgently, desperately needed help and for the last time decided to begin the emotional healing process. I would get it right, this time. I had to. I contacted the Veterans hospital in Prescott, Arizona, just outside of Flagstaff and made arrangements for the onsite recovery program two months after the car accident in May of 2007 and moved out my Scottsdale, Arizona apartment. As mentioned, I put my furniture in storage, made arrangements for my ex-boyfriend to keep my vehicle and was optimistic.

After he helped me clean out the apartment, he explained that he had contacted a friend of his who had an extra empty bedroom. He was involved with an attorney by then and she visited him regularly and randomly from Chicago. I did not have a problem with staying with his friend and was grateful for 3 days. A bed would be ready for me in at the Prescott Veteran's hospital Domiciliary after which.

When we pulled up to his friend's home a stocky jovial African American man walked over to greet us who had been working in the front yard. They exchanged greetings then I was introduced. I shook hands with the guy saying hello and thank you. We then all headed toward his front door following him through the house to kitchen where a woman was preparing dinner. We were introduced and I on crutches hobbled over to the couch in the adjoining family room to the kitchen taking a seat. I was now in a soft cast and relying heavily on crutches to walk on my newly restructured ankle with permanent pins, plates and screws. It was far from healed. I was told that it would be a long and slow process by my physician.

I sat on the couch in the family room looking around the nicely furnished home and observed a pool just outside the patio door. My friend and his friend immediately became engrossed in a debate over sports. I listened to the bantering between the two men while the woman quietly continued dinner preparation. I was offered a beer of which I declined, with no desire, as they both twisted the caps off their bottles and began drinking. I was on the wagon and on my way to the Prescott, Arizona VA facility for the help I needed after the inability to cope with what has happening around me contributed to my weakened spirit.

My friend was a cross between, streetwise, or so he thought, and a tastefully dressed professional. He had on many occasions told me that he wanted me to meet the attorney he was now dating to see if he and I could work together in some sort of way with her. When I asked him how this idiot amusingly told me for a ménage à trios. My response, "You're joking right." There were things I did not like about his character but overall, he had proven to me there whenever I needed him, he was always there at the drop of a dime. The day that I moved from the Scottsdale apartment, he had left her at his place and came to help me.

I just did not get it when he tried to sound tough and bragged that he was from the mean streets of Cleveland, Ohio, saying life there was hardcore. He did not look the role of a player. If so, I would not have been attracted to him in the first place. I thought it was cute that he wanted to be thought of that way. The only hustling he did was in real estate, by profession, and of which he was in the million-dollar-a-year sales bracket for Century 21 Realty. So, when he continually tried to portray himself in this manner, I would just laugh and tease him about it.

The woman put the roast she was preparing dinner in the oven and joined us. We both sat quietly, feeling each other out, listening to the debate on why, or how the game was won. What floored me, as the conversation made it way around to me, was the ridiculous remark my friend made out of nowhere to his friend.

"Hey man, if you have any problems out of her just tell her to get you're 'a—' over there and sit down," he said pointing to the couch.

My ears could not believe what I had just heard. He had never talked to me in this manner. Realizing that he possibly was just showing off for his friend, trying to make his reputation off me, I ignored him thinking, okay, I give you that one as I laughed along with them. He apparently wanted to pretend that I was some silly woman that would allow a man to talk to me that way which was dead wrong. I did not like him or anyone else that much. I treat people the way I want to be treated. Because it was out of character for him, I let the comment pass though I did feel a slight temperature rise. There was no real harm in him trying to show off for what now appeared to be his loudmouth friend. So, I laughed along with the two of them, as the woman grunted, and we gave each other one of those woman-to-woman looks as I nodded to her. After about an hour visit, my friend stood, saying he had better get moving heading towards the door. Just as he stood, his cell phone rang.

I stood with him following him to the door on crutches. I heard his voice change to softness, which indicated to me that he was indeed talking to a woman. I asked him who he was talking to after he hung up out of nosiness and he said, to my surprise, "How dare you ask me who I'm talking to," very rude. I was surprised again for the second time that day by something he had said that was out of character though this really offended by the remark. It was the tone of his voice when he snapped at me that successfully struck a nerve. I knew he had always liked my older model car and had on one occasion acted like he wanted it and that he would take it from me if he could. I felt this strongly one day but brushed it off finding the likelihood of that happening more comical than anything else. I thought he must be joking when he hinted at it. When I told him that I was still making payments, his response was, "Oh, I did not know that. I don't want it now" which was even funnier.

He could not be serious. However, his behavior overall would turn out to be no joke and it became apparent that he was now recruited in the effort around me. I looked at him as we both stood in the door, just before he headed out and said,

"Look, you can't talk to me like that. I just asked you a simple question."

He surprised me again saying, "And I told you," he said. "It's none of your business," he snapped.

I was confused and dumbfounded. Why was he still playing some sort of player role? I turned and noticed that his friend was standing in the kitchen doorway absorbing the whole scene. I had never seen this side of him before. Added to my confusion, while standing at the door with him was his again demeanor changed. This time his voice softened returning back to the person I had always known.

"Call me later," he said as he headed toward my vehicle.

"I have a house to show. I will be home later in the evening." With that said he drove off.

I watched him as pulled away from the curb then walked back into the kitchen and sat back on the couch. The couple was watching television.

The man had his head laid in his girlfriend's lap on the couch as they both watched. He sat up when I entered the room. The woman stood and told me to follow her. She would show me where I was going to sleep. Apparently, my friend was connected with these people as tenants for the homeowner who now lived in California. I was shown to a bedroom that was comfortable. I told her that I was tired and wanted to rest a while. It had been a long, arduous day with me hobbling along trying to help him clean out my apartment. She smiled saying she understood and told me that she would call me when dinner was ready. I thanked her as she quietly closed the door behind her saying,

"If you need anything just call me," as she returned to the kitchen.

I still was a bit confused and slightly hurt by my friend's behavior in the quiet of the room. I tried to call him for an explanation before I nodded off to sleep. He did not answer his phone. I decided to call him later. For now, I needed rest.

The next day I called and waited for him to call me back; he did not respond. I left a message that I needed to get to the VA hospital for a prescription refill before going on to Prescott, Arizona. The refill was factually something I had truly needed having neglected due to being wrapped up in moving. It was now Monday morning. When he did call me back I mentioned this to him, for the third time and was really shocked by his response this time. He said, "Do I look like your taxi cab?" When he said this, this time, I went left and told him to bring me my car back, and bring it right now! I can do it myself I told him. He said that he would do no such thing and hung up in my face. I called and called his cell phone, and he did not answer. I was now livid demanding he bring me my car back leaving messages.

When the guy whose home I was staying heard all the commotion, he appeared in the doorway of my room as my friend hung up on me once again after answering briefly. I tried to redial his number and of course it just rang after that. I explained the situation to his friend then asked him if he could take me to pick up my vehicle. He said that he would take me but he and his girlfriend only had one car that they shared and she was at work and not expected home until later. He did however agree to call my friend for me to see if he could get through to him. When he called and left a message, his phone rang back within seconds. I listened as he said, "Hey, man, she's asking for her car and she's upset." After seeing how upset I was when he came to the door, I explained to him that I was only leaving my car with my ex temporarily. He then told me that he and his girlfriend could have kept it for me saying that a second car, even if temporary, would help them out a lot. After all, he said, they were helping me out by letting me stay there. I was angry at my friend and began to consider his offer. With my leg in the condition it was in, I did not need to be driving. Because of my consideration of the possibility of now leaving the vehicle with him, his friend was now motivated to help me get the car back.

It was Friday evening when he dropped me off at his friend's home. It was Monday morning when I called him requesting my vehicle back since he declared, "I am not your taxi cab." It was Tuesday afternoon before he finally pulled up, not in my care but in his. He came only after talking with his friend who asked him to at least come by and calm me down. I had been watching out the window all morning waiting for his arrival. I thought we had agreed that he would bring my vehicle. However, when he showed up in his car, I concluded that he had no intention of giving me my car back. His friend, probably already knowing this, and I hatched a plan. He told me he knew how I could get the car. He told me that what I should do is to call the cops and have the police present when he got there.

So, there I sat at the window waiting for him to pull up. As soon as he pulled up, I dialed 911 explaining the situation knowing there would be an argument. I watched out the window as he exited his vehicle and slowly walked to the door and rang the doorbell. When I hung up with the police, I grabbed my crutches and quickly made my way to the family room where his friend was cleaning, telling him that he was here. When I said that, I anxiously turned as the doorbell rang to go to the door to open it myself as the man yelled out, "Hey, wait a minute, you do not, and I repeat do not answer my door." Was I imagining it? Was his tone now extremely aggressive also? I was now a bit surprised by him now too. Maybe he had bought into what my friend had told him that first night when he told me he could disrespect me and tell me to sit down and shut up and I would obey. He walked pass me to the door, opened it, greeted our friend,

"Hey man," as he came in and both stood whispering while standing in the front door way. If he were explaining to him that I was very upset this would be an understatement.

And there it was again my friend switching into the role of a player, then saying, "I'll take care of her."

He headed toward me brushing past me heading into the family room as I turned around to follow him saying, "I thought you were going to bring my car," as we now stood facing each other.

He looked at me with a condescending look on his face and, in his voice, said, "You thought wrong" as he sat down.

When I realized that he was there to give me more of the same crap, the last I saw was red. I slammed down my crutches balancing myself on my one good leg.

"You had better go and get my car," I said.

He just looked and said, smiling smugly, "I am not bringing that car to you."

I became incensed and got in his face bending over him; he was now sitting down and I holding on to the arm of the loveseat where he sat. Who was this Dr. Jekyll-Mr. Hyde? Again, I had never seen this person before. The change in behavior could only now be related to the effort around me, I was absolutely sure now. I knew that I was not going to allow someone to treat me this way. I had had my fill. I had taken the high road with my ex-husband. That was because I was emotionally weakened and damaged. He won by default in the divorce by me doing what I thought was best for our children at the time. It now appeared that this man now thought that he could just take something away from me that belonged to me, and that I would not protest. I don't know where he got that idea but it was untrue. Now there I was with this now, "so-called" friend talking down to me like I was some silly woman while I stood over him yelling and screaming at the top of my lungs to go get my car. He sat patiently, calmly, and was nearly laughing in my face. I was further shocked by his next words.

In what appeared to be a final act to prove his player status, and to my total disbelief he then said, "Get you're An-- over there and sit down!" If anyone has ever seen the original movie of the Exorcist, imagine me, my head turning slowly and completely around on my neck. When it resumed it normal position, non-literally, my face was distorted with anger. But instead of yelling, I spit in his face. Okay, bear with me now reader. It was not a gross amount, more like sprinkles, but just enough to get the message and effect across. He had to be shown that I was serious. All of a sudden, the smirk and smooth player persona disappeared from his face. As he sprung up off the couch, his keys, which were sitting in his lap, fell to the floor. He stood there, shocked and now in his own disbelief, "She spit it my face!" then "She spit in my face" said again.

Now mind you, his friend had deposited himself immediately outside after we walked into the family room, walking past us both to the patio in the pool area. He closed the door, and began washing the patio glass door repeatedly spaying window cleaner and wiping what appeared to be the same spot over and over again. As loud as I had gotten demanding my car, he had to have heard every word I said.

As my ex friend now stood wiping the shower off his face, before I could say another word, the doorbell rang. His friend, heard the doorbell, and watched as I again anxiously turned to hop to the door forgetting my crutches which I had earlier thrown to the floor in rage.

When he saw me again heading to the door he opened the door and said, firmly "Hey, I told you, no one answers the door but me." There it was again, that same tone now from him. The only person in the room who did know who was at the door was my friend who was still standing with a dumbfounded look on his face. When he opened the front door, there stood two police officers. By then, I had grabbed my crutches, and limped over to the door where his friend stood talking with the cops. I anxiously began telling the two policemen without so much as breathing what was happening. I turned and saw my friend watching from the family room doorway, quietly listening to it all with the same stupid look on his face.

The two cops listened patiently to every word I said trying to first calm me down telling me to breath. I told them how I had agreed to let my friend keep my car while I went into recovery at the Prescott Veteran's Hospital. When I told him that I needed him to take me to the Phoenix VA hospital for a medication refill before I left, he told me no. Seeing my cast, I told them I was recently in a major car accident and had just bought the vehicle. I told them that when I asked him to take me for the prescription refill, he told me that he was not my taxi. I told him at that point he refused to bring my vehicle to me so I could go on my own. He refused.

When I spoke with him on the phone, I hoped that he would show up with my car, but he had not. I asked him why, and he said, flat out, that he was not going to give it back to me. I was so highly agitated at that point that it was impossible for me to easily calm down and they requested that I try several times. I was at maximum agitation though I tried taking a few deep breaths.

They separated each of us and asked my friend to step outside to talk with one of them. The last question one of them asked me was who is the registered owner of the vehicle? I told them me and only me. I watched as they talked first with my "so called" who now was standing by the curb leaning on his car now looking frustrated. Then they talked again briefly with the tenant of the home who was standing midway between us and them on his lawn. I stood in the doorway.

After they finished talking with each of us, they then approached me saying that he had agreed to give me the car back. It had been suggested that his friend, ride with him back to his house to pick it up, and his friend agreed. With that, they got into his car and drove off. I closed the door and peeked out the blinds as the police sat for a few minutes writing their report before driving off themselves. Relieved, I walked back into my bedroom. About an hour or so later, the friend pulled up with my car, but little did I know it was for Act II. Bear in mind that I was under 24/7 satellite surveillance and that everyone around me had or were being manipulated and influenced in my environment to include wherever I went.

As I watched him drive up with my vehicle, I had an omen that many more problems were on the horizon with this old classic car. I sat and watched him proudly exit the car with his chest poked out and head toward his door. Although the car was an older model, it was a good pick for me and was well maintained.

When he came in with the keys, I immediately asked for them. He looked at me and said that he did not think that giving them to me was a good idea. He then said that he had promised our friend that he would not give them back to me. In disbelief, I exploded again although a bit more restrained than earlier. Here now was a complete stranger, yes, in whose house I was staying temporarily, now refusing to now give me my property for a second time. After he realized that I was not playing, and after witnessing what had occurred earlier, he threw the keys to me and they landed on the floor at my feet. He then said that if I picked them up, then you will have to leave. I said "fine," grabbed my keys, and on crutches walked past him to the bedroom to get my suitcase. I began throwing my things back into it and hobbled out to my car. I sat in the car, trying to digest everything that had happened, wanting to cry but did not knowing where I could go. I had moved out of my apartment and was now homeless.

My bed was not ready at the Prescott VA hospital for another few days. I was lost; severely depressed, and shaken. I sat there feeling completely alone. The girlfriend arrived home about forty-five minutes later from work. I saw her pull up and get out of their SUV heading inside. I waved at her thinking good, balancing hormones. She went inside first to get a briefing about the day's activities probably. After getting the run down, she came out saying that she needed to go to the grocery store. We went to the grocery store for a few things she needed for dinner. I was shocked and could not believe the whole situation. So, what did I do? Naturally, I made a beeline to the liquor department and grabbed a beer. When we got back, she went inside and I sat in outside in the car and drank it. It was starting to get dark as the sun began to set.

When the guy came out and told me that I could not sit in front of his house and if I did not move he was going to call the cops on me, I started the engine and realized that I did not know where I was going. I also did not have my prescription glasses and am blind at night without them. Driving realistically was a chance I should not take but I had no choice. My driver's license said "with glasses." So, without them, it would mean, literally unforeseeable trouble driving at night. I knew that it would be unwise to go far. I could not read the street signs. I did not know where I was going or having any specific place to go, I started the engine and slowly pulled away from the front of this man's house. I had not paid any attention when we drove to the unfamiliar neighborhood when I arrived with my friend a few days earlier. I noticed a large apartment complex on my left after turning the corner and after I had driven about three blocks. It was now about 7:30 p.m. I turned into the apartment complex hoping to find a secluded place to park for the night. I parked the car so that it would not be obvious that I was inside it. I did not buy anything to drink for fear of it making me have to use the restroom. This was how I had become accustomed to handling any and all storms in my life and the only way I knew to cope with pain, sadness, depression, and disappointment by programmed habit. I knew that I would have to stay there at least until daylight, before I could see exactly where I was or needed to go. I turned off the ignition and tried to settle down and rest. When I would nod off, I would wake startled by someone going to or from their vehicles or just walking by in the parking lot. I would immediately become hyper vigilante and watched to see if anyone saw me sitting in the car before trying to sleep. I was in danger, or worse as my thoughts went haywire racing in my head tangled in confusion and pain. I had had a horrible few days, but there was some light. The light was that I was at least heading to recovery at the Prescott VA.

At the first sign of daylight, I started the engine and drove slowly out of the complex. I had to use the restroom. When I looked at the clock in the car it read 4:45 a.m. There was just enough sun on the horizon for me to see. My psychological and emotional state had taken yet another severe and harsh beating. It was also compacted by the undercurrent of the covert harassment and terrorism from an unknown source and for unknown reasons in the mix. In the strain, I was again beginning to feel like I did not want to go on as I tried to position the large boot so that I could drive. As I started the engine and slowly drove out of the complex, I searched for signs searching for something familiar which would give me an indication of where I was. I saw a sign giving directions for the I-17 freeway and knew that it would take me to the Phoenix VA hospital.

I was admitted and stayed there a few days. The staff confirmed that a bed was now available for me at the domiciliary in Prescott. I pulled out of the Phoenix VA around 2:30 p.m., a day later, heading to what I thought would be the ever-evading new hope and new beginning I constantly sought and refused to relinquish the hope. This was the first week in June of 2007. After this and a brief say in Prescott, I moved back to California.

***

I now sat in jail in Arizona on the DUI charges now for three weeks in April of 2009, two years after the car accident unable to reach my ex-boyfriend who was supposedly waiting on my arrival. He had told me he would drive the U-Haul with my furniture on to Albuquerque, New Mexico for me. He lived there once and had free time. He was now engaged to be married. I told myself that I should not be surprised or confused by his behavior or why I had not seen hide or hair of him since being incarcerated. I was now coming up on the third week of being in jail and the strain was taking its toll on me.

What ultimately got a response from him and got him to the jail was an official call from an attorney. A young Hispanic lady who I laughed and talked with gave me the name and number of someone she used to work for saying he was the best in town. When I called the number the next day, during phone privileges hours, in the open bay jail holding area the law office took my collect call, and the attorney agreed to try and contact him for me.

As I spoke on the jailhouse phone, I could still hear the familiar voices of some official unknown agents every time I used the payphone. They were talking as the phone rang in the background taunting me, laughing, "We got her, ha, ha, ha, ha..."

I was greatly surprised when I heard my name over the intercom "You have a visitor." Three week later, it had taken an official call from a possible legal representative to get results from him and to get him the jail to bail me out. He showed up with his daughter, in tow. I had met her once, and then only briefly at a ballgame he invited me to for his grandson when we first began dating. I could not shake the feeling that he had her with him especially, as some sort of safety net due specifically to his knowledge of the full picture of what was happening around me. Thank God he did show up at all. However, after our connection whenever I needed to call him there was now additional money added to his phone carrier from my bank account for the calls. I could now call him when needed.

With the agency listening in the background as we made arrangements to post bail, one said, almost sounding disappointed "Oh, so he 'is' going to get her out" emphasis on 'is.' "Yep" said the other. I guess somewhere in his conscious he decided to help me in spite of his involvement. The way it was said felt like it was intentionally to give the impression that he was in on everything also. There would be other red flags later that would prove this as a great possibility later on for the second time.

Yes, there was definite gratitude overall. I could have been laying in a ditch somewhere. It appeared he likely already knew where I was. When he asked how I found the attorney, saying that he was impressed with him and that he sounded sharp, I knew that it was the attorney who had blessed me even though his services were too rich for my blood. One last thing that was glaring about my friend that created distrust and which nearly caused an argument with him after we began talking in the jail.

While preparations were being made for my bond and release there was the ever-present relentless request by him asking me for artwork I had hanging in my Scottsdale apartment when he helped me move out in May of 2007. He decided that two of my very favorite, beautiful pictures on my wall should be his. I did admittedly tell him that he could have them initially. However, this was before the incident with my car. By the time he came to help me finish cleaning everything was already in storage.

He bugged me about those pictures nearly every time we spoke over the phone for the next two years after I left Arizona in 2007 saying,

"Where are my pictures?"

I was honest with him telling him, "You forfeited those pictures when you acted how you did about my car."

This man was a real piece of work. Here I was incarcerated and he still two years later believed that he should have the pictures. And, he had the gall to put his daughter up to asking me if she could get my storage key. Her excuse was to take some of the things out of my packed down car to the storage. Typical of some women the ones who bend over backwards to satisfy some men he could not handle the fact that I was adamant, not fascinated with him much, and that I was not going to give him the pictures two years later. Being who I am I argued with him about it before bail was placed over the phone angry about her even asking for a key to my storage. Fortunately, the things were stored not in a walk-in storage unit but storage crates so they would not have been able to get anything out of storage anyway after being stored for two years and numerous other crates packed on top of mine.

By 2011, he had married and divorced the attorney after only six months. Her daddy, the judge, picked up on his deceptive character quickly. We still talked a bit from time to time although he was down after the real estate market decline. Broke due to the real estate market crash and out of the only profession he had known all of his life; he asked to borrow $500. I sent him what I could afford $300 in consideration for helping me that time.

I was now in California when he called asking me to be his Valentine in February of 2011.

"I bet you look so good."

This revealed to me a very possible continued connection to those targeting me I felt instinctually. I remembered he did not like how I was now wearing my hair, in the beginning stage of growing locks, when he arrived at the jail that day or think it attractive at all and told me so sounding disappointed. When he called and begin laying on the compliments before Valentine's Day, sounding just like those targeting me during the same time with compliments of how I look, I emailed him, on a hunch, testing the water, saying that I was now convinced he had always been working with them. Expecting to hear immediately back from him, saying I was wrong. I got no response. When I finally phoned him, after leaving several messages for him to call me, his voice was cautious, and over the phone, his overall manner had significantly changed and spoke volumes regarding my likely accuracy of his 100% involvement.

THE CAT WAS AGAIN OUT OF THE BAG AND THANK GOD FOR CLEAR VISION!

CHAPTER SIX

"Don't accept that others know you better than yourself. Work joyfully and peacefully, knowing that right thoughts and right efforts will inevitably bring about right results."

— **James Allen**

Thank goodness that in mist of life's trials, good people continually showed up in my life.

In Arizona, it was in the form of three people, an Arizona Superior Court Commissioner/judge, a court appointed doctor and the assigned probation officer in Pretrial Services. The Rule 11 court necessitating a full mental health evaluation was the typical result of me speaking up about the satellite surveillance and the "black bag" technologies being used on me and again, typical disbelief.

As a result, it became necessary for the court to rule out psyche issues and determine my capacity to stand trial on the DUI and related charges. These three individuals were a Godsend. Due to being isolated and having to cope with the continued around the clock psychological badgering, degradation, energy weapon attacks and threats, at least I had someone I could talk to and vent meaning the Pretrial services officer I checked in with once a week. It did not matter if either believed me or not. These three individuals appeared sincere, and showed ethical concern. In an environment where my trust was completely shattered regarding law enforcement or those connected to law enforcement. These three good men were rays of light in darkness.

Their involvement with me provided the necessary coping mechanism and comfort of knowing that I would be treated fairly under the tremendous strain of the continued covert abuse and two could check and verify that an effort had factually evolved around me. Everyone and I do mean everyone, it appeared had either been questioned or approached and it was evidenced in conversations by odd remarks and personality changes.

I continued to hold onto to the truth and refused to let go. What I was enduring was very real and technologically very possible, and I was not going to let anyone convince me the truth was unreal even if it meant dismissal of the three felony charges by the Rule 11 court determining as me being delusional. I would take my chances and continue to speak up about what was factually happening.

After being pulled over just outside of Phoenix, Arizona, as I stated, I was stunned to learn that their threat of, "You will not make it to your destination," New Mexico, and "You are going to jail," said by those targeting me before I left Oakland and the fact that it speared to have become reality.

To my great surprise, after being stopped for switching lanes without a blinker on at 2:30 a.m., with no other cars on the road, I was being handcuffed and hauled off to jail. Again, in 2007, I left Arizona homeward bound after the accident and severe damage to my ankle.

I was now just two years sober and I struggled to remember exactly what the officer was telling me, in 2009, in disbelief that there factually were warrants for my arrest. I had no prior knowledge of any charges officially nor was notified after the accident although I did leave the state incapacitated. I was even more shocked to learn that the charges became active eight months after the accident official in November of 2007.

I had no choice but return to California needing assistance with my basic needs which included even entering and exiting the shower, grocery shopping, house cleaning, cooking and transportation. My sports utility vehicle had been completely demolished after a small flame ignited on impact and it grew after I foolishly tried to restart the engine after the crash and engulf the entire vehicle when police and firemen arrived.

I had two major surgeries to the ankle. Holes were drilled into the bone of the right leg for fitting of the uncomfortable metal external fixation device that I wore for a month. I spent months in a hard cast, a soft case, a wheel chair, crutches, and a boot.

When the officer placed me in handcuffs then sat me in the back of his squad car almost twelve hours later after leaving Oakland, with my repeatedly telling him there had to be a mistake, he showed me on the car computer the charges. I was speechless. It took me a while to register what he was saying, connect the warrant to the car accident in 2007, then digest everything along with the fact that I was actually being arrested and factually had been forewarned. Yes, the charges were real, but the situation overall was the obvious machination of and agency. This was true in 2007 when the car accident happened, and again very true at that moment in 2009.

I had been talking on the phone right before running out of gas that morning after passing up gas station after gas station during the final stretch into Phoenix, Arizona without a thought to the ex-boyfriend. I had taken the batteries out of my cell phone due to repeated threats before I left Oakland and its use as a tracking device. This was only because I was unsure of what to expect or what, "She's gone" actually meant as someone watched and listen to my preparations for the trip and move. I was also travelling alone.

When I saw the gas tank extremely low, after getting off the phone with him letting him know my location, I panicked and pulled off the road and dialed 911. When the operator told me that there was not much she could do I remembered Roadside Assistance. During the call to the 911 operator, I heard a familiar voice in the background of the call say "We found her" discerning my locations by cell phone after putting the batteries back in. Tired, burnt out, and frustrated, I began yelling into to phone at them.

I was immediately cautioned after the operator questioned whom I was talking to forgetting for a moment that she was still on the line and listening. I regained composure and told her I was arguing with someone sitting inside the car with me.

When I arrived at the jail, it became obvious that the group targeting me factually had their hands involved. During the processing, and also just before being handcuffed while standing beside my car, I listened to a second backup officer, say "Dang, they really, really want her" said within earshot although he did not know I heard him. This was said right after the back-up officer got off his cell phone sounding as if confirming to someone that I had been apprehended.

With my head spinning, I ignored his comment at that time as I stood in disbelief that I was actually going to jail on something I had not a clue existed.

When we reached the Estrella Jail on the outskirts of Phoenix, I was instructed to take a seat not far from where the arresting officers began processing my information into the computer. As he did the second officer walked up behind him peering over his shoulder. I watched them still hoping a mistake had been made still. I astounded when I heard the second officer say again, this time, "Wow! They want her" with emphasis this time. After he said this a second time, I spoke up. I asked, "What do you mean they want me?" They both looked up from the computer surprised that I heard the comment. The arresting officer quickly regrouped telling me that his partner just meant the warrants, at the highest level, and nothing more downplaying the comment and leaving it at that. The one who made the statement said nothing. However, an impression of official tampering was given by his making this statement twice.

I also could not negate the fact of their showing up when they did with no other vehicles in sight, the arrest, the charges, and everything else. I also could not negate the fact that the situation was being covertly influenced by those one called "They" by the second officer.

You Are Not My Big Brother

After the initial processing, both officers, gave me a compassionate, sincere look, saying, "We wish you the best of luck" then said goodbye before handing me over to the jail staff. I mustered up a smile to the both of them and a thank you before they departed. I was then led away to another area to begin additional paper work. What happened next cemented the idea that it was the feds likely tracking me. Doing nothing wrong had afforded me the luxury of believing I could travel through Arizona without issues and carry on to my destination.

There were two of us being processed together, myself and another female that night in the quiet of the jail as everyone slept in the early morning hours. We were led to a room inside a secure holding area and told to wait for the clerk at the window to finish paperwork processing. As I stood at the window waiting for someone to come, a man whom I thought was the clerk slid into the seat at the desk. He said,

"So, you are a Veteran huh?"

"I replied, "yes" proudly.

"How much money do veterans receive nowadays?" I told him.

He then stood and left without saying another word leaving behind the apparent hope by "They" to created doubt, and fear, again monitored from the operation center. Immediately after he left the area a woman whose position it was to assist with the final processing sat down and began asking questions, name, social security number, address, etc., then handed me papers to sign. With this process complete, I and the other lady, after she was processed, were given jail clothing and moved into an open bay type area housing approximately two hundred females of all ages and races sleeping in rows of bunk beds just as dawn approached.

During my three weeks stay at the jail, whenever I walked by the guard booth, I occasionally heard one of the guards say, as if I was some sort of circus attraction, "The Feds are after her" pointing me out to a coworker. On another occasion, "That's her right there" was said as I walked past as the intimidation effort continued with everyone now playing their role. From the way, they sounded when referencing me, I was some sort of big-time crime lord, or a powerful person of interest. Or were they just impressed to be involved with something they perceived bigger than their typical normal day-to-day county jail activities of watching over a large group of hormonal female inmates. One thing was sure the comments were said for me to hear them by the guards intentionally.

Jail clothing colors, designated by the Sheriff of Phoenix, Arizona, are gray and white stripes with pink accessories–pink socks, pink t-shirts, and pink underwear. This is also true also for male inmates a choice of the Sheriff Joe Arpaio. Never having been incarcerated except overnight, by my ex-husband a few times after my initial divorce filing, the reality of the experience had not completely sunk in yet. The whole thing was surreal and admittedly I wanted to stay in the lightheaded place of disbelief believing it was a nightmare which I would eventually awaken from. Had this really happened? Instinctually I knew that when the disorientated feeling dissipated, I would likely feel the full brunt, force and shocking reality of where I was in a matter of hours.

I was excited for the new experience leaving a two- bedroom apartment in Oakland, California I shared with my middle daughter. I was paying for rent there twice what I would be paying in New Mexico and getting a very nice living space. I found a beautiful, eight-hundred-square foot apartment with a fireplace, a mountain view, including a garage in a brand new complex. On top of this it was connected to a golf course landscape, although I do not golf, and for only seven hundred dollars a month.

I had been taking online spiritual advancement courses from a program headquartered in Albuquerque and wanted to be around others studying what I learning. The courses, I believed, would contribute to my overall spiritual well-being helping to heal me. And after an argument and parting of ways with this daughter, I realized it was time to let my girls grow up and have their own life experiences and stop babysitting them. They were young women now with smart and disrespectful mouths to go along with their adulthood, and did not need my advice anymore. They were grown. I had to turn them over to God's care.

Although my ex-boyfriend and I managed to remain a friendship, the fact still remained that we had had that major argument right. I had to consider this but I did not know another soul in Arizona to call. Our personalities under right circumstances had always clicked and we could always laugh and joke around easily with each other.

Now fully processed into the women's unit, I tried to acclimate to the environment. The disbelief lingered acting as cushion for the blow and shattering of my plans for spiritual advancement to take myself above what was happening.

Sleep did not come easy. I tossed and turned dreading waking. I was assigned to a top bunk. This became a major issue for me due to the screws and pins in my ankle. I could not put the necessary pressure on my right foot to hoist myself up. One of the ladies saw me struggling and was kind enough to find a lower bunk for me.

"Hey," she said, "I noticed that bed number 124 is open. It is a bottom bunk too."

I then approached one of the guards and explained my dilemma and was gratefully moved.

Throughout the next few days at the designated times for telephone privileges, I tried to phone the only person I knew in town, the ex-boyfriend. Typically, in the background of my calls were the continued taunting and now laughter and sounds of victory,

"We've got her" was repeated over and over.

That this same group was listening to my every call was no great surprise. It had been a daily occurrence for three years. I also was not surprised when I heard comments using the technological ability to beam their voices to the back of my neck as they watched me walk around in the limited area of the open bay cell. They continued to follow my every move by real time from the operation center in there.

I tried to distract my thoughts fearing the grip of intense depression and mingled with some of the female inmates who I perceived not hardcore. I have always been a likable person and in there it appeared to no exception thankfully due to my sincerity. Although I did not have much, I shared it with other females who had nothing at all. I watched their sad faces when it was time to purchase goodies from the canteen and the excitement when the guards later handed out the goodies. Those who had caring families on the outside knew they were loved and I suspect it helped them to cope when somewhat put money on the books for them. The ones who had nothing or no one would sit quietly watching the others dig into their large bags full of potato chips, candy bars, lotion, shampoo, makeup and various other items. I had about twenty dollars in my pocket when I was pulled over which was put on the books for me to make small purchases. However, doing for others when things are bad for you can bring joy and lift your spirits I had always known.

The fact that I am this way, however, would later create a minor problem for me with one of the women by giving the appearance of me being vulnerable, weak, or perhaps someone easily manipulated, pushed around, or to be taken advantage of by jailhouse standards. Although I am not stupid, nor do I think I am bad or tough, I am human and had to prove it during the short incarceration.

I knew that I needed legal help but did not know how to go about getting it from inside the jail. And no one, as far as I knew, knew where I was. I repeatedly tried to contact my friend who was supposedly waiting for me to call him as soon as I made it to Chandler, Arizona where he now lived in the early morning hours. I kept trying and trying his phone number. His phone would ring. I would hear him pick up and say "hello, hello, hello," and then the line would go dead.

I was frantic. I did not know if he was disconnecting my calls intentionally or not. I chastised myself for being so trusting and considered the very real possibility that he might still harbored resentment toward me along with his recruitment. Why not him everyone else had been used it appeared?

I recalled how conveniently he had shown up the night we met with his roommate at the supper club I had gone to eat and socialize. His roommate, a young handsome white male, at the African American social location was a tad odd. He was the only non-black person there that night or any other night that I would go there at times to eat. He told me they had come all the way from another town specifically to order food after sitting down in the two vacant chairs at my table where I sat alone. He introduced himself, and his roommate. We started a general friendly conversation. I would later learn that he and his roommate had bought an investment property, a house, which they shared on the outskirts of Phoenix, in Queen Creek which he called their bachelor pad. The thought did cross my mind that it was a little late to be ordering dinner especially after he told me they had driven so far. His excuse was that he wanted to turn his buddy on to real soul food. It was around 10:45 p.m.

I continued trying to call his cell phone from the jail. Later I was told by an inmate that I was being disconnected because I was calling a cell phone number. I was somewhat relieved to hear this. The sinking feeling in my heart lifted and I realized that all hope was not completely lost and I could give him the benefit of the doubt. In order to call a cell phone, she explained, money needed to first be added in advance to the cell phone holder's account.

The protective fog of the reality of where I was lifting and I was beginning to get frustrated and sick to my stomach. If I walked to the restroom, "She's going to the restroom" was said by Synthetic Telepathy and Psy Ops mimicry. I still could not believe how this could have happen. I was driving along, happy go lucky, about a new life, then wham I had been blind sighted and sucker punched.

A week after incarceration, on March 26, 2009, there was a Statutory Hearing. I and about ten other females were woken around 3:00 a.m.

to shower, dress, and prepare for the bus ride at 5 a.m. to the courthouse in Mesa, Arizona. Once there, we were handcuffed to each other and sat waiting in the holding area in the back of the courtroom with an armed guard watching over us until our appointed court times.

As I sat waiting for my name to be called, I watched as a female public defender slowly make her way in my direction for my interview. During the time I waited, I caught bits and pieces of the reasons other inmates were there and they were there for many reasons. Listening to their stories kept me preoccupied and helped me by distraction to stay calm. I wanted to scream. My anxiety level was excessively critically high but I had to suppress it. If I flipped out due to the enormity of everything, that would not be good for me.

When the public defender's office personnel first entered the room, there were three attorneys, two men, one younger one and one older. The older male appeared to be a supervisor, and then a woman. During the two-hour wait, for my turn, I listened to the younger male standing near the door talking to the guard. I looked up when I overheard him say to the guard, "The Feds are after her." When I did they both were looking directly at me. After he had gotten my attention he then turned around and left the room proving another individual playing a role while the operation center kept deciphering my thoughts for any useful fear. I knew I had done nothing wrong and nothing they could do would change this. There was neither fear nor guilt in me.

The guard busied himself with paperwork on the desk where he sat trying to nonchalantly look over at me as I sat now staring at him. When the female public defender finally made it to me, I asked to speak with her outside in the hallway. Just prior to her walking into the room, I observed her being approached by a man in the doorway who attempted to hand her a very small file folder with a few sheets of paper in it. She looked from me to him then shook her head no without uttering a word indicating that she would not take what he was trying to put into her hands. As I watched the scene, the man glanced over at me briefly then turned and walked away. I had a feeling that he was somehow connected to my situation. Later, back at the jail, it crossed my mind he was trying to hand her information on me.

After he left, I stood face to face with the public defender attorney in the hallway as she read the charges. I was officially told that I had been charged with three felony DUIs, along with a $100,000 property damage charge. I now completely understood what the second arresting officer meant during the jail processing when he said, "Dang, they really want her." Apparently, "They" really, really did. She told me that I could take a plea agreement then explained it meant four months of mandatory jail time and loss of my driving privileges for a year. As she spoke, I could see her lips moving but did hear a word she said. I was still stuck in disbelief of $100,000 property damage. Coming back to reality I said,

"Property damage, property damage, what for?" I asked surprised. Not believing what I had heard,

"Did you say property damage of $100,000? For what," I asked again?

"It was reported that you ran into a brick wall," she told me.

This was when the reality hit me of absolute entrapment and nearly knocked me over.

"I had not hit a brick wall. What I hit was a small brick medium in a construction site which was without lighting when I tried to turn around to get back onto the freeway lost" to go back home. I told her. The drive had substantially calmed me down after fleeing my home late that night running from the two male voices coming from the ceiling of my bathroom directly over the bathtub after I got out of the bathtub around 8:40 p.m.," I told her.

"I was only going about thirty miles an hour or less, at best, when I crossed the railroad tracks straining to see ahead of me on the unlit street hoping to turn around and get back on the freeway. Out of nowhere a small brick medium appeared. It was unseen due to it being so small and the high seating of my Sports Utility Vehicle (SUV.) I was on a street blocked off by several mediums due to being a construction site with no markings. I immediately slammed on the breaks as the medium appeared within inches before impact, but was too late."

Overwhelmed, I made it out of my vehicle first noticing my grossly distorted ankle dangling from my leg, crawling, before collapsing in the middle of the road on the side street now lit only by the small flame ignited. Later a man and woman out walking around 11:30 p.m. would find me and carry me to safety. The last thing I remembered was a request to God of why before I passed out on the ground.

After I returned home to stay with my oldest daughter in June of 2007, in Los Angeles over the phone, I told family and friends that I had run into a non-literal brick wall. Yes, I had described the situation as hitting a brick wall. However, it was the brick wall of realization and awakening. The brick wall was an image used to indicate that I needed to rethink my life because it could not go on the way it was. I had to toughen up emotionally. If I were to go on, or find any happiness in life, I realized that I would have to get the help and support I needed once and for all described as the impenetrable brick wall I denied I needed. As I listened to the public defender talking, a silent alarm sounded in my head.

I regained my composure and told her that my hitting a brick wall absolutely not true. I then told her what had happened as stated above. After I finished recanting to her vividly the night in question, I then told her,

"I am being tracked everywhere by satellite surveillance and by technology provided to my neighbors called X-ray Vision which can see through the walls." And, this I told her anxiously this has been going on for quite some time, and around the clock. She was now watching me closely with a skeptical look on her face. Of course, she did not believe me. As I talked to her, the guard now stood nearby listening. She asked me if I had any diagnosis. I told her about the VA trauma diagnosis after which she then told me to take my seat saying that she wanted another court to take a look at my case. I sat down hearing the same guard say "Yep, she's a nutcase" quietly to her.

I did not know what other court she meant. I later learned that it was the Rule 11 Court responsible for psychological evaluations and my case was going to be moved to downtown Phoenix, Arizona from Mesa.

After I told my story of what sounded like a science fiction movie plot of government satellite surveillance, and high-tech advanced technology following me from state to state no less, her demeanor softened from the stern expression she had when we first began talking now believing me in need of mental help. I took my seat, but just I did, I heard her say to the same guard the young public defender had told, "The Feds are after her," that something just did not feel right about my situation.

After the Statutory Hearing, I waited in line with the other inmates waiting to board the bus to take us all back to the jail house. While I stood in line waiting to board the bus, a now different man of similar appearance to the one in the hallway with the public defender earlier stood watching me a short distance away. When I realized that he was staring at me I started watching him. He then quickly glanced away then turned and left. He looked officially federal. We arrived back at the jail just before dinner.

After putting in administrative order after order hoping for help with finding an attorney, it was my buddy on the top bunk who gave me the name of an attorney she used to work for. She claimed he was the best in Arizona but also very expensive. I could not afford him either, however he accepted my collect calls and then contacted my friend for me.

I noticed that on one of the administrative orders I filled out seeking information on how to get an attorney through the jail when my carbon copy was returned to me there was a special handwritten note at the top of the order that said, "Do Not Release." I tried to question one of the guards about what exactly this meant after noticing it. She would not give me a straight answer and rudely told me not ask anymore and get away from the guard booth. However, with all the whispering among them, about the feds, it was obvious, they were trying to deny my rights.

My friend finally was able to contact me after the attorney contacted him. Along with the little money I had saved for my move I was able to scrape up the bail amount of $2,700. I had been there just over three weeks. However, getting out of there, even after the bail was posted, would become a challenge. The guards having seen the note in the computer really thought that if the Feds said, "Do not release" then they weren't going to let me out even if bail was posted. During the timeframe, the area that originally housed my group of women was changed due to plumbing issues and we were moved from one location to another. After we were resettled, a male sergeant came in to talk with us hoping to calm the irritation that had surfaced from the move. As far as I knew my bond had been posted but I could not get a definite answer from any of the guards. When I got my turn to speak with the male sergeant, I told him of my dilemma and the guard's anger at me for asking for any definite information. I asked him if he could check to see if officially the bond had been posted in the computer for me. I now sat at a table not far from the guard booth with him where he was holding his meetings. He got up and walked over to the guard booth and spoke to the guard on shift as I sat watching. I then saw her stand, go to the computer, type in my name and point to something on the computer screen. She was obviously showing him the "'Do Not Release" note which also must have been entered into the computer. When I heard him tell her,

"They can't do that" sounding annoyed, I was relieved. It felt like the weight of the world had been lifted. Had he not come in, I probably would have imploded. I was grateful when he returned to me saying yes, the bond had been posted and that I would be released in a few hours. I could not sleep wondering when they would call my name. Around 2:30 a.m., my name was finally called just as I dozed off to sleep.

You Are Not My Big Brother

After out-processing, I was released early the next morning just at sunrise. I contacted my friend telling him that I was at a 7 Eleven not far from the jail. He told me to sit tight that he was on the way. I would have to reluctantly make Arizona my home for the second time in April of 2009.

Staying at my friend's apartment for one night, the next day I searched the Internet and found an apartment manager who decided that she would take a chance with me as a tenant even with the three felonies and the $100,000 property-damage charges showed up my credit report. I moved in April 18th of 2009.

A year later, I sat listening to the noises above now from the newly rented apartment and a new tenant apparently following me from room to room with the microwave pain beam.

My friend and I lost contact eventually. He was now engaged, which I already knew even before the agreement for him to help me move to New Mexico. I was not interested in him in that way anyway. I forgave but did not completely forget literally having to have the police make him give me back my car.

I settled into my new apartment. I had no intention of making Arizona my permanent residence this time as I had from 2006 to 2007. Because of this, I did not get my furniture out of storage. I purchased the necessities: an air mattress bed and supplies for the bathroom, and kitchen and I was comfortably set. I had a roof over my head, and a bed of my own. I was content. I had a small television in my car when I was pulled over and my laptop computer among other things.

The precarious, ominous situation, with the felony DUIs loomed overhead menacingly with uncertainty. Ironically it would be the truth that would set me free as disbelief in what was happening around me.

> "You never really know a man until you have divorced him."
> Zaa Zaa Gabor

Approximately three months after receiving military orders and after three years in Stuttgart, West Germany, my then husband, along with myself and the kids, reported to Fort Carson, Colorado. It was January of 1989. We settled into base housing on the facility and he reported to his assigned unit, and I sought employment. The kids were enrolled in the elementary school on the facility, and I found a position at the Army hospital. We had met at Fort Riley, Kansas in November of 1982.

We left for Seoul, Korea, in late December of 1983 a few months after getting married on September 3, 1983. Shortly after leaving Fort Riley, Kansas now stationed in Seoul, Korea, signs rose that even my ex could not deny and would later confirmed as definite signs of the beginning stages of issues for me. I recall one incident of an unexplained outburst specifically shortly after arriving in Korea. We invited a group of friends over for a barbeque at our off-post residence one weekend. However, for unexplained reasons, I became upset and angrily put everyone out.

This would be the incident my ex would recant to my oldest daughter as a sign of me having issues immediately after the marriage, using this outburst as evidence that I was the one messed up and not he. I will never forget waking the next morning ashamed and confused by my unexplainable reaction and behavior to our guests. This and similar incident would be the tell- tale signs of erratic, uncontrollable outbursts which continued to grow impacting my psyche in many ways. What he witnessed would reveal that after leaving Fort Riley and now in Korea. I just was not the same. And, so intense were these episodes, along with other symptoms, that it began to contribute to the quality of what was once exceptional job performance as a young soldier. My concentration suffered along with sleep, anxiety, and increased agitation, along with serious bouts of depression. Feelings and the intensity of my unexplained reactions resulted in drinking after arrival in Seoul, Korea.

During our tour in Seoul, Korea, I was assigned to the personal staff of the highest-ranking military officer for the United States government, a four-star general. When these specific issues began to impact my job performance, it ultimately cut short a promising military career.

When my job performance began to falter, instead of being relieved of my position due to decreased of my quality work, I opted to get out of the military instead. I had just re-enlisted for another tour of duty. I also had gotten an Army Commendation Medal after only a year of service, as a Private First Class, and other conduct awards. By appearance my military career was on the fast track with steady promotions. However, when the issues began to surface and take its toll on me impacting my job performance and a few weeks pregnant with my first daughter, I opted to take a Chapter 8 Pregnancy Discharge, and got out of the military. The military as a career was no longer my reality. I then took a job in a civilian capacity on base.

We left, Seoul, Korea for Stuttgart, West Germany after a two-year tour, stay three years in Germany before heading to the final military installation of Fort Carson, Colorado. Through all the changes, highs and lows and marital upheaval, the marriage appeared to be surviving. This was in spite of an act of infidelity by my husband which I initially thought I could forgive after his tearful apology during our stay in Germany. However, the reality of broken trust would be more than I could handle in the long run. His infidelity left insecurity and doubt in the relationship. Whenever we argued, the ever- present act of his violation of the marital trust was ever present and an angry emotional topic especially for me. As a result, I would always threaten to divorce him. It was after my threats of divorce that he first began calling me names. I was first confused why he chose to call me a specific degrading name for quite some time. When the reality hit me that he was referring to the traumatic incident in so the military, it cut deeply that I knew that the marriage was over.

We had been a military family for ten years by the early 90s. At that point and we had lived in two countries, Korea and Germany, with daughters born in each of these two countries. I was pregnant again with our third and youngest daughter, the last of the three when we arrived at Fort Carson back in the United States in 1986. After a medical discharge for severe recurring migraines, necessitating taking heavy duty pain medication, my ex was discharged from the military. The youngest born in 1992 was still a newborn when we moved into the home in a newly built suburb in Denver, Colorado. We were both in agreement that we did not want our children raised in California where both he and I were born choosing to make Colorado our home.

Through my dad I learned that I had a family member in Denver whom I had never met. He was a distant cousin who was a police officer with the Denver Police Department and he was also a recruiter for the department. As a result, we learned he was on Fort Carson, Colorado regularly as part of the recruiting effort. As soon as my ex was released from active duty, he tested and passed first the sheriff department's test, worked briefly as a Denver County Sheriff before switching to the Denver Police Department.

I started working temp-to-perm positions around town and was continually having typical issues of unexplained obvious dysfunction. It goes without saying that whatever was going on with me had prevailed and reflected in all areas of my life by then. On the weekends, after putting our kids to sleep, it was our time with each other. We would crank up the oldies, and drink. Alcohol, however, did not have the same effect on him that it did on him. He apparently could handle it.

I had always been able to land really good jobs, with promotion potential, but somehow keeping them was an unexplainable problem for me as I sabotaged myself. Because of this, I began to feel worthless, insecure and doubtful. My confidence continued to plummet and although alcohol was not helping, it had becoming a crutch for me.

Of the little family I did have, I maintained contact with one of my great aunts in Oklahoma City who was a rock in my life. I adored her. She believed in me, and when I sent her a sample of the moisturizing cream I had made in my kitchen, she invested $5,000 in the endeavor. However, during this time my marriage was slowly crumbling. Bills needed to be paid, and we needed two incomes. We also had three small children to support. My husband and I argued frequently about money although this are typical in marriages. Added to this equation was alcohol.

The great aunt I adored passed and I, shocked and emotional, was upstairs on Christmas 1994 morning in a heated emotional debate with my great uncle regarding her belongings instead of being downstairs with my ex and the girls opening gifts. He came upstairs heard me arguing with my uncle then called me a malicious name. Devastated, I knew at that very moment that we were done and that I would not be able to stay in the marriage as his wife any longer. Our first unofficial separation would be the result of this incident and he first moving in with his parents. I later filed officially for divorce.

I was so deeply hurt by him that at that time that I just wanted the situation over. I guess he decided that it was time for him to come back home after realizing he technically had abandoned his family and after he closed out the joint bank account. He must have learned from associates in law enforcement that he now stood the risk of losing the house, losing custody of the kids, child support, and likely alimony. He probably was also told that moving out and leaving us without even money for food would cost him big time.

This is when I believe he hatched a plan along with his mother to get me out of the house and get the kids and house. It started with a bouquet of flowers when I dropped the baby off at his mom's in the mornings heading to school. I had enrolled in Court Reporting School. Another morning it was a stuffed animal.

The next morning, he was teary eyed and almost begged for forgiveness and to come back home. He persisted asking to come home until finally, one night we decided to ask his mother to keep the girls, and we went out for a night of dinner and dancing in an attempt at reconciliation. When we arrived back at our home, he turned up the pressure saying he wanted nothing but to come home saying he loved me and was sorry.

I was cooking something before turning in for the night and was distracted by his repeated requests. I let the oil get too hot after taking out what I had cooked. I took the pan off the stove and headed to the patio to dump the hot oil into the dirt outside when the handle shifted and the hot oil rolled back over my hand causing a major, third-degree burn.

The next morning, I woke up with a huge, massive blister on my right hand. I went to the hospital, was bandaged and was told that I would not be able to use my right hand for quite a while. With this incapacitation, and needing help with the girls, the reality of needing help materialized. He moved back home the next day. To this day when I look at the scar, though barely recognizable, I call it "Learn from the burn."

It was not even a day or two after he had gotten settled back in that I realized that he had an ulterior motive and plan. The argument initially began with him learning that a guy had called the house for me while he was gone told to him by my oldest girl who apparently was his little spy. There was bitter anger and tension in the air as a result of this knowledge and the malicious verbal assault. Because he was in a cast, he lay in our bedroom upstairs, drinking and making malicious and sarcastic remarks about the unimportant person calling the house for me one time but overall, he had been acting really crappy to me officially since his return in general.

I was livid as the perception of his insincere motives materialized. A heated argument began which started upstairs from his post in the bedroom. As we argued, he got up and started heading down the stairs. I shoved him slightly as he hopped down the last two stairs while we were arguing, and told him that I should take his gun and shoot him. I had had three children by this man and had never cheated on him.

After the threat and the slight shove, he looked at me with rage in his eyes and said,

"I am going to get you out of here. And, I am going to get you out right now" his plan now fully realized.

With that said, he then called 911. We lived in a cop, fireman, and sheriff department neighborhood on the outskirts of Denver. City employees were required to live within city limits. When the cops arrived, I heard him talking with them in a low tone and then I standing in the living room watched them head upstairs to ask my kids, who were now in their rooms, if they saw mommy push or hit daddy. They said they had. The next thing I knew, I was being arrested and marched out of my home barefoot. I spent the night in jail before he came and bailed me out the next morning.

The kids were at his mom's place when I returned. I think we both knew, painfully, that the marriage was finally was over. He brought the kids back home later that night and went back to his mother's house after that and stayed there from that point on. The next few weeks were a nightmare. The kids started to act out, especially my oldest. I was an emotional wreck.

The court-ordered Guardian Ad Litem was appointed for the children during the restraining order hearing that we both applied for in 1995 after several incidents of anger. One day after taking the kids to court ordered therapy my oldest became angry with me swiping her food off the table onto the floor later. When I sent her upstairs to her room, she started destroying her room, tearing posters off the wall and throwing things around. I spanked her lightly and told her to stay there. I went downstairs and began cleaning up the mess of spaghetti splatters on the wall and floor, sending the other two girls upstairs to watch television.

The next thing I knew the police were outside wanting to come in. My oldest had taken the other two kids and locked themselves inside of one of the other upstairs bedrooms and called her dad who in turn called the police on me for child abuse. She had learned to do this during the mandatory group therapy by the court that I had taken her and her siblings to earlier that day. She was told that if someone was threatening to harm her and she feared for her safety, find a safe place, lock the door, and call for help. At nine years old, she cleverly did just that. In reality, she was upset that her dad was no longer in the home and blaming me. I watched helplessly as the cops turned the kids over to him who waited outside. Two of his cop coworkers who had visited our home for dinner, on football night responded to the call. I began to feel like I could not fight, due to the tremendous emotional burden, City Hall or the Denver Police Department.

However, later, this mentality, after realizing the, unjust, bogus effort to take my life technologically, did not apply to the machinations of Big Brother puppets!

CHAPTER SEVEN

"Nothing great has ever been achieved except by those who dared believe something inside them was superior to circumstances."

— Bruce Barton

I received a phone call from an administrative clerk in the Central District Court of California courthouse who read the letter I had sent and wanted to guide me. I had written the district court hoping to find the courtroom involved in the approval of the satellite surveillance around me believing California where the situation originated. I was not sure if the approval for the high-tech electronic surveillance was given in Los Angeles or Orange County initially so I wrote both district courts before moving to Scottsdale Arizona of that year with renewed hope to find happiness.

"If you still lived in Los Angeles now, help is available for filing in district court here," she explained. "We have a Pro Se Clinic in downtown Los Angeles. They assist with formatting and basic guidelines for filing a civil complaint on your own behalf."

I was grateful for the call and the fact that someone cared enough to call me all the way in Arizona. I had checked with private attorneys. After explaining the surveillance and each time I was told that a case like mine carried a hefty start-up price of approximately $10, 000 to $20,000 against Big Brother and that was just for starters, one told me.

"However, you now lived in Arizona," the clerk said. "This means that you have to file in the area where you live." As we talked I could hear the typical noises of someone listening to the conversation in the background and this person did not sound pleased with the call from the courthouse. About a week later, I called her back with questions on my filing in Los Angeles and the possibility of flying there for court appearances. She told me that she could no longer provide any information or assistance for me. Those listening in the background of my phone had obviously silenced her and it showed in her voice.

The first week of August of 2009, after three years of steady stalking and harassment, I filed a case in the Federal District Court of Arizona on my own behalf.

It is needless to say that I was out of my league, and apparently somebody's joke as noted in one of the court documented responses from the United States Attorney, but this fact did not dim my enthusiasm. Just alerting someone, if anything at all, would help me in the long run I reasoned. The complaint was naively filed against the Department of Homeland Security, the Federal Bureau of Investigation, the Drug Enforcement Agency, the National Security Agency and every police department in every city I had lived beginning in 2006 from Orange County, California to Arizona. Unsure exactly who was responsible for the type of surveillance around me, at that time, I naively used the formatted case below:"

(American Civil Liberties Union, et al., vs. National Security Agency Central, et al., 493 F.3d 644 (6th Cir. 2007).

It was a case decided July 6, 2007, in which the United States Court of Appeals for the Sixth Circuit held that the plaintiffs in the case did not have the standing to bring the suit against the NSA, because they could not present evidence that they were the targets of the so called "Terrorist Surveillance Program (TSP).

I copied the names of the defendants in this case as my defendants who as far as I knew were the major players involved in the satellite surveillance initiative within the United States. I purposely did not include the Department of Veterans Affairs who logically, if any issue surrounding my veteran's compensation would be the likely investigating agency because I did not think it was the VA. Later I would learn and understand that fusion centers are factually investigative centers for fused agencies which includes the Veterans Administration.

I believed the Veterans Administration Special Agent when I received a call from the Office of the Inspector General (OIG) in 2008 from the West Los Angeles campus saying that the Office of the Inspector General unequivocally were not involved in any investigation surrounding me nor to the best of her knowledge, the female special agent explained, were any other agency. Especially regarding another agency, this was not true at all. Later in 2011, I called to the OIG headquarters in Washington, D.C. I would be told again it was not the VA but this time factually told likely another agency. The fact is that everything around me indicated that some agency was factually involved 100 percent.

Interestingly, in April of 2012, as I began the final process of attempting to edit this manuscript, among ongoing tampering, of typographical errors, additional comments, in certain sections, etc., I would carry my laptop everywhere I went to work in my spare time. I had set a deadline of late spring to early summer 2012 for book release which resulted in fall due to ongoing tampering with the manuscript with subtle misspelling and erroneous punctuation of which I had to correct several times. The operation centers had become the offsite administrator of my laptop.

While editing specific information regarding the Department of Veterans Affairs' likely involvement while waiting on a dental appointment one day, on this facility, an entire paragraph detailing the phone conversation above between myself and the Office of the Inspector General female, Special Agent in 2008 was highlighted then immediately deleted from my computer.

The West Los Angeles, California Veterans facility is one of the largest in the country. On this facility, if anywhere, a possible technological location of operation could be the large building, Building 258, the OIG headquarters. This building was not far from where I sat in the main hospital in Building 500 that day waiting to see the dentist.

However, again, state fusion centers include active participation by federal, tribal, state and local law enforcement partners along with state departments of Military, Veterans Affairs and the Department of Corrections respectively.

Satellite surveillance at one time was spearheaded by the NSA as one of the many high-level federal agencies involvement during initial surveillance efforts related to global interests of the United States. However, at the time of my filing a Civil Complaint in Arizona, I did not understand the mechanics of Electronic Surveillance Laws or that across the board they are now being applied in the United States, not only by highly placed federal agencies but also, as again state and local authorities such as the Los Angeles Police Department.

The United States Attorney plays a pivotal role in Electronic Surveillance approval for law enforcement working through fusion centers and the attorney for the defense in civil filings.

However, there are numerous programs such as the High Intensity Drug Trafficking Area (HIDTA) task force operations, described later, for example also working out of state-of-the-art mega computer centers too. HIDTA appears to be connection to District Attorney Office which oversees internal initiative and reviews.

If my hunch was right, a bogus narcotic trafficking allegation was used to gain approval of Electronic Surveillance of me in its full capacity masquerading as a covert technological ideation to get inside my head with mind control technology and use me as a test subject.

Four months after filing in district court in August of 2009, in December of 2009 the case was dismissed "With Prejudice" for Lack of Subject Matter Jurisdiction. However, I had done what I could, though inexperienced and outgunned. And more importantly, a lot of people had been alerted, to include the Attorney General in Washington D.C., along with the United States Attorney offices in both Phoenix and Los Angeles, and numerous defendants, via mandatory mailing, depicting the heinous and merciless abuse if anyone cared which likely, no one did.

This fact of so many agencies notified via procedure mailings related to my civil case, alone made the continuous death threats of immediate death ridiculous. However, it did not make slow, undetectable kill not an option, and this method ultimately being chosen as the method of operation around me as a slow decisive process deteriorating one area of my body before moving on to the next.

I continued my aggressive letter writing campaign to judges, the Inspector General for both the, VA, FBI and DEA, in California and Washington, D.C., Congressmen and women, and numerous others government officials to include the Department of Justice Special Investigation Unit of Civil Rights. If the pen is mightier than the sword, I was aiming to find out.

The court appointed doctor, a Neuropsychologist, was not easily convinced of my experiences. When I told him of the real-time surveillance, especially the use of Synthetic Telepathy he did not want accept to the possibility it was being directed at me. He preferred to believe in the "Hearing Voices" effect of the textbook phenomenon resulting from fraudulent chemical imbalance in the brain instead of which they are intentionally taught which today many believe deceptively taught in light of this technology's advancement for decades. I was court ordered to see him after telling my story to two other court ordered psychologists during the evaluation process for the Rule 11 court. After meeting with the first two, one reported that I was capable of standing trial and the other reported that I was not. This last doctor was supposed to be the deciding factor as a third opinion.

One day I showed up for an appointment with him with wet tissue balls in my ears. In my desperation to drown out the constant verbal chatter, from the technological telepathy, I was willing to try anything to keep my thoughts focused. I explained to him that the wet tissue drowned out, to some degree, the voices of law enforcement by muffling their constant remarks when directing the radar laser around the crown of my head or the back of the neck.

During my next visit, I watched him watching me as I checked in. He was trying not to laugh as he pointed out to one of his colleagues standing near him the tissue in my ears. She then looked away trying not to laugh herself. This just had no concept of patented technology as a reality for consideration. I could see how it would be humorous but could care less. My objective was to find anything that worked knowing that what helped me would help others if it did.

While most were trying to convince Court appointed doctors that they were crazy hoping to get charges dropped, I was trying to convince the court and others that what I was experiencing was very real, the technology exists and that it is highly advanced today.

I tried everything to convince the third doctor. I brought in patent information, copies of articles and studies on related specific subjects printed from online, directed him to my website, and showing him the beginning stages of this manuscript as proof of a clear mind able to formulate clear thought. It would prove to be a formidable task convincing him that I would lose but would gain, ironically and officially, by the dismissal of all charges regarding the DUIs and property damage.

As a result of perception, the Martha Mitchell Effect was repeatedly applied to my life.

The Martha Mitchell Effect is a common term in psychiatry related psychotic diagnoses applied to patients when the clinician's is unable to verify if what the patient is telling them is an actual experience.

The term originated in context with Martha Mitchell, the wife of John Mitchell, the United States Attorney General during the presidency of Richard Nixon. John Mitchell's wife, Martha, claimed that illegal activity was happening in the White house. She was repeatedly determined to be delusional by doctors. Watergate later exonerated her claims as accurate. John Mitchell and Martha separated and divorced after the incident.

This woman had brought down a presidency. She later died at the age of 57 due to Multiple Myeloma, a rare bone cancer. I mention this here interestingly due to one of the causes of this type of rare cancer being ionizing radiation.

I often wondered if the fact that the bones in my legs and later shoulders were being repeatedly targeted specifically, though non-ionizing, for a specific reason or outcome. Later in the terrorism, as mentioned, they began to target my breast and eyes also.

The inability of the court appointed doctor to verify my claims of satellite tracking and technological verbal harassment in a twist of fate would be my benefactor. The end result was the fact that I could not be forced to take anti-psychotic medication against my will although the prosecutor had unofficially threatened to jail me to force me to do so if she could. The medication was supposed to make me suitable to stand trial. To my chagrin, I lost in district court by an overall assessment of bizarre claims against the government or, bizarre claims of a government conspiracy stated in one of the court documents. But, in Superior Court, I won through my unyielding truth. An attorney told me that a lot of judges are not even aware of the availability of certain technologies in use today until it is publicized or brought into their courtroom.

The court doctor was a hard sell. It was a little disappointing but easily forgiven with him. This was a genuinely good human being I felt. The doctor, the probation officer and the Commissioner were not naive by any means either. Even though the court appointed doctor told me that he contacted his brother who is knowledgeable of many high-tech advancements, employed as an engineer, and his brother confirmed knowledge of a lot of advance technology in use today, the doctor still was by the book. Many years of programmed education and assessments in his profession attributing certain traits across the board to specific disorders, without exceptions would be his reality.

The torment continued at home, each day in my now small apartment in Glendale Arizona beginning in 2009.

"She's going to jail," said repeatedly.

"Hey, man, we are ready to get her today," or,

"We've got her," were some of the statements of choice.

They begin to role play. One would say,

"Hey man, she's gone."

Then the other would say, "Yep."

Or, "Hey man, I know how we can get her."

"How?" another would respond. The other would then say,

"We can get her through her medication."

(I took mild pain medication. Later medication for depression became mandatory and a personal choice for me along with a non-narcotic sleeping aid.)

The other would then say, "Yep" again.

They began to sound like bad actors in a low-budget film.

I received an inbox email from a social network friend explaining her similar situation to me and the horror in which she and her family were being subjected. She lived in Oregon. She told me that she felt she had become a target after a pain medication addiction. Instead of recovery, many were being used to test technology instead and keeping the person with an addiction, through nudging, is beneficial to these efforts due to the usefulness of discrediting easily if they learn they are factually being manipulated, influenced, and targeted.

Creating debilitating pain with me became a strategic issue as they watched me continue to take normal doses of pain medication careful to take it appropriately which weakened the full effect of their intentional creation of pain in my body. Taking it any other way would result in its ineffectiveness and I needed it for pain management. I was sober, and determined to remain sober and not trade anything for my sobriety. A person consumed by any substance is in a weakened state and is unable to fight off outside forces in the game of mind control. I took my normal dosage and the medication made me only sleepy which I did not like during the day.

One day I heard one of the men in the program ask another, "How many pain pills did she take" the next morning after this, I suffered an all-night attack of the microwave pain beam leaving me crippled which could have resulted in me increasing the dosage had I not decided to grit and bear it. When I heard him ask this, I recognized that creating pain, then nudging me to take more pain medication, could also be used as a possible Psy Ops. In an altered state, I would be more pliable.

The social network friend writing me was sober but the targeting continued. She was grateful to have someone to talk to and said she could not wait to read this book. She asked what I thought about taking anti-depressants. She said those targeting and harassing her through synthetic telepathy and electronic torture told her to stop taking the anti-depressants. I told her not to listen to them.

I had learned their object first and far-most is literally to control a person. I told her, as I had learned that an anti-depressant and something to help you sleep is vital I felt. A person does not have a fighting chance in my opinion, without these two because of man psychophysical torture. The targeting and the effects of microwave in and of itself creates depression along with a great sadness, change of chemistry, and recognition that there are monsters out there in human form who are coldblooded and ruthless in the darkness of a center miles away. Sleep deprivation is also an effective means of breaking a person down and a logical strategy for obvious reasons.

As for me, the fact that their initial purpose around me may have been the result of my substance abuse resulting from my intent to self-destruct, and unable to cope after divorce, was also a reminder of human weakness and frailty at times in life and not a bad person. It would take years for me to get to a healthy place of understanding and acceptance. Self-medicating did not help me and only served to increase and intensify the emotional pain. I would still suffer with regret regarding the youngest years. However, I eventually learned how to cope in a positive manner.

I had to dig deep for my emotional and psychological survival and know that I made an unselfish decision in the best interest of my children, at that time, and know that love was the foundation for my actions. Admittedly, I did not know how much grief would follow the decision or how it would impact me emotionally. Who does? I did know one thing and that was that I would not have my girls around me providing an image of a mother, unable to cope with life by her example. Also contributing to my decision was the fact that I had no real destination to go to after the divorce, was unemployed, and basically no family to speak of. I would have to first get healthy, mentally and physically myself before I could be of any use to anyone much less my children.

I was sober heading into three years at that point as this group watched my every move inside my home in Arizona in 2009 and pretended that the surveillance was for substance abuse. At times, unexplainably, my body would jerk randomly as I lay watching television. It scared me when this first happened. I thought it was some sort of spasm, due to the great amount of stress, or possibly a stroke. I would later learn this as being the effect of satellite radar laser energy weapons attacks to the body. I found videos on You Tube of people who had actually taped the space-based weapon attacks on them inside their homes. The videos showed them having identical jerking episodes of the body as was happening to me.

During a visit to Los Angeles in spring 2010, after Court approval for the visit, three of these older, tired-looking African American men watched us inside my daughter's apartment during my seven-day visit then decided to follow us out to a social event one night as proof of their inability to separate themselves from their male organs. They had a field day now watching us shower, during the visit, and focused on the oldest girl making comments for my ears to agitate me about her nudity.

Feeling tired, I left the reggae social location we had gone to for entertainment just after midnight and went home. This was after my daughters met up with friends who said that they would bring the three of them home safely.

I immediately, instinctively, recognized who these two might be as soon as they walked into the club. It was not because I had seen them before as I had some of them, at various times, but something about their presence. They looked officially, unofficially out of place and were dressed sort of shabbily in my opinion. And they were older men among a majority of younger, attractive men there that night. They both had on hats which reminded me of the old style "Apple Hat" of the 70s. From the looks of these two characters they probably still had them from that period and today wore the hates due to receding hair lines and balding. All three girls left briefly to walk to McDonalds across the street. I watched the two men enter setting themselves up at the bar with clear view of our table. Because the light was dim where I sat, they could not see me observing them as they apparently plotted, whispering and giggling like two school-girls among themselves.

After a while, I walked outside looking for the girls spotting them as they slowly returned oblivious back to the club laughing and talking amongst themselves eating French Fries. As we all entered the room together, the oldest leading, and me picking up the rear, one of these creatures, believing that I did not suspect who they were, had the gall to reach out his hand to my oldest daughter as we passed them by. This was just unbelievable and outrageous and I was ready to implode but remained calm. They want you to react.

As we made our way back to the table we had been sitting, it was all I could do to not go completely off. I actually had to breathe deeply to calm myself down. How dare this old, worn out looking character, and his partner, dressed in clothing from the 70s, have the gall to think that a young beautiful girl would look at or want them in a room full of young, handsome men. Talk about deranged egos.

It had to be connected to the illusion of law enforcement superiority glamorized on television as the culprit. Or perhaps it was the false reality of a perception of power to destroy lives, right or wrong, given to some misguided souls and delusions. She did not even see him reach out his hand to her as she passed, but I did and glared at him as I walked by. He was so ignorant that he still did not suspect that I knew who his dumb behind was. I then heard their colleague at the operation center speaking when we took our seats. He typically had a front row real time seat, as usual, to the whole scene played out via satellite surveillance and asked if she was as good looking as they "ALL" thought.

The question, though directed at the two men standing at the bar, was heard clearly by me possibly because I was already biometrically tuned in or because they wanted me to hear it strategically.

This old, beat-up, tired looking egotist, were apparently so out of touch with reality they must not have taken a good long look in the mirror when they woke that morning. The one who reached out his hand was about my age and I would not have been interested in him myself. He looked sloppy. The one with him had on a pair of tight fitting orange polyester pants, a white shirt and white cap to match. This one, as I watched him, seemed to me to have feminine mannerisms and gestures by his hand movements. They stood at the bar glancing our way periodically, still thinking themselves clever, grinning from ear to ear and that I had no clue who they really were or did they?

It was not until later that I noticed a third one who had not walked in with the first two. When I stood to dance, I inadvertently ended up next to this him. I then heard, "She's gone." When this was said, I knew who he was. I turned around and looked him squarely in the eyes. He turned his head quickly avoiding eye contact and changed locations immediately walking to the far end of the dance floor. I was brave enough to approach them but it really would have been fruitless and a manipulated bad reflection on me. These deviants would not admit anything even if I did make accusations and I ran the risk of looking very foolish or even insane if I made a scene. Undoubtedly, they would pretend they had no idea what I was talking about and must be crazy. I was so upset that I could not trust myself not to go off. One thing was sure, I knew that my daughter would never be interested in these men nor would she get into any vehicle with any of them. They looked more like someone's aging father drooling at the mouths.

After pointing them out to her when we sat down, and telling her to stay clear of them, exhausted, I decided that they were in good hands with their friends and in a group. Tired and needing to redirect or else, I decided to call it a night.

Why is it that our offspring think parents are dumb when they get older? When I told her what was happening, she brushed it off. Even if she did not believe me, I knew for certain she would do as I asked and stay clear of them. There also was no interest there at all. Before leaving, I said to her,

"See those to older men standing over there at the bar?"

"Yeah," she said a little more relaxed by the wine she had in her hand.

"Stay away from them. They are involved in the situation around me or are connected to it."

I then left avoiding walking past them out the door and back to my daughter's apartment.

At around 4:00 a.m., the three girls had not gotten in. I had dozed off, and when I woke, I panicked after seeing the time. I reached for my cell phone and dialed the middle daughter's cell phone number.

When she answered, cheerfully, I asked where they were. They were at a restaurant eating breakfast she told me and would be heading in shortly.

The next morning, I questioned them about the situation after I left and if there was any further contact with either the three men. The oldest then told me that as they were leaving one of them tried to entice her into his privately-owned vehicle asking her if she wanted him to take her to breakfast instead of her friends. I asked her what type of car they drove. She told me that one drove a black Mercedes and the other drove a tan colored Sports Utility Vehicle.

When I returned back to Arizona, seven days later, I immediately filed a complaint with the Los Angeles County District Attorney's office detailing everything that happened that night to include their vehicles after calling around to find who to report this incident to.

Later they would declare, "We got your daughter," I shuddered to think what could have happened to her had one of them successfully gotten her into his vehicle that night. Without a doubt, I believe they would have set her up to be sexually exploited by these unethical pathetic hounds. We were dealing with a group of men, who would do easily in the dark unheard of things, although sworn by oath to uphold the law.

Someone had foolishly entrusted these men, with this brilliant technology and they appeared to be of such lowly character with little integrity that they would use others unethically. I had expected them that night, so it was not difficult to spot them when they factually showed up. As we turned off the lights leaving the apartment heading out, one of them declared how fine my daughter, then saying unbelievably, that he wanted her and was going to get her with certainty in his voice as we left. And these scummy men had definitely shown up and tried it appeared with the breakfast request to entice her. One would hope or expect more from them.

While telling this story to the court appointed probation officer during my mandatory check in now back to Arizona, he told me, from a man's point of view, that he knew of very few men who could have the discipline or restraint after watching an attractive woman in the buff regularly to not get aroused. Apparently, the male genitalia have a mind all of its own.

If this is the case, then they do not need to be in the positions they are in or have available technology to corrupt their small minds! In this specific case, it obviously had manifested itself as definite criminal behavior.

Los Angeles is no stranger to corruption, and unethical behavior specifically in the Los Angeles Police Department for example, the publicized scandal involving the Rampart Division.

The Rampart scandal refers to widespread corruption in the Community Resources against Street Hoodlums (CRASH) anti-gang unit of the Los Angeles Police Department Rampart Division in the late 1990s. More than 70 police officers either assigned to or associated with the Rampart CRASH unit were implicated in some form of misconduct, making it one of the most widespread cases of documented police misconduct in United States history. The convicted offenses include unprovoked shootings, unprovoked beatings, planting of false evidence, framing of suspects, stealing, and dealing narcotics, bank robbery, perjury, and the covering up of evidence regarding these activities. And, three of these law men were also found to be on the payroll of an infamous Hip Hop mogul with ties to the Los Angeles street gang known as the Bloods and possible ties to the murder of a famous rapper from the East Coast.

The question is where did these disgraced officers go? Could some have materialized into spearheading covert harassment programs for hire, private citizen groups, or even security businesses with police connections and availability of advanced technology? One thing is certain "The Program" works hand in hand with official personnel working in operation centers overseeing everything.

Following the oldest girl and I one day to an audition a reality television about struggling singers in the music industry, those targeting me watched her audition commenting how good she looks, and how well she had done during the audition and the possibility of her and becoming famous. Based on what the show producer told us, she was also a favorite. After I dropped her off and headed home, I was threatened,

"If you do not stop book publication, we will mess that opportunity up for your daughter."

How low were they willing to go to silence someone after their consciously chosen immoral behavior? With secretive, covert technology in hand today, it appeared they were willing to go to levels that were once thought impossible

I thanked God for the discerning spirit in my life once thought of by me as over and extreme sensitivity. However, this overly sensitivity nature was now the source of my saving grace and of which had spared my life. God does not give help, love, protection, or insight, or guidance then take it away.

One day, a group of friends and I, huddled around a fortune teller for amusement at the Venice beach getting our palm's read. I did not take seriously what the woman said. There was no one trying anything around me or with me so I brushed it off. I was on my way to Arizona for a fresh start and new beginning believing now sober I would be left alone.

"There will be a car accident in March she told me. Be very careful" she warned. When nothing happened in March of 2006, I knew she was a fraud.

Later, I would realize that this woman had accurately depicted the car accident in which I would be involved which resulted in the annihilation of my right ankle. It did not happen in march of 2006, but it did happen exactly one year to the day in march of 2007.

> To the courts of Sedgwick County Kansas.
>
> I James Walbert am filing with the courts of Sedgwick County of Kansas.
>
> For a protection from Stalking under these request's. That any and all parties that related Jeremiah Redford of 2614 N. Wedgewood be restrained from using these listed devices for stalking harassment and or bodily harm, eavesdropping, electronic forms of harassment and stalking. As I have retained an attorney for this matter and an investigator that has provided reading that are indicative to these weapons and or devices that are currently being used to perform the above achievements as they are intended to propagate the said doings to the human body and the human nervous system by way of electromagnetic and or said forms as listed in the attached documents that are provided to the courts. That these devices be withheld from being used upon my person and other persons that are related to myself and family. The documentation that is attached to this protection from stalking clearly provide the courts the means and the ways for this type of harassment and stalking.
>
> This Request is per James R. Walbert
>
> Of this said address of Wichita Ks
>
> 3607 west 13th st apt B-9
>
> Wichita ks 67213
>
> 330 S.Tyler apt 605
>
> Wichita, Ks 67209
>
> Respectfully James Walbert

James Walbert won the first and only ruling to date against Covert Electronic Harassment after petitioning the court for the restraining order above.

Today, Mr. Walbert is in court proceeding regarding the implantation of the Verichip / microchip implant. Some are the size of a coin or as small as a grain of rice, and getting even smaller.

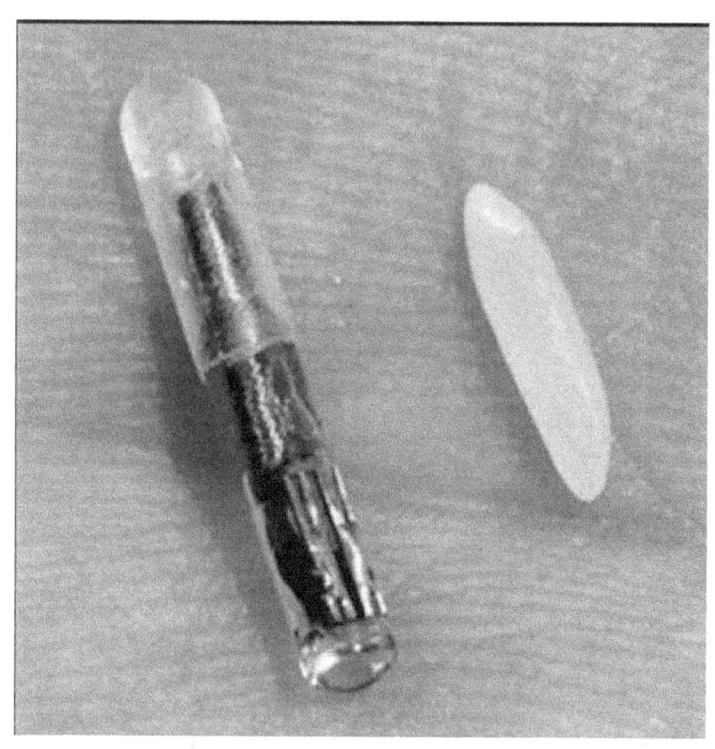
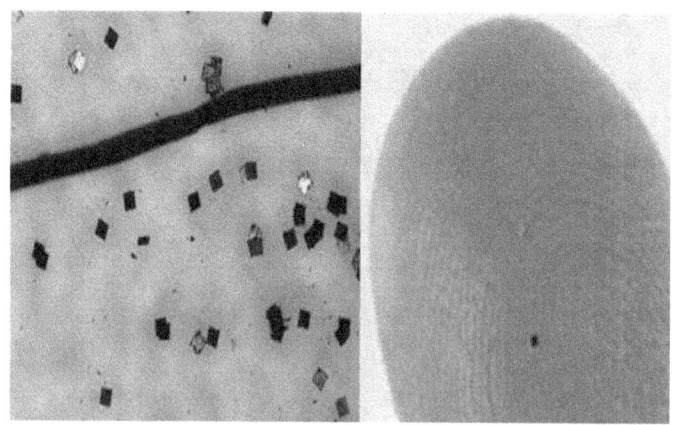

Miniscule RFID chips have the power to communicate with satellites for tracking and are incorporated into everything from bank cards to merchandise.

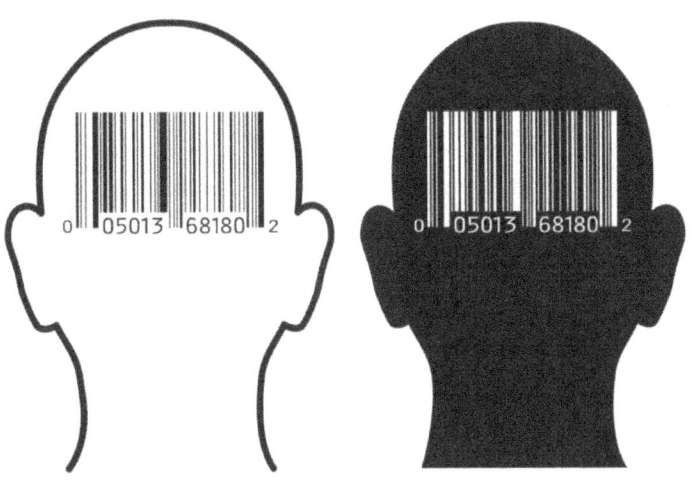

Radio Frequency Identification (RFID) tagging is the use of very small electronic devices (called RFID tags) which are applied to or incorporated into a product, animal, or person for the purpose of identification and tracking using radio waves. The aggressive, growing use of passive, semi-passive and active RFID chips are even implanted in new clothing, Gillette Fusion blades, and in countless other products that become one's personal belongings. These RFID chips, many of which are as small, or smaller, than the tip of a sharp pencil, also are embedded in all new U.S. passports, some medical cards, a growing number of credit and debit cards and so on. More than two billion of them were sold in 2007.

U.S. Patent 5,878,155 was issued to Houston inventor Thomas W. Heeter, described as a "Method for verifying human identity during electronic sale transactions" — by tattooing a bar code on an individual!

U.S. Patent number 4,706,689 was issued for a human implantable homing device. The patent abstract reads, "A new apparatus for location and monitoring of humans has been developed. The device employs a unique programmable signal generator and detection system to locate and monitor the movement of individuals…The device is small enough to be implanted in young children as well as adults."

You Are Not My Big Brother

JAMES O. GUEST
STATE REPRESENTATIVE
DISTRICT 5

P.O. Box 412
KING CITY, MO 64463

Tele: 660-535-6664

CAPITOL OFFICE
State Capitol - Room 233 B
201 West Capitol Avenue
Jefferson City, MO 65101-6806
Tele: 573-751-0246
Fax: 573-526-7740
E-Mail:
jim.guest@house.mo.gov

MISSOURI
HOUSE OF REPRESENTATIVES

March 22, 2010

Re: Mr. James Walbert, Implant of Foreign Device

To Whom It May Concern

I have been acquainted with Mr. James Walbert for over three years and his personal struggle to get relief from the continuing electronic harassment, physical abuse and intimidation he is subjected to. I have complete confidence in the honesty and character of Mr. Walbert. He is an individual who is exhausting all avenues to get the RFID implanted device removed from his body.

There is sound medical evidence and medical evaluation to verify that an implanted device does exist in the body of Mr. Walbert. Dr. John Hall, who is experienced in reading MRIs, has confirmed that a foreign body, and most likely a microchip, is present in his body. The type of foreign bodies in Mr James Walbert has also been confirmed by Dr. Hildigard Staninger, Industrial Toxicologist, of the Integrative Health Systems, LLC. Their evaluation confirms that it is a severe medical necessity to have these foreign bodies removed for the safety of Mr. Walbert. This has also all been confirmed by William Taylor, a recognized expert in the field of Technical Surveillance and Counter Measures.

Ms. Melinda Kidder, owner of Columbia Investigations, has investigated the claim and has been professionally involved in this matter and has found all reports, materials and claims to be factual and credible.

To summarize, technicians, medical clinicians and physicians, private detective agencies and other mental health professionals have verified the accuracy of reports and MRI scans about James Walbert. This leaves us with one decision to be made and that is to have the implanted microchip removed from James Walbert's body. I implore those who have the experience and authority to remove this device or devices from the body of Mr. James Walbert as soon as possible. It is a humanitarian issue to let Mr. James Walbert return to a normal life.

Sincerely,

Jim Guest
State Representative, 5th District

JG/pc

COMMITTEES
Chairman – Real ID and Personal Privacy
Member – Agri-Business and
Health Care Policy
Interim Committee on State Intelligence Analysis Oversight

Renee Pittman

October 10, 2007

Dear Member of the Legislature and Friends:

This letter is to ask for your help for the many constituents in our country who are being affected unjustly by electronic weapons torture and covert harassment groups. Serious privacy rights violations and physical injuries have been caused by the activities of these groups and their use of so-called non-lethal weapons on men, women, and even children.

I am asking you to play a role in helping these victims and also stopping the massive movement in the use of Veri-chip and RFID technologies in tracking Americans.

Long before Veri-chip was known we were testing these devices on Americans, many without their knowledge or consent.

With the new revelations of the cancer risk besides the privacy and human rights problems with the use of Veri-chip and RF signals,

I am asking for your help in stopping these abuses and aiding those already affected.

Sincerely,
Rep. Jim Guest
District Office: 660-535-6664
Canitol Office: 573-751-0246

NOTICE: Please do not call Rep. Jim Guest. He donated this letter for you to ask other legislators to do the same. He is being inundated and it may cause negative backlash to the endorsement with too many phone calls. This is an image I have used also in the other books for substantiation.

This is an example of a state-of-the-art fusion, high tech operation center.

Video monitoring can be accomplished by both CCTV and satellite imagery.

On October 25, 2011, U.S. Deputy Chief of Mission Ted Osius announced the United States funded and completion of the $57 million U.S. Government Integrated Maritime Surveillance System (IMSS) project with the Indonesian Navy. The system includes eighteen coastal surveillance stations, eleven ship-based radars, and four command centers (in Batam, Manado, Jakarta, and Surabaya). [U.S. State Dept.]. The IMSS is a tightly integrated network of ship and shore-based sensors, communications devices and computing resources that collect, transmit, analyze and display a broad array of disparate data including automatic information system (AIS), radar, surveillance cameras, global positioning system (GPS), equipment health monitors and radio transmissions of maritime traffic in a wide operating area.

Surveillance cameras also work as video cameras for observing an area. They are often connected to a recording device, IP network, and watched by law enforcement officer or security personnel. This image of cameras is similar to a 'nest' of surveillance cameras at the Gillette Stadium in Foxborough, Massachusetts.

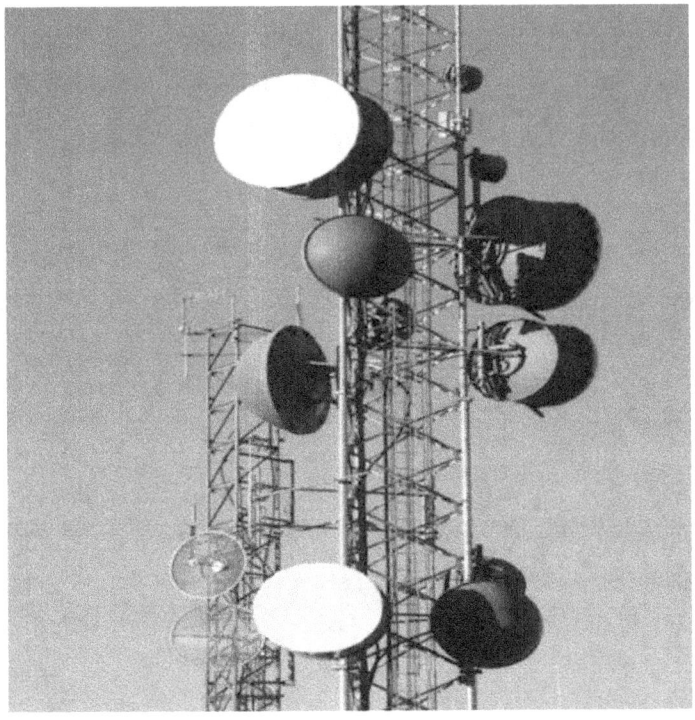

Microwaves Towers are widely used for point to point communications because their small wavelength allows conveniently sized antennas to direct them in narrow beams, which can be pointed directly at the receiving antenna. This allows nearby microwave equipment to use the same frequencies without interfering with each other, as lower frequency radio waves do. Microwave towers through the radio waves, connected with patented subliminal message carrying technology allow Synthetic Telepathy.

Numerous clusters of microwave communication towers behind the famous Hollywood sign.

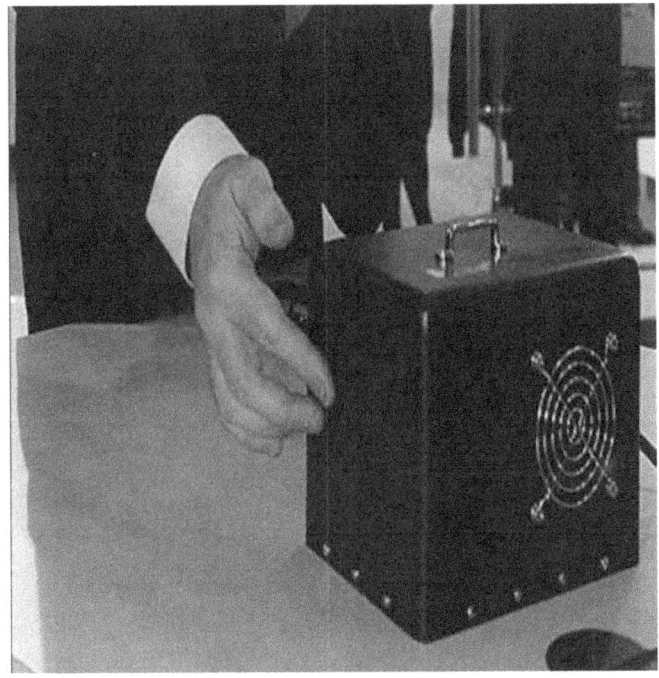

One of Raytheon's smallest but very powerful portable microwave pain beam (Silent Guardian)

EXCERPT

"Silent Guardian is making waves in defense circles. Built by U.S. firm, Raytheon, it is part of its "Directed Energy Solutions" program. What it amounts to is a way of making people run away, very fast, without killing them, or even permanently harming them. That's what the company says, anyway. The reality may turn out to more horrific. different."

Source:

http://www.sonicyouth.com/gossip/showthread.php?t=16491

Note: Image for educational purposes only.

The phone number no longer valid.

The "Silent Guardian Box" (portable microwave energy weapon) above demonstrated at an advanced scientific weaponry and technology expo. This small, portable version is a scaled down version and useful from neighboring apartments when compared with similar technology mounted on the back of Army trucks. Basically, it emits a focused beam of radiation tuned to a precise frequency that stimulates human nerves in the leaving behind instant excruciating pain. The rays only penetrate a human's skin 1/64th of an inch, so it allegedly doesn't cause permanent damage. However, when used consistently, it can and will likely cause eventual organ damage.

The portable "Microwave Pain Beams" works the same way that a microwave oven heats food at 2.45GHz. The millimeter waves heat the water and fat molecules in the body, instantly heating them via dielectric heating causing intense pain. One of the many first stage symptoms is blurred vision and eventual cataract.

First Stage: feeling a shock as one drifts off to sleep, or seeing, seeing lights as one drifts off to sleep, unaccountable increased heart rate, nervousness, irritability, aggravation reactions, erection dysfunction, compressing the vertebrae noted upon waking, sensitivity to sound, depression, minor spasms and Charlie horses, inability to concentrate, loss of memory, night sweats, sensitive ear to touch, upon waking finding that the muscles of the back are tingling as if electrified, ringing in one or both ears and or hear tone bursts, GERD (Difficulty in Swallowing), Arthritis, eye sight becomes blurred, teeth snap together when drowsy, loss of sleep, nails become wavy, water weight and cellulite accumulations on the upper thigh, and buttocks from cellular fluids displaced generally from the head and upper body especially in women, where those fluids find ready redistribution in those areas, changes in the tone of the internal voice, waking up in extreme pain, and arthritis condition, spontaneous tearing without emotional thinking, mild pressure in the head, a cloudy feeling, increased need to urinate during the night, feeling puffs of air on the face and back, such may be a demodulation of energy on the skins surface, sensation that blood is trickling into localized areas of the brain and other parts of the body, this feeling is akin to the impression that these areas were devoid of blood, unaccountable increased heart rate just before drifting off to sleep causing the person to wake up

Second Stage: burning sensation on the skin, loss of hair, feeling of temporary heating of the head (demodulating RF effect), rashes, narcoleptic reactions, sleepiness, sleep only after exhaustion, virtual insomnia, miscarriage, gaunt face, facial wrinkles, losing skin turgor, hair breaks from rapid microwave heat on hair causing increase fracturing of hair shafts from expansion of water via humidity, losing control (unexplained anger), heating of body (body feeling as if it is being cooked), waking after sleep feeling as though you did not sleep, children's symptoms can manifest themselves as ADD and Hyperactivity

Third Stage: effects of exposure, loss of coordination, accidents from sleeplessness, damage to eyesight, atrophy of the muscles, heart valve damage, loss of weight and/or weight gain, nausea, sensitivity to sound, decreased dexterity, seizure, choking, vivid dreams, lost time (Alzheimer type symptoms), change of mood, heart attack, the personality becomes quiet, a lack of thought takes place, decrease in mental activity, limbs jerk typically as one is trying to sleep, weakness, lethargy or hyperactivity, forgetfulness, constipation

A World of Hurt (Image by Darren Hope)

Fourth Stage: Syndromes, disease, insanity, heart attack, stroke and death

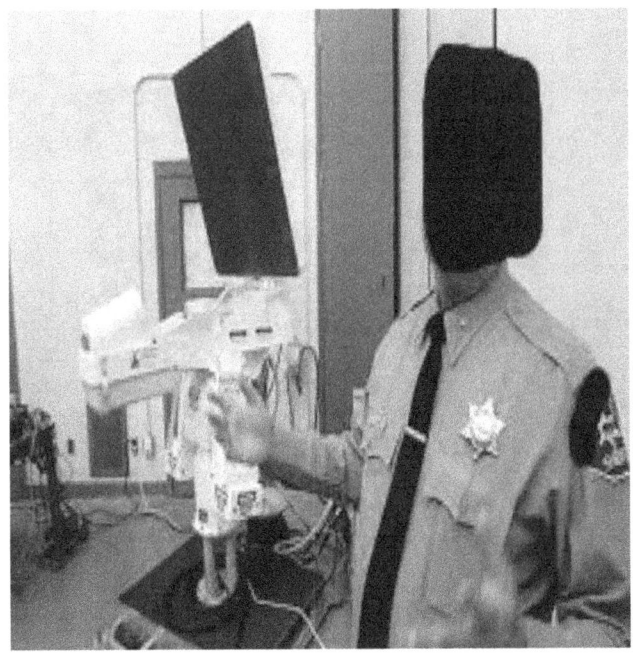

This is the portable microwave pain beam / Active Denial System available to law enforcement.

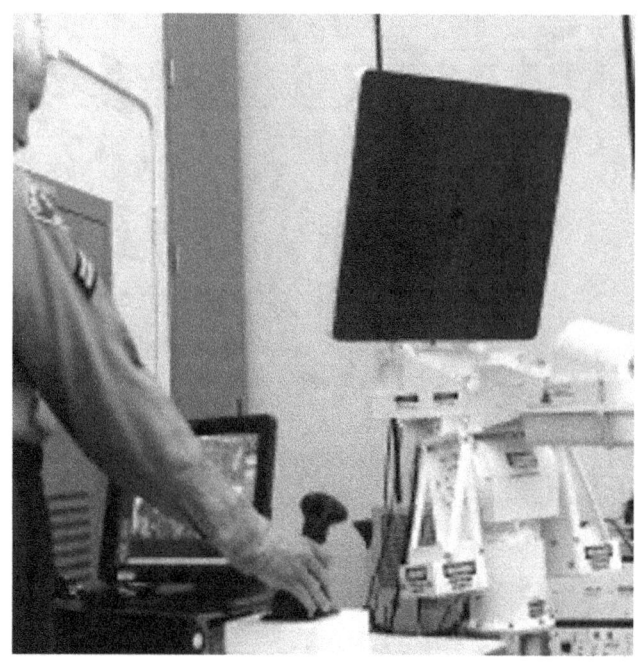

Active Denial System mounted on a Humvee used for crowd dispersal.

Great Caesar's Ghost! Cambridge Consultants (Cambridge, UK, and Boston, MA, USA) has just brought to market a portable system, dubbed prism 200, that employs ultra-wide band (UWB) radar pulses to see through walls, giving users a high-tech equivalent of Superman's X-ray vision.

Developed over the last two years, the system would allow military, security, and emergency personnel to see whether or not there are people inside a room before entering it. The unit weighs 5.4 kg and its design — modified since the prototype was unveiled in 2005 — lets users hold it against a wall with one arm. Videos of the unit in use can be seen at Cambridge Consultants' website.

One of many military weapon technologies which as trickled down to civilian law enforcement is the Radar Flashlight – It is through the wall detection of stationary human targets using Doppler radar and also a portable weapon able to detect a heartbeat.

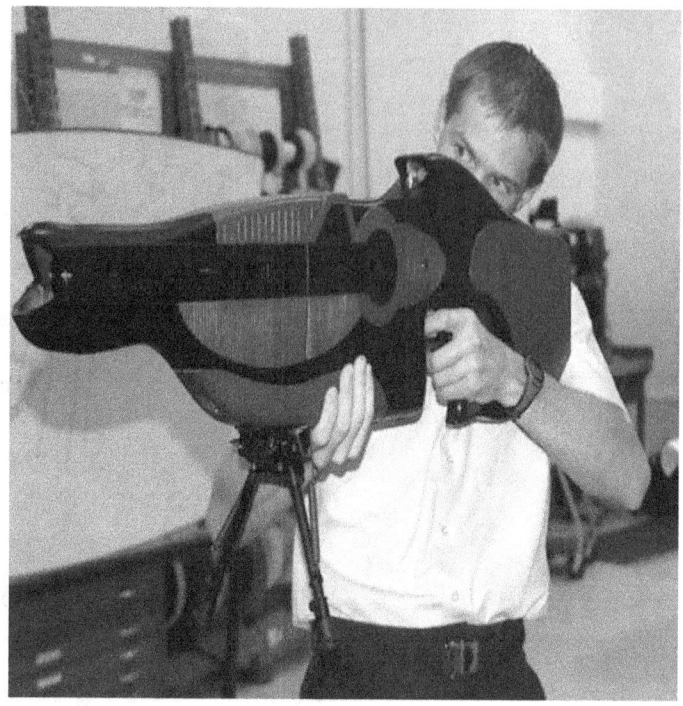

The Active Denial System handheld PHASR is also called the Army Telepathic Ray gun. The PHASR rifle above is a U.S. military working prototype dazzler laser beam weapon.

"In the past, the problem with lasers of this type has been that they often permanently blind human targets," says an expert at Bradford University's Non-Lethal Weapons Research Project in the United Kingdom.

The Rasputnik VI mind-control pistol: The psychotron core (A) is housed inside a containment tube (B) and is connected to the integrated engramputer and power supply module (C) through a ring of back-scatter nubbins (D) to protect the user from self-inflicted brain-washing. The business end of the psychotron is capped with a removable psychotronic polarizing plate (B) which keeps the mind-control ray focused along a narrow path, allowing for single-brain targeting. The ruggedized design uses only passive cooling fins (E), thereby limiting moving parts. A unique feature of Russian portable psychotron technology is the perpendicular transceiver channel (G), which allows the pistol to deflectively relay inductively amplified satellite signals to targets hidden under aluminum roofs.

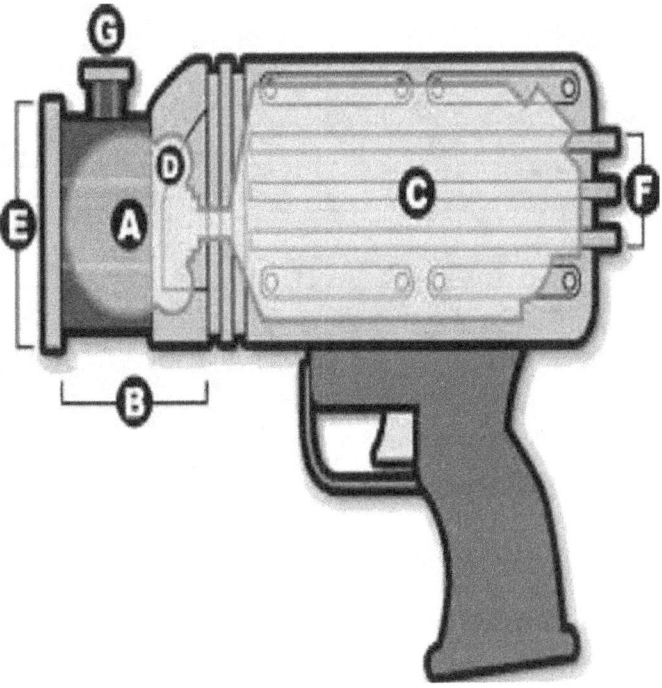

Note: Apparently this alleged mind control beam weapon relays a remotely generated electronic signal beamed to it from a satellite. This electronic signal that is beamed at the target after being relayed to the beam weapon by satellite is presumably managed by a computer in an office and created using computer controlled electronic signal generator technology and electronic signal modulator technology.

Satellite imagery - On May 25, 2007 the U.S. Director of National Intelligence, authorized the National Applications Office (NAO) of the Department of Homeland Security to allow local, state, and domestic Federal agencies to access imagery from military intelligence satellites and aircraft sensors which can now be used to observe the activities of U.S. citizens initially.

You Are Not My Big Brother

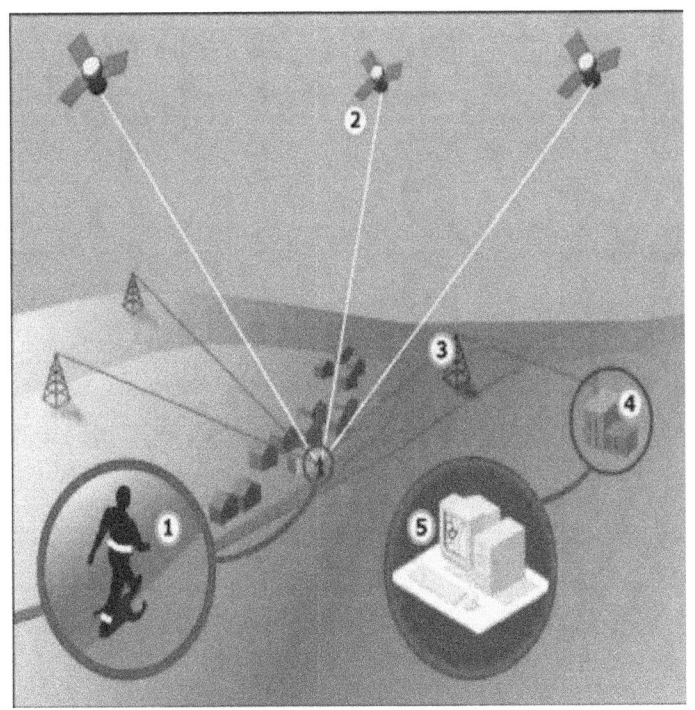

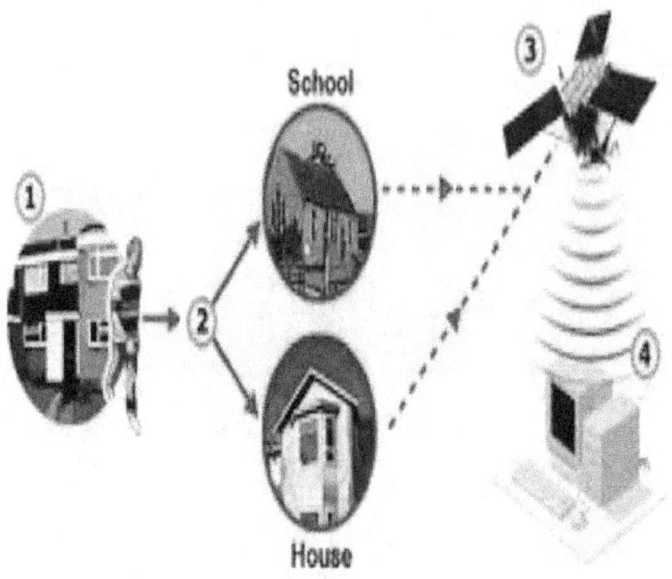

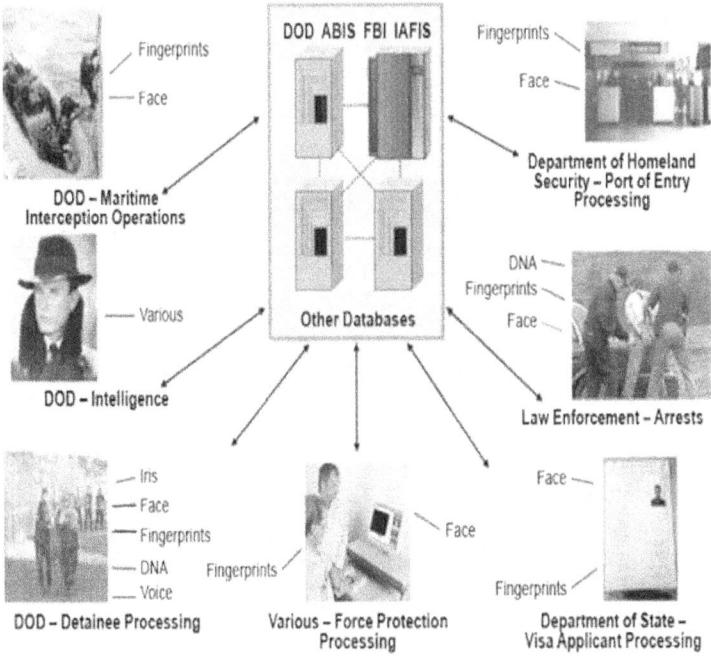

Figure 1. Identity dominance.

Example of satellite real time biometric surveillance / targeting and the capability to report directly back to a mega computer system found in advanced fusion / intelligence /operation centers.

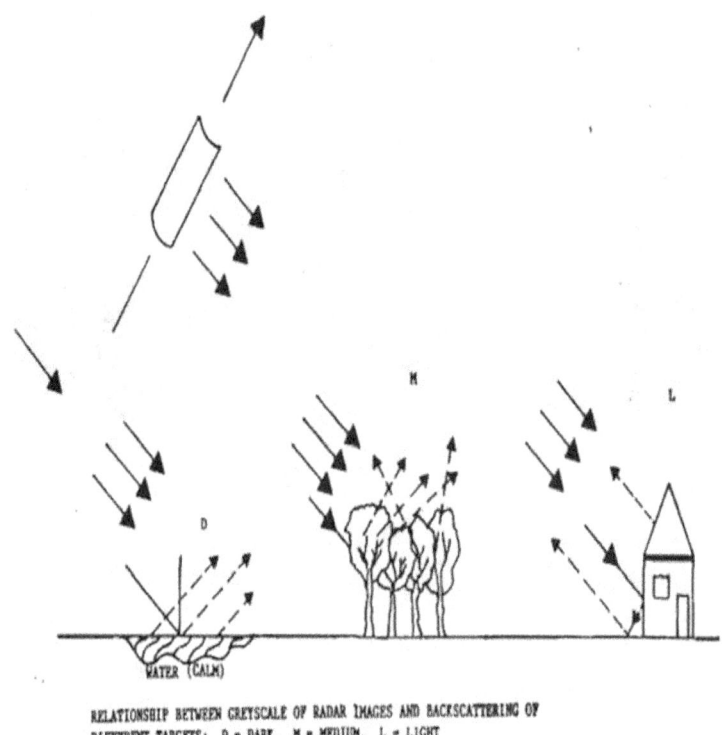

Diagram of satellite delivered radar laser energy weapon attacks.

A satellite delivered energy weapon laser beam can be delivered into a residence with pinpoint accuracy.

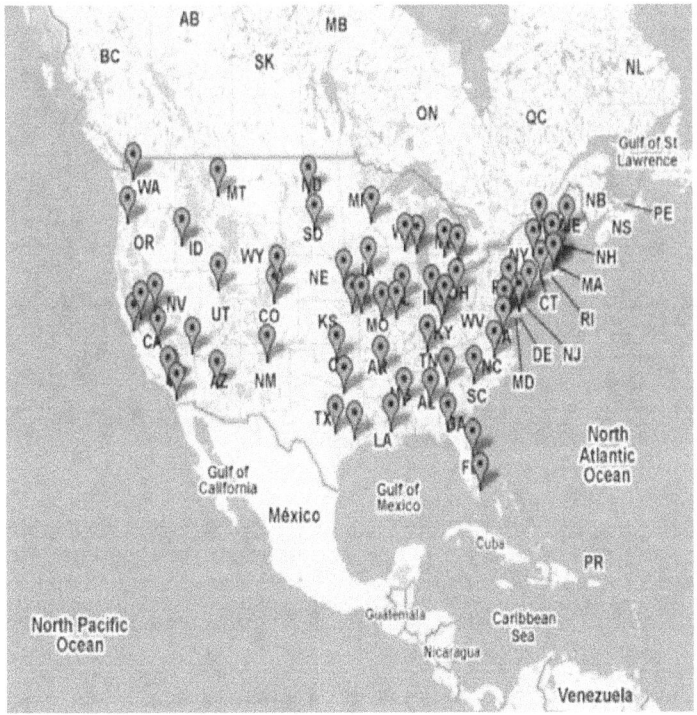

Originally there were 72 state-of-the-art fusion centers across the U.S. Today there are approximately 120 and growing. Fusion centers are centralized locations housing Federal, state and local government agencies to include all levels of law enforcement agencies. Within these centers is the availability of mega computer systems using advanced technologies (energy weapons and psychological electronic "black bag" technology.) For example, these centers include representation by the Department of Homeland Security and Immigrations of 14 or more total agencies working under one roof.

Joint Resource Intelligence Center (fusion center) in Norwalk, California

Arizona "fusion" center

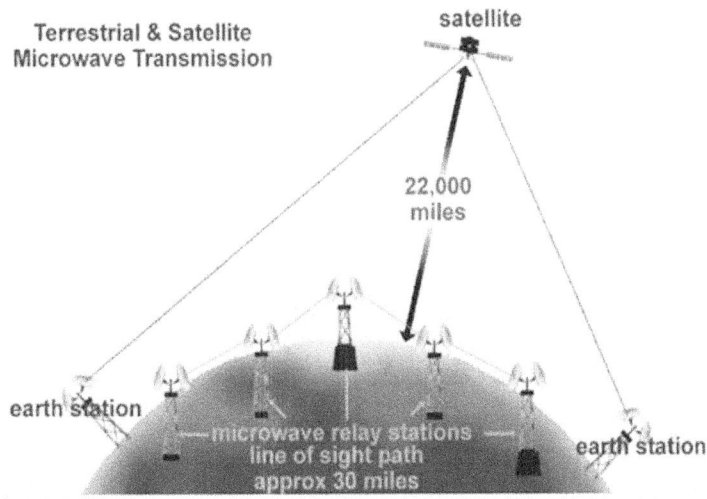

Satellite to microwave towers is capable of microwave energy weapon attacks and also microwave synthetic telepathy.

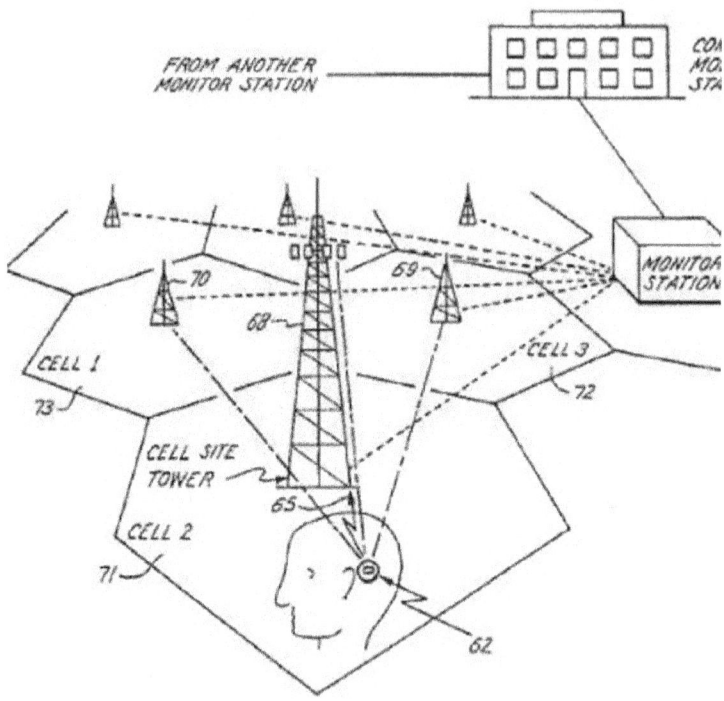

Microwave communication tower radar laser can be deployed directly to the human brain of a target.

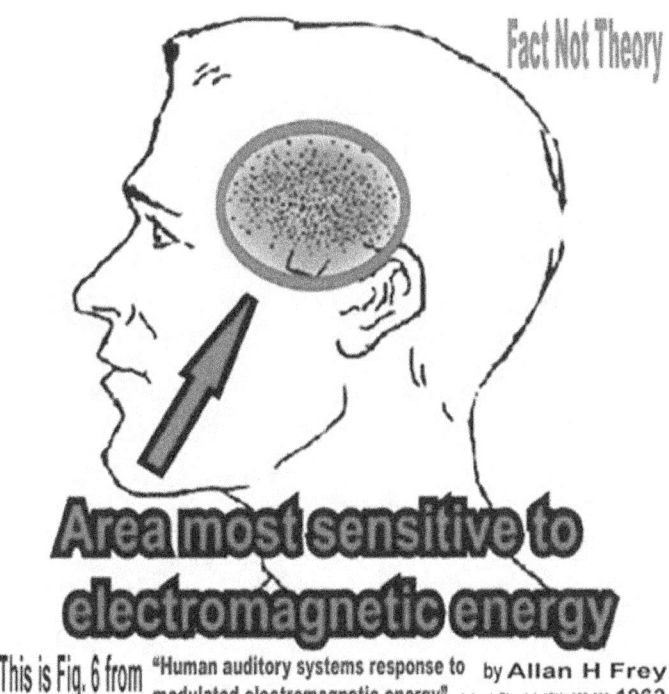

Note: The Neurophone accomplishes Voice to Skull (Artificial Telepathy) and is satellite delivered. (See the Mind Control Patent section for details, http://bigbrotherwatchingus.com.)

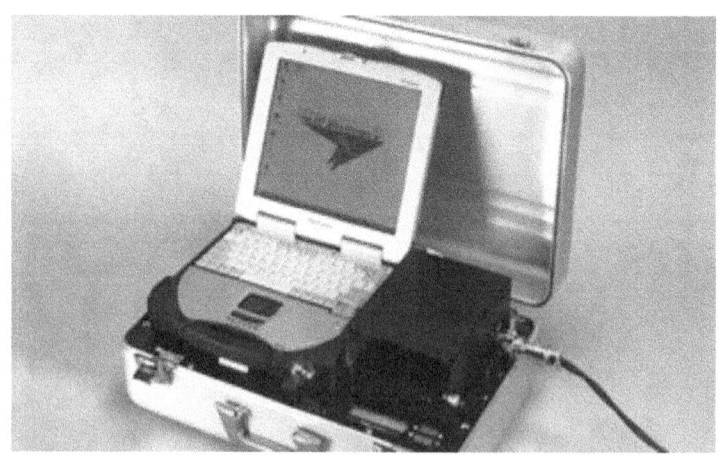

The Panasonic "Tough Book" laptop computer includes all of the system control software used in operation centers but as a smaller portable version. It also is a real time viewing system using a live video display screen. This portable system disseminates energy weaponry with from neighboring locations effectively. It includes a joystick for directing the acoustic beam which is deployed as if the user is simply playing a video game.

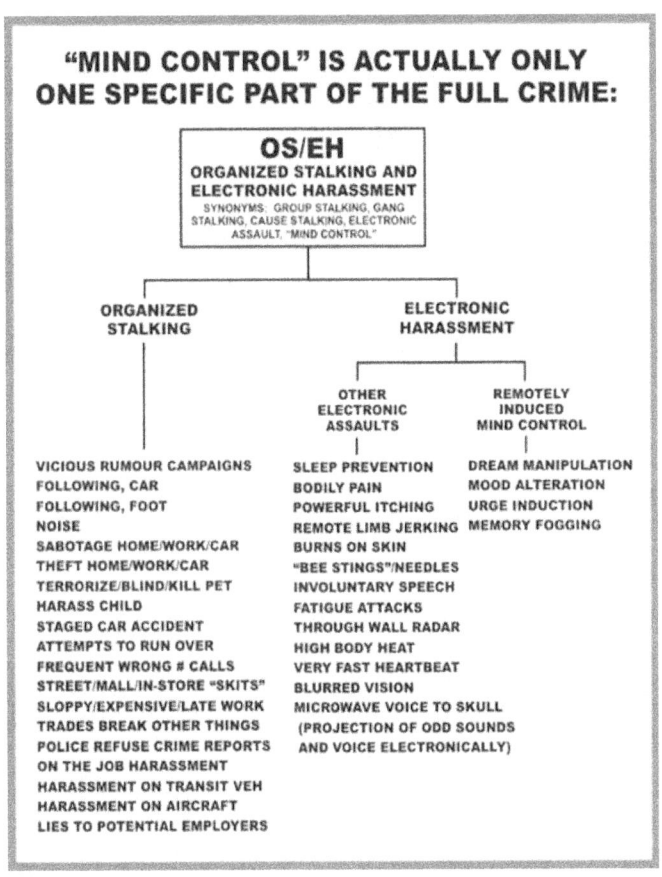

A Global Paradigm

Website Taken Over by Disinformation Agents

Renee Pittman

Houston Chronicle – June 10, 2005

Renee Pittman

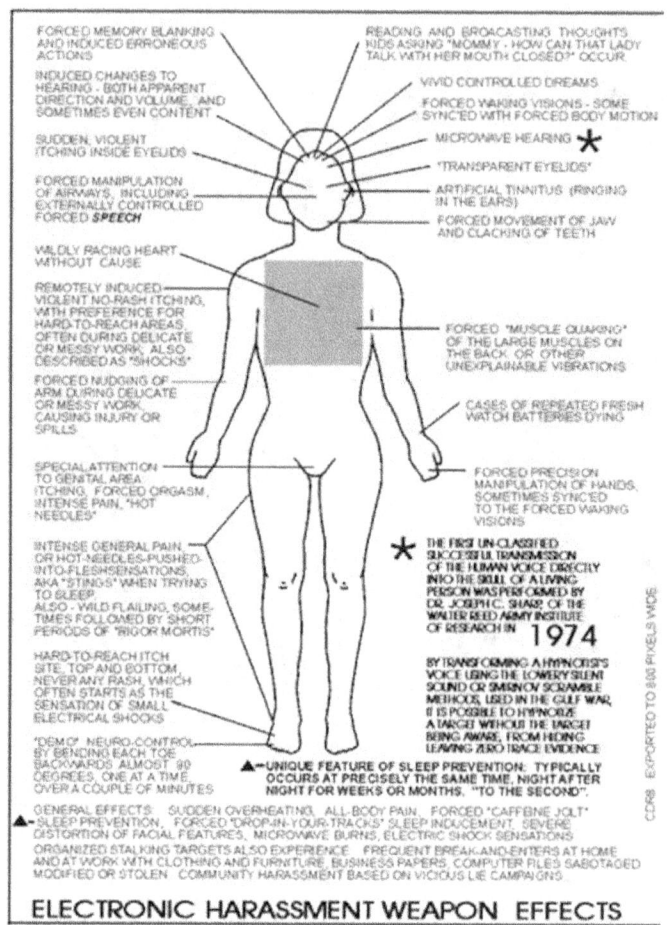

You Are Not My Big Brother

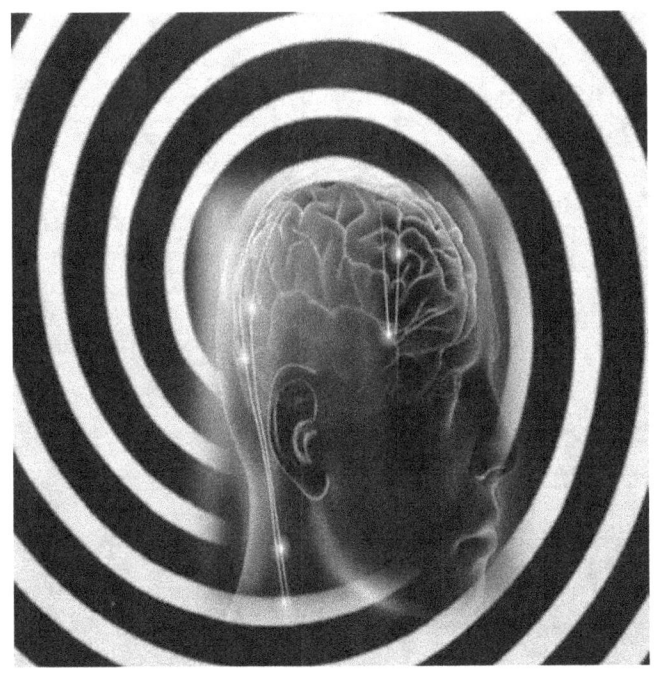

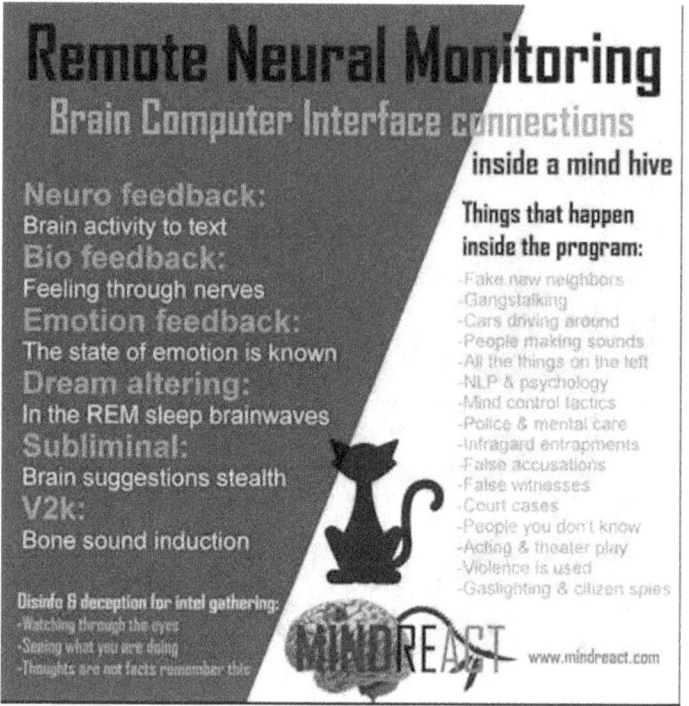

CHAPTER EIGHT

"Love all, trust a few, do wrong to none."

— **William Shakespeare**

A similar incident as far back as 2008 would cement my realization of the fraudulent practices in these operations by men of little ethics and some even obviously, decisively 100% evil and mean spirited. The reality is that these characteristics must be vital to do this type of work and likely traits sought specifically for employment.

I sat in my new apartment and tossed over the events of the weeks prior with a renewed spirit of hope. I had just left the Renew Program in early June of 2008, on the offsite Long Beach, California, VA facility and the therapeutic groups had really done me a world of good

Monday afternoon while leaving the Long Beach Veterans Administration (VA) Medical Center, I met a guy who seemed to be nice and possibly someone I thought I might be interested in at first. It was his approach that I liked immediately. He winked, smiled, and then blew me a kiss, which made me giggle like a school girl. I had just pulled into an empty parking space. He appeared to be leaving.

I had not been involved with anyone for a few years after returning from Arizona. The car accident, and subsequent long healing process, played a role along with the targeting and the operation center destroying even hopeful relationships. Always alone overall, there was room for companionship in my life. I was open to it, but not with just any one. There would be no harm in at least exchanging phone numbers with him I thought as we talked in the parking lot that day. He looked and seemed like a very decent human being and appeared to have a sense of humor that was a big plus. Before I could even get back home to my apartment, he had phoned three times. I was flattered. Most women, including myself, love being pursued, especially by someone we might be interested in. Admittedly I was intrigued. Before I could say no, his aggressiveness, which I also took as flattery, placed him parked within a matter of hours after meeting at the VA outside my apartment complex. He now sat in his highly polished black truck with the shiny rims sparkling in the sun of the warm summer day as I walked over to meet with him. I had already told him in advance that he could not come inside my apartment but that I had no problem with meeting him outside to talk. He told me his name when we exchanged numbers in the parking lot at the Long Beach VA hospital. However later, the thought hit me that what he first said was his name, in a very low tone; sounded totally different from the name he actually gave me. The reason for the name discrepancy would be revealed later.

His vibe and energy felt good. It was not until I began to get suspicious that I questioned if he was actually who he was portraying himself to be or if anything about him told to me was true. Suspicion rose subtly as he guided me expertly into a question and answer session after I agreed to sit on the passenger side of his vehicle "so we could chat." I saw no harm in sitting down as he reach for the door unlocking it as I walked around the truck and slid into the passenger's seat. By appearance he did not look like a serial killer, though, in most cases, serial killers do not look like serial killers, I thought later that night back inside the safety of my apartment. However, I had no reason to be fearful. I was caught up in meeting someone whom I thought was genuine.

While sitting inside his vehicle the conversation was general in nature with social questions, children, branch of service, etc. However, before I realized it he had expertly steered the conversation into a question and answer session surrounding how to obtain VA benefits. Expertly, he engaged me in what appeared to be some sort of unofficial interrogation.

His questions were odd, yes, but I had no reason to be suspicious of him. I was still under the belief that I was being targeted due to substance abuse and was now proudly sober for life. The manager of the apartment also hinted at this subject by telling me he worked personally for the police department that from experience meant Neighborhood Watch. In two months, I would soon have a year of sobriety and I was learning to feel feelings, understand them process them properly and cope. Although AA recommends getting a plant first, I thought dating was harmless.

There were other red flags that I chose to ignore and of which would go completely over my head as danger signals. For example, while directing him over the phone to my exact apartment complex, I told him to use my car parked outside of the building as a marker that he had arrived at my address. What struck me as odd was that after I mentioned my car he seemed to go out of his way to convince me that he did not even know what it looked like. Had it not been the same vehicle I sat in while he and I talked when we met? I also watched his eyes, typical of men, surveying the vehicle. However, when I mentioned it as an indicator for being at the right location, he acted as if he had never noticed it and did not know how it looked.

The deceptive tone in his voice should have also been a giveaway. The way he said, "Your car, I didn't see your car, I don't even know what kind of car you drive" seemed oddly exaggerated. This was something that would later strike a note with me? There was an undefined something in his voice that registered but I could not put my finger on exactly what it was. Later that night, while thinking back over the day's events, his remark about my car was one of the first things that stood out in my mind.

He began by first telling me that he was a service connected veteran like me emphasizing just like me. He then began to lead the conversation around to the reason he had obtained his benefits, and then asked me how I obtained mine. I listened and responded to his questions innocently. It appeared that he was trying to extract specific details on how to go about getting service connection benefits from the Veterans Administration. What struck me as odd was that he had already told me that he was service connected himself for some sort of back injury. For this reason, he did not need to be guided on the procedure. If he were service connection, he already knew the long, detailed, process having gone through it himself.

Whenever I tried to switch the direction of the conversation into something more interesting like his only daughter's name, or marital status, he answered briefly, then led the conversation back to the two of us trading information or pointers on how to get compensation and anything I did specifically to obtain mine. I told him that I was service connected because of an assault and another documented injury in my typical, matter of fact, honest fashion. After I said this, I silently chastised myself for being so forthright with personal information to a stranger for now he seemed amped up wanting to dwell on nothing else except this subject exclusively. His reaction surprised me; after I mentioned the assault, he then insinuated immediately that my ex-husband was responsible, after learning I was divorced from a cop,

"Who assaulted you?" He then said sounding angered, then answered the question himself, "I'll bet it was your ex-husband."

He was leading the question and answer session hoping for me to volunteer correct information I later understood, which I did.

"Your ex-husband must have done that to you, didn't he!" he repeated, feigning disgust and concern.

"Was he responsible?" he asked me point blank.

"No, it happened before he asked me to marry him."

I did not realize it but this is a very common interrogative technique used by law enforcement in this case LAPD. Ask a question that you already know the answer to, but ask it using wrong information. The person being interrogated has to correct you with accurate information. For example, a person would say, "I heard you hurt your left ankle," and then you would respond, correcting, "No it was my right ankle."

It seemed that a light bulb must have gone off in his head when he said,

"So, that happened before you were married?" emphasizing "before." This I would later learn was something my ex-husband had conveniently left out when they spoke with him it appears.

I replied "Yes, months before to be exact," I said. "And no, my ex-husband was not the perpetrator," I said.

At this time, he must have felt that he had a clear opening and was ready to go in for the kill. He redirected the conversation back to obtaining veteran service benefits, which I thought we had already discussed. There was no information to give him. It is a step by step extensive process based on everything to include your military files and health records. Finally, when his repetitive excessive prodding was becoming a one-track bore, I decided I did not want to talk about my personal life or personal business with him any longer. What was the point? It was my impression that the purpose for his visit was for us to get to know each other. I was becoming annoyed with his focused, invasive questioning, and started to feel that something else may be the real foundation for his persistence.

"I did not want to trade information regarding my veteran status nor yours," I said. He then quickly changed the subject switching immediately to sex. He told me that he found me very attractive and that I looked Caribbean with the short, curly locks hairstyle and a mole on my face. He rubbed the back of his hand on my cheek as I pulled my face back to avoid his touch.

"Your skin's so soft too," he said.

"Nice breasts, are they were real?"

He then reached his hand over trying to feel them as I brushed his hand away. Something about the way he complimented my breast struck another note with me and I began to get nauseated. The nagging feeling, along with several red flags I had optimistically overlooked slowly began to paint a picture and registered an undercurrent and motivation of something else afoot. His compliment of my breasts seemed more like a confirmation. It was said as if he had somehow already seen my breast before. Was my mind playing tricks on me? Each morning right before showering, I could hear what sounded like the faint voices of several men emanating from the ceiling right above me.

"Yes, of course they are real," I said, annoyed that his focus changed to my breasts. I was now immediately ready to get out of his vehicle looking for an easy excuse to make my exit politely. No one had ever asked me that before. Also, because I did not routinely expose cleavage, most people did not know that I had decent sized breast under the loose-fitting clothing I wore.

My mind began to play back a comment I heard inside my kitchen about a week or so prior to meeting him and what appeared to be this chance meeting. The comment would later confirm that what I thought was a random meeting was actually an intentionally orchestrated meeting for him to make connection with me.

About a week prior, I was standing in my kitchen making a veggie burger for dinner. As I sliced the onion and laid it on the bun, I heard a distinct male voice say, from what I learned was an optical entry point, in real time in the ceiling, with again nothing above but the upstairs concrete patio, say,

"I am going to f--- her."

I then heard another person, laughing, "Man, she's going smell like onions when you get there!"

Now, based on what had just transpired within the first fifteen minutes of me sitting in his car, immediately, I realized that this man could even, quite possibly be the man who had made the comment. The inside of his car was beginning to get smaller and smaller by the minute as the situation continued to get increasingly more and more uneasy for me. As he continued, talking, my mind wondered off into space. It was now apparent that he possibly, 100%, was not at all whom he had portrayed himself as "just a regular ole guy and veteran like you" as he put it. His actions and questions slowly revealed that he was not just a regular guy at all.

During the three months that I had lived in the apartment, based I managed to establish that definitely some type of surveillance was happening around me and occurring inside my residence. It appeared now undeniable that this person may be connected. Initially I felt it due to someone searching for now nonexistent drug use. However, I was sober, coping with my issues, and determined to stay this way having made a lifelong decision. I was much stronger and had grown. Various occurrences made it increasingly obvious that I was definitely being watched while undressing to include showering each day and at times by what appeared to be a whole audience of men making my life a real-time reality via satellite surveillance. As further confirmation, right before my normal shower time each day, I would listen minutes before to a scratching noise enter the apartment from the outer ceiling, scratch its way across the concrete roof above me then appear to stop in the bathroom just over my bathtub and shower waiting for me un hop in.

I now sat in this man's vehicle digesting everything and the uneasiness rose along with strong, overpowering feelings of caution and even possible danger if I were wrong. These feeling filled my mind and were based on the realization that he might be one of these men? Yes, it appeared that I was definitely under surveillance, and that targeting me in the nude and 24/7 was a fringe benefit. One of these men now sat beside me apparently wanting to take the voyeurism to a whole new level. One thing was sure, I was now very glad that I had made the decision to not allow him inside my apartment deciding to meet him outside immensely. He dwelled on my breast and a sex theme for a while apparently searching for anything to get an exchange of information between us on now this subject.

There was no secret information, tactic, strategy or skilled craft or magic trick to teach him regarding VA compensation. Now dazed, and half listening to him, I plotted my casual exit from his vehicle as he now maneuvered the conversation around to his penis size. He told me that he had a big one and asked if I wanted to see it. I then considered that if he was law enforcement that he surely would not pull his penis out and if he did this could indicate that he was not I thought naively. However, to my astonishment, in a matter of seconds, he did just that. He unzipped his pants, reached in, and pulled out his penis, flashing all five inches of it or less. He then looked over at me, confidently, dead serious and asked,

"Is this big enough for you?" while holding his obvious pride and joystick in his hand, waiting for validation.

Utterly shocked and dumbfounded, I lamely mumbled, barely getting a word out. What else was I supposed to say? And more importantly, what would have happened if I said no. That just did not seem like a smart at that time.

My mind began to race a hundred miles a minute. I did not believe that he had actually done this. I began to feel cornered, and knew it was time to make my exit expediently. I began to perspire. Red flags were now numerous and flying all around inside my head, now with flashing red lights and a siren rang out in the back of my mind. Instinctually I knew that I should not show fear. Although I was guessing, I still was not completely sure exactly who he was especially after this move. I couldn't take the chance to exciting him. I was nervous and shaking as the foreboding feeling increased and intensified. I repeated to myself, stay calm. Just stay calm.

"Do you want to touch it?" he asked, looking at me still holding his erect penis in his hand. Before I could answer, he grabbed my left hand and forcibly pulled it toward his penis. When I resisted, he tugged my arm harder indicating that he was not going to accept no for an answer.

He guided my hand to his penis with a firm grip. As my hand met his penis, I cuffed my hand around it, and he let go of my arm briefly feeling victorious. He then made a beeline straight to my breast trying to work his hand under my blouse again. At this point, I was thinking that there was not much he could do to me as long as I had his precious body part in my hand. I could yank it off if I wanted to, I thought. I let go of and brushed his hand away from the top of my blouse. Getting out of his truck safely and in one piece was my first and only priority.

I could not believe that the stranger sitting next to me had dragged my hand over to his penis and attempted to hold my hand on it while bragging about its size. "Is this big enough for you?" this butthead asked a second.

I assumed that he probably wanted me to massage it or something that was just not going to happen. I was repulsed. Did this idiot think that we after having just met a few hours earlier that we would be sit outside my residence getting freaky inside his truck? Apparently, he thought just that. I made an excuse that he was making me very excited, as beads of sweat rolled off my forehead as proof, and that I had better get out of his car before he got into trouble. With that said, I guess he felt that he would eventually score, if not this time, surely during another encounter. I reached for the door handle, opened the car door and hopped out of his truck quickly. The whole thing was surreal, and my moves felt robotic. I was in what seemed like a trance with everything in slow motion heading across the street to my apartment complex entrance.

Admittedly I can be vulnerable and naive at times, but stupid I was not any more. I was an older woman now and had learned a little. He set watching me as I crossed the street heading into my building, leaving him with anticipation. "Let get together later" he said after me as I crossed the street. "I will call you." Later, as proven by his phone calls he actually thought that we would be getting together again and very soon for Scene II.

He started his engine as I climbed the stairs. I lived in one of the apartments in the very back. When he said I'm going to call you so we can get together again, soon, I turned and waved without saying a word and ducked inside my building. However, one thing, I knew, and knew for sure, that would never happen again or would I ever see him again in person.

I glanced back as his truck made a U-turn slowly picking up speed then driving down the street. His expression read that he was on cloud nine. He was in. He must have made this team effort proud.

Thinking back over the whole ordeal, I reasoned that if he was factually law enforcement another strategy may have possibly have been to portray me as promiscuous. Later that evening, as I thought back over what had transpired, there was the distinct impression that someone was telling him what to ask me possibly by Synthetic Telepathy beamed from the operation center I observed. Law enforcement from operation centers use this capability to communicate with those in the field I had learned and among themselves. Again, this was while the operation watches over everything for situational awareness along with thought deciphering of parties involved for possible danger.

While sitting in the truck his expression gave the appearance of listening to someone distinctly right before asking specific questions. He was obviously being directed what to say by Synthetic Telepathy when he kept trying to delve into my personal life I later felt? Because of my fighting back rightfully for my life, and knowing I had done nothing wrong, I had become a challenge to ego driven men who perceived themselves masters of Psy Ops games. In reality, it is the technology that is brilliant and not their foolishness.

I chastised myself as a precaution about being too trusting realizing how dangerous the situation could have gotten for me. There I had been sitting in a strange man's truck that I did not know at all, holding his body part briefly in my hand. I shuttered to think that what could have happened if he had been a serious maniac, murderer, or any number of types of perverted deviants. He personality switched so quickly from pleasant to bizarre.

By appearance he was deviant law enforcement, and typical of these men in these operations, I had learned, seeking to take advantage of single women after being technologically projected in lives around the clock, via real time, and developing an abnormal attraction and attachment because of this. Fortunately, I had managed to get out of his vehicle fast, not knowing what to expect or what was in store next.

My heart still pounding, I now sat on edge of my bed reviewing the incident as the beat slowly started to return to normal. I realized that my mind had left the building briefly.

I recalled him telling me a story about something, but I could not tell you what he said. In fact, he asked me did I hear him. Again, I had been staring off into space with one thought and one thought, only "Get out!" of that vehicle. Knowing that a repeat of this episode would never happen again, inside the safety of my residence, I now was extremely curious to find out if he was who I now thought he was. I searched for clarity to the continued mounting evidence of some type of official covert effort around me which continued to reveal itself step by step and it as being a highly technologically advanced effort and also in a way that I would not completely understand in early 2008.

Later that night, he began phoning repeatedly. Before I could even say hello after picking up the line,

"Can I come over?"

Still trying to play coy and not insult him, remembering you can catch more flies with honey than vinegar, I told him no with a light, playful tone to my voice. My excuse being that I could not trust myself around him that I later felt was dangerous also. This must have been too much for him because he kept asking, which led to nearly begging at some point.

"Please," he said as he continued with, "Just let me come over just for a minute.

"Let's just talk," the spider said to the fly. "We do not have to do anything," he said.

His voice tone betrayed him reading he was extremely and abnormally anxious. Wanting to redirect his attention to something else, I decided to try a different approach saying,

"Let's just talk and get to know each other a little better over the phone first" I told him. "What type of work do you do?" I asked. His wanting to come over to just talk in person as he put it was a farce. I knew this was an excuse for him to get inside the privacy of my apartment. I knew that I would not be cornered inside my apartment under any circumstances with him. He obviously felt that if he could at least get inside my apartment, that there would be a very good chance that we would have a sexual encounter or pick up where he left off earlier in his vehicle. I tried to steer the conversation away several times from sex unsuccessfully and his repeated request to come over. He was not having any of it and kept asking persistently refusing to be redirected.

There was a sense of urgency in his voice that again disturbed me. It sounded like desperation. He briefly changed the subject changing his strategy, outrageously, questioning me about possible vacancies in the apartment complex where I lived. To my disbelief, he incredulously even mentioned that we could live together. I could not believe this guy; we had known each other all of about six or seven hours at this point. He then totally switched tactics saying that he was not happy with the mother of his daughter with whom he currently lived and that he wanted to move out anyway emphasizing that they were just friends after getting out of the service a few months prior he said. Trying to sound convincing, he then added to his voice tone element which he hoped projected as his dislike for her.

Regarding the two of us being roommates in my studio apartment, I told him what the manager of the building had told me when I signed the lease that he frowned on two adults living in the small studio apartments. I told him that there were several vacancies in the complex, about four to be exact. He then asked for the manager's phone number. He said that he would give the manager a call about possibly moves in since I was not going to take him up on rooming together.

I gave him the phone number knowing that the manager never, and I mean never, answered their business phone and respond only if you leave a message. Since I had been married to a cop, I also knew that policemen routinely have access to free rent at some apartment complexes. A cop living on the premises provides free security with just their presence being a crime deterrent. I hung up with him, with him saying that he would call me back later. This was after hearing a female's voice calling for him in the background of his line I assume his daughter's mother and not his wife as he had mentioned.

A cardinal rule of mine is that I never knowingly, get involved with another woman's husband, etc. After I hung up this time, I was totally convinced that he was connected with law enforcement in some way or in another way in some capacity. And, if anything his interest in living close to me would mean that his apartment could be used as a surveillance unit I thought. Was this the new plan along with a hopeful fringe benefit of neighborly sex? Again, no matter what he thought, I knew that sex was out of the question and it would never transpire between us. If he was factually law enforcement his living close did not frighten me. They say keep you friends close and enemy's closer. I had done nothing wrong, and there was no additional information to give to anyone about the VA. However, I realized that in his egotism he must have thought that it would be the perfect setup for him. This man was literally poised and hoped to position himself to screw me over royally and in every way he could which meant mentally and physically.

We got off the phone, after the woman's beckoning voice called out to him the background. I turned the television up as an episode of "Law and Order" began. I was ready to call it a night. I had had enough for one day.

A short while later, the phone rang again and to my surprise, it was him calling me right back. I questioned him about the woman voice I had heard. Before he could respond, apparently another call came in on his line. I was put on hold for a moment when he switched over to speak with whoever it was calling him. When he came back on the line, ignoring my question of the woman in the background earlier, he began to once again to question me, yet again, about my veteran's status and how to obtain service-connection. Someone was trying to send me a message with the repeated questioning it now appeared. He aggressively continued this avenue sounding more and more determined than ever now. I had already told him that I did not want to discuss my personal business with him earlier. However, he continued to completely ignore my request as if I had not said anything at all. This began to drive home the reality that he was factually not who I thought he might be played out as a subtle intimidation effort to create fear and doubt in myself.

Lately whenever I talked on my cellular phone, it was obvious that the calls were being monitored by someone who was making various comments obviously for me to hear said in the background. So, I had no reason to doubt this was also being done during my conversation with him. I again told him that there was no magical information or formula to give to him. He was relentlessness in his questioning. However, this time, when I again asked him to stop, my voice was stern. When he still continued, I told him that I had something I needed to do and would talk with him later in mid-sentence to his questioning; I abruptly cut him off hanging up in his face.

The next afternoon around 10:30 a.m., the phone rang and he for the umpteen times went directly into his line of questioning about my benefits, unbelievably. He was determined, and undoubtedly his actions were being played out for the group listening in the background and probably recording every word. I could sometimes hear what sounded like a voice activated recorder at times click on when no one was there physically listening to my phone calls it seemed. The sound it made appeared to click on and off by voice activation of me talking.

Again, technology was definitely being used to gage my emotional state from what I learned is factual voice stress analyzing computer software in my search for answers. Someone was definitely hoping to scare me. This was apparent by the comments "She's not scared" said frequently in the background as this party listened in.

Substance abuse was no longer an issue for me after I decided that my life was worth living which left any investigative effort empty handed with me in this area. Trying to attach to something else was now the objective, by this group, and after this encounter, the beginning of book publication became a possibility and my focus. His continued his quest to come over with each phone call. He egotistically left after our first and only meeting feeling sure of himself undoubtedly. His tactics repeatedly changed to whatever he thought would work at a given moment.

"I thought we could compare notes to see if you could help me out," he said after picking up the conversation at the same place when he phoned yet again never missing a beat. I was done and my anger was slowly rising at the unjust effort now obvious.

Losing what little patience I had left, I finally asked him "Why do you consistently, repeatedly, want to talk about benefits?" I wanted a direct answer from him.

"I told you earlier this is personal information that I did not want to discuss over and over again. What is the point?"

"You do not hear me questioning you about your personal affairs repeatedly, do you" I asked.

I then told him that I was not the expert.

"You should speak with someone from the VA." I then told him to contact a benefit's counselor at the VA hospital in Long Beach, California or even someone at Regional Headquarters in West Los Angeles, California for help.

After getting nowhere, he again expertly switched the conversation back amazingly to sex and his sexual stamina. This man had not a one-track mind, but two tracks. And unbelievably he was still trying to promote the image that, he was just a regular ole guy with big gonads. This man was not a regular ole guy. He was a spider and I the fly for his web. I was angered by how, if I were right, he had tried to use me sexually also but I kept this anger under wraps though not far from the surface emotionally ready to release it if he pushed the wrong button. I guess the plan was for him to have his way with me sexually, use me up, and I guess after gaining my trust under false pretense hope to prove the truth a lie by gaining information to use, as part of an unethical the agenda. In reality, I would later learn that these are not legitimate investigations but psychological electronic radio frequency technology testing efforts. Hoping to ingratiate himself with me, was also the reason for the weak-minded compliments from this group overall on my phone line.

We talked for a short while longer and hung up. Later when he called me back, now around 11:00 a.m., I had decided to now try to probe his mind to see if I could get any definite information out of him. There is always the benefit of the doubt for a person and sometimes things are not always what they seem I reasoned. I began the conversation by saying

"You know when I first met you, I heard the people who listen in the background of my phone say,

"Oh, she met somebody" during our first phone call.

"Someone is listening in the background" he asked. I ignored him.

"Lately it seems that on the rare occasion that I meet people they end up mysteriously missing in action," I told him. "I never hear from them again. This is after positive phone conversations and no explanation at all. The reason for this, I could not explain at first. However, it now it appears that it may be due to people either connected from the operation around me or being recruited to assist in it."

"Huh" he said, "Is that what you think about me?"

"No one has ever informed me of being under any official investigation which should be a legal requirement or so I thought." I told him. He listened patiently as I remembered other situations in my life that reflected my now growing belief that people were intentionally being used and placed around me to ingratiate themselves into my life and environment for a reason and cause. Determined to get my point across that something was up, and convince him that I was aware, and also trying to confirm reality, I started to remember other situations that were slowly adding up. Surprisingly he listened as I began to recall several suspect incidents.

This was 2008, however, later, while working at the library on my laptop in Glendale, Arizona in 2009, a professional, well dressed, looking African American man began popping up coincidentally every time I was there. This would not be out of the ordinary except he appeared to be moving closer and closer to where I would sit each time. If I glanced up, absentmindedly, from what I was working on, I noticed he would be watching me before quickly turning his head. During this time thoughts began to materialize in my mind that even though I did not know him, this man was a nice person, harmless, and that I should get to him likely beamed, after understanding this technology, from this operation via radio waves. This was also along with suggestions that he was far more attractive than what he really was although not bad looking. This was followed by a strong urge to connect with him which I resisted.

Later after I became more and more knowledgeable and indoctrinated into the capabilities of the influence technology in the "The Program," I would come to understand that people can be tailored made, fit to order, to your likes and dislikes, after mind reading software use on you, and in my case tastefully dressed professional looking men appearing to be about something. But what could not be made to order is strength of character which is my preference overall.

The ordering these specific types for me if anything at all fell short. This man, each day continued his gradual dissent moving closer and closer to me until one day when I arrived at the library he was sitting at the same table where I normally sat and directly across from me. Immediately, apprehension filled my senses as I pulled out the chair to sit so much that I even considered moving to another location. But there it was again, just a thought it seemed saying, "It's no big deal. This is just your imagination. He is an okay guy." He looked up at me appearing to be surprised to see me when I walked up, then gave me a reassuring smile, nodded, then continued reading the book he held in his hand. I sat down and connected my laptop computer to the library website, then shuffled through the handwritten notes I had brought with me and prepared to begin working on this book.

After I was settled in, he looked up again from the book this time asking me what I was working on. I told him a book. He then introduced himself. A cordial conversation began first about the subject, which gradually led somehow to religion and religious beliefs in general. More than likely, believing he had found his niche with me using religion and portrayal of himself as a sanctified man, he began quoting scripture after scripture to impress me. This was amusing since my beliefs are metaphysical. So intense was his religious views and force of conviction that I asked him if he was actually a preacher by profession. After learning he wasn't, I told him he truly missed his calling saying "If you are not you should have been," then, "It is not too late to consider it."

Although he seemed genuine after seeing and talking with him several times afterwards I could not shake the initial feeling of apprehension about him also. After arriving early one day, and having worked non-stop for quite a few hours, around lunchtime he asked if I wanted to grab a bite to eat saying he had a favorite restaurant in the area. Needing the break and hungry I agreed to follow him in my car.

When we arrived at the restaurant, I did not immediately notice the official looking group when they sat down behind me at their table. My back was turned. However, sitting in the restaurant in the booth right next to ours were three FBI agents, two men, one black, one white, along with a tall, thin, white female. When the waiter came to take our orders, I turned around looking for the waiter to add something to my order then seeing them for the first time. I immediately recognized the African American man. On my mission to find out who, what and why from anyone and any agency two years prior, due to a beam focusing on my shower, I visited the FBI headquarters in Phoenix, Arizona. This was also after a judge's letter in 2006 confirming basically the Warrantless Spying Program. The African American man I spoke with that day had been one of two agents, himself and another female.

Being married to a cop for thirteen years, the appearance of those following me around at that time did not have the feel of the typical regular police persona except for the black men. This was a feeling I often felt. There was a definite air to these men and woman. Eventually, the focus on me would leave me totally in the hands of whatever agency the African American men were connected to in Los Angeles likely LAPD. It would be this group in which I would later suffer the most inhumane of tactics and victimization and sexual overtures. I began to feel that they were connected to HIDTA though still unsure. They tried to convince me that they were from the VA of which the VA vehemently denied.

As explained, standing outside my residence the day I packed out for the move to Scottsdale, Arizona in March of 2006 was a person of similar presence to the individuals now sitting in the booth next to us that day. The dress slacks and dress shirt the man wore a revelation.

It was by direct intention that the man moved closer and closer to me during each visit to the library, I would later learn again stupidly. Later it would appear that many strategically would be sent to ingratiate themselves with me as part of the machinations. It appeared that someone felt that I was vulnerable due to being a single female and due also to their expertly crafted isolation through tampering with any and everyone around me while sitting comfortably at a desk in the operation center via radio frequencies. The constant deciphering of my thoughts must have revealed a perception of vulnerability for companionship, a void it appeared these men hoped they could fill with one of their own.

Returning back to the persistent man on the phone, still trying to come over, I told him, "You would be surprised how many people find it exciting being involved in these types of efforts." He listened to my rationale that people were likely being placed around me by intent. I actually was amazed that I now had his full attention, and that his continued requests to come over temporarily on the back burner. For that moment, he was letting me explain myself fully and my rationale why I felt the way I did. I was beginning to think his now silence was also for those listening in the background of my phone.

"You would be surprised how many people can be manipulated into anything. You would be even more so surprised that effective manipulation can be done without the person knowing it and from miles away, technologically. Today, a person can be manipulated effectively, subliminally, and technologically without a clue." I continued waiting for him to redirect the conversation back to my VA benefits or sex, but he was quiet.

"Excuse me, I take that back, you probably do know," I added sarcastically.

"Someone is after you?" he said again as if this was a new revelation. Tired of games, I did not respond and told him I was getting off the phone. As I did I again heard the distinct sound in the background of something sounding as if a tape recorder stopped just after I made this declaration and prepared to hang up.

This person I now felt was an undercover cop, and part of the effort following me when I was lost, and in deep emotional crisis, but now recovered, continued to listen intently to my every word as I recanted story after story of people I now felt sent to get some type of non-existent information from me. He listened as I sought to prove that something was going on around me. All talked out, I told him I was sleepy and hung up for the night.

When the phone rang again early the next morning, I was tired of the nonsense and decided to cut straight to the chase saying that "they" are definitely watching me inside my home shower and some agency was also following me I around.

"They, who are "They?" He asked sounding amused but stern.

"They," I said, "are the obvious group targeting me by satellite surveillance and hiding in the storage apartment next door to me. They are also listening in the background of this phone call at this very moment." And "They," most importantly, can't seem to stay out of my bathroom while I shower!" I felt that it now time to rattle his cage. I told him point blank, "I think that you are either an undercover cop or yet another person "They" are using." I would have loved to have seen his face when I said this to him.

"No, I am not!" he quickly shot back, defensively, with an exaggerated hint of sounding offended in his words. I caught him off guard and he had to regroup with something so he said,

"You're paranoid," then, "You're crazy!"

When he said this, I began to get angry. I guess that on top of it all he felt that I was supposed put up with insults, and his assessment of me regarding a now glaringly obvious situation. Was I supposed to accept insults coming from a stranger whom I had only known a few days?

"Whatever. You are a cop," I said. "I am sure of it," going in for the kill, then hung up.

The next morning, the phone rang again. Guess who? It was him again, waking me up. I looked at the clock which showed just after 6:45 a.m. Grumpy, my patience completely gone by now. Even before I could answer the phone, I watched his number flash on the caller ID and could feel my temperature rising from zero to one hundred immediately. I pondered if I should even take the call. However, curiosity got the best of me. Before he could get his joyful sounding, morning greeting out, I let him have it with both barrels.

"What the heck, do you want?" I said with obvious agitation to his calling with more of his nonsense.

"I guess you did not get the message I gave you yesterday about who I think you are."

I could not believe this man. He obviously did not care what I told him before. My beliefs and my accusations were completely ignored. And unbelievably he insanely rewound the tape back to, "Can I come over?" I could not believe my ears. Was he intentionally trying to agitate me? Was he completely insane? How could he be so silly not being led by his organ? Perhaps he believed that I would involve myself foolishly with him or perhaps he just wanted an opportunity to intimidate me as he began to drop hints of my demise through veiled threats. He also possibly wanted sex also after still watching me undress and shower propelling him forward. Although I tried to remain as calm as I possibly could, I was unsuccessful. I was at a boiling point and shouted at him,

"Why do you keep calling and asking me to come over after I told you my suspicions? Did not you hear me when I told you last night that I believe, you definitely are either directly involved with this group around me or you are definitely connected in some way? This group, I said, incidentally, continue to refuse to accept that I am now sober for a year. "You," I repeated, again, "are 100 percent involved with them in some way."

"No, I'm not," he protested, trying to restrain the undertone of sarcasm in his voice that did not escape by me.

I listened to the change in his tone which reflected that he had begun to realize that he had lost the edge he mistakenly felt he had with me while sitting in his vehicle.

"How dare you even ask me can you come over or even think I would consider it?" I asked him point blank,

"Aren't you working with them?" I wanted to hear his response, although the truth was definitely not an option for him.

"I can't believe you just asked me that," he said instead.

"I am just a veteran just like you."

"Listen," I said, "You must think I'm really dumb."

"I guess I should not be surprised, whatever is factually going on, that "They" operate would like this.

"They," he said, "You, don't even know who they are".

He then, to my very own disbelief said, "If you have sex with me "they" will leave you alone and we will stop stalking you."

I cannot tell you how outraged I was by this statement. I am sure this is likely what many women are being told trapped into sexual liaison with these pathetic frauds. At that point I said,

"Bye!" yelling into the phone and, "Lose my phone number. And, don't you ever call me again!" I then hung up again.

These programs do not care whose lives they destroy and human lives appear to be toys, non-consensual test subjects backed by highly advanced technology in covert use.

Many around me would be used and one prominent life almost destroyed.

Because I was in the military and worked for senior military personnel at the highest echelon, an old and dear friend, an Air Force Lieutenant Colonel needing a new clearance was odd to me even when he said it.

In the positions in which he held he would have had to be cleared before he even could stand even in the doorway of any classified area in the Air Force and he had been in the military for over 20 years. A clearance would have been mandatory immediately in his career as it was with mine.

I did not think that his questioning was out of the ordinary at first because I had no reason too. Plus, he always prefaced his questions with as "only wanting my opinion" or to compare my answer with how he had responded when asked similar questions as part of the lie detector test, to renew his clearance, he said he had recently taken.

After we hung up one night, I began to tossed over a lot of the questions he had begun asking me over several weeks. Habitual with me the internal alarm clock would sound when things were just not right or sounded out of place. In fact, everything in my life at that point I had the feeling of some type of undercurrent around me and again, this undercurrent made known their presence during all phone calls by remarks as very real.

When I began to feel like his questions were for the benefit of those in the background of the line, hurt would give way to anger, as the possibility arose of his involvement in something greater than simply wanting my opinion. To compare my answer to what he had said during the polygraph made no real sense. This was a competent, highly intelligent man whom I had known since he was a Major, about ten years. Even though he lived in another state, we still spoke regularly.

I considered that he had recently endured a heated divorce where his ex-wife had stuck it to him and stuck it to him good. As a result, he was bitter, which I knew all too well as being typical during and after divorces. It was after his divorce that we reestablished friendship. Factually when we met, years back, he had been separated and having marital problems then. Part of the reason he told me that he liked and respected me was that I would not involve myself with him if he was still married or be his "chick on the side," he told me amusingly, of I had told him in the beginning.

In the heat of the quest for any type of negative information from me, a few days after his odd questioning on incest of all things, angered that he was possibly connected, I called a girlfriend of mine who was with me the night that I first met him. I told her what he had asked me, about the test he said he took. I told her the line of questioning was likely for the benefit of someone listening in the background of the call apparently waiting for my responses.

I am not stupid I told her. For no other reasons except being insulted, hurt, disappointed and angry that he apparently was even asking these insulting questions, I then insinuated to her that he was possibly in the closet. I mentioned his love of strip clubs implying to her that it appeared to be at an addiction level for him. To substantiate his possible hiding in the closet, I told her that once when I phoned him he had a male visitor from out of town at his home. Something he said to the person while I was on the line with him, stuck me as odd for a brief moment and I felt that they quite possibly may be having some type of relationship based on the unusual playfulness they appeared to have with each other also which felt girly to me as I listened to them speaking while on the line with him.

Whether this was true or not, I did not know. What was said to her was motivated from a place of emotional disappointment for me of his involvement in something completely negative in my life seeking to destroy with vicious insinuations I later realized were designed to change the perception of me and isolate me from people close to me.

An image of pure disgust was associated with abusive heinous deviance inflicted on innocent children came to mine, and I was sickened and insulted by the mere thought of anyone even remotely connecting me with any involvement!

What I said to this girlfriend was to insult him to those listening closely to everything in my life and phone line. Again, I did not think that what I was saying was officially credible or would impact anything significantly. However, little did I know that this information now in the hands of the unscrupulous eavesdropping team, looking for anyone to target, possibly may have used the information to go after this man's honorable military career as a promotable Lieutenant Colonel seeking promotion to the rank of Colonel?

A few months passed, after this conversation with not so much as a word from him. Then, one day he called me sounding like he was nearly in tears with his voice shaking.

"I thought you were my friend," he said before I could get a greeting of hello to him,

"I thought you said you loved me" he said.

"What do you mean?" I asked, proceeding cautiously.

He did not elaborate on exactly what he meant. He then told me that he was getting out of the Air Force. I was stunned. Based on several conversations between us over the years, and specifically after his divorce, I knew that he was planning to retire at around twenty-five years. He was now had just under twenty-two.

After this revelation, and the sadness in his voice, my heart sank. I instantly began to believe that the people listening on my line that day, who had tried to use him against me, had possibly used the information, I said to out of anger and to insult him only, to assist in destroying this man's outstanding military career. At this time, I naively did not realize how vicious these efforts are in the hands of these psychopaths. His career would end due to being a casualty of this war centered on me. This too, I reasoned, if I were right, was the reason possibly for the lie detector test for him. The objective is to hear allegations then start targeting the individuals by psychological electronic technology to see if there is any validity, by manipulating even the person's thoughts in this area or brainwashing. If a Lieutenant Colonel in the United States Air Force was gay or addicted to strip clubs, it obviously would become an issue for any senior officer.

Although this could not be, again, substantiated, my gut feeling told me that this was quite possibly what had happened in his case. The last time I saw him, I observed he was taking medication, during a brief visit to a military installation in Arizona, where we met up, but did not see exactly what it was. He also was not himself, likely due to now being under the gun himself. He had already complained of a lot of racial issues in his positions over the years.

I don't remember how the subject came up regarding my compensation, as we spoke that night after he told me of his retirement. I do clearly remember that he then tried to attack me saying that getting my VA benefits was some kind disinformation or wrong doing on my part.

When he said this, I knew for sure that he was involved, voluntarily or involuntarily, and that those using him had cost him dearly not giving a dam about anyone or whether allegations were fact or fiction.

I told him what happened to me as a young, female soldier of 22 years of age. I told him that I also told my then boyfriend, who later became my husband and now ex-husband. I told him that he at that time had been compassionate and nurturing of me during a difficult period. As proof, of his belief in me, a few months afterwards, in complete trust, he had proposed marriage.

With this said, it clicked with him against obviously what he may had been told. His demeanor changed, when I told him the story, and he then said,

"Oh, I did not know that" then, "so, you say this happened before he asked you to marry him?"

"Yes." I said with great sadness for him and the entire situation overall and how we had been played against each other by this deceitful program looking for human guinea pigs.

This conversation that night between this old, dear friend of mine would be the last time we would ever have until toward the end of this manuscript when I phoned him. He had regrouped and now had a high paying job and position in a civilian capacity on the same air base in Ohio where he had retired. You can't keep a good man down.

I had hoped that I could get him to substantiate what I felt strongly had happened and its likely connection with my situation and also the attempt to use everyone one around me. As with most people, he could not and would not substantiate my beliefs or even possibly due to the perception of covert harassment turning on them again.

I remember being taunted numerous times, by the group targeting me that people I thought could substantiate my veracity and their bragging, by Synthetic Telepathy "This person" or, "that person is not going to help you." This was said as if in The Program many could and were easily being systematically manipulated and controlled by technology which could instill fear, doubt, sadness, by frequencies, etc., without the monitor, again, ever leaving the operation center building. And I found the manipulation of people to be on a massive scale for years to come around me to include my neighborhoods.

He would not confirm any involvement but did say, "You can't fight the government." The government was said without me specifically even mentioning any agency or who exactly was targeting me to him and this was not the first time this reference had been made specifically related to a likely government agency.

This proved his involvement by at least his awareness that something was happening around me and connecting the government as involved. He then told me that I should be fearful saying that they were too powerful to take on as an adversary. I did not, nor do I believe this to this day and resent anyone discouraging me from fighting rightfully for my life no matter how big the foe. Did not David take on Goliath and win?

If any entity is abusing you, or attempting to use you, no matter who they are, you are not required to sit back and just take it. I had heard this statement a few times during my fight for justice, "you can't win against the government." Accepting this was not even option for me. I was unafraid. I was not trying to win. I was trying to get these beyond ignorant, immoral men, with whatever agency they were representing, or jointly, to include combined military operations, to move on or come into the open ethically. They, however, had latched onto me through biometric signature download and became technological super glue. And by 2015 were still there now five books later focused on this subject attempting to destroy me covertly!

CHAPTER NINE

"There is nothing more beautiful than believing in you."

— Sam Kao

I stumbled onto the diagnosis in the VA computer system of me quite by accident. I was sitting in the office of a medical doctor after complaining of an upset stomach and nausea while in the Veterans Village Recovery Center (VVRC) in 2007. She began to check the computer, as I stood behind her glancing over her shoulder, searching for any previous lab work. As the computer screen flipped from screen to screen, pausing briefly for her to see if she had found the information, I noticed that a diagnosis had been entered into the computer by the director of the VVRC regarding me. He was also the chief psychiatrist. I could not believe my eyes. When I saw the diagnosis, it was upsetting. I questioned the medical doctor why the diagnosis was there. She told me that she could not explain another doctor's diagnosis then said, that those in the psychiatric field were quick to routinely label African Americans as having psyche issues. This fact conveniently opens the door for all types of bogus testing and use as test subjects, as well as medication test, I would later learn. Confused, and becoming angry I abruptly excused myself. I now urgently needed to speak with the director of the program and headed to where I knew his office was.

When I reached his office, his door was open and he sat engrossed in reading something on his computer. I immediately told him, how dare he diagnose me with, something, anything, and not even talking to me about it. I told him that I had not come to the VVRC for a diagnosis; I came for help in finding work, getting a place of my own only and more importantly to get my children. I did not believe any diagnosis would help in this effort. He sat calmly watching me. I told him that if anything my symptoms were related to Premenstrual Stress and demanded that he take the diagnosis out of the computer at that very moment. He hardly said a word as he listened to my ranting and raving.

"How dare you after only meeting with me twice and for less than 30 minutes" I told him.

He reluctantly told me he would remove the diagnosis seeing how upset I was or because no one had informed me. However, before he changed what he had written, he said,

"I have been at this for many, many years, and we, (meaning he and the young residents, trained with the same belief, he was responsible for training) have rarely been wrong."

"Something is going on with you. And in nearly all cases people in recovery most often are dually diagnosed," he added. This meant substance abuse issues which are motivated from some other issue as its foundation and core with a person. And adding insult to injury, he then said, "most people with issues do not think anything is wrong."

In other words, he echoed what I would learn later is a typical doctrine in psychology, "Crazy people do not think they are crazy." When he said this, it was a further slap in the face. I then told him,

"Well, I don't care what kind of brilliant doctor you perceive yourself as being, but in my case, you are wrong! I said nearly yelling."

My behavior problems, agitation, anxiety and emotional outbursts, I felt, were the result, if anything, of the harassment of being and outnumbered on the predominantly male facility, in the recovery program and in the environment overall. My reactions I also felt were the definite end result of the sexual harassment from the men that no one chose to believe was factually happening. One staff member even went so far as to blame me for the behavior of the men around me in the program. It had become apparent to some that my reactions had reached a crisis stage it seemed.

I would later learn in therapy that a reaction and definite symptom of Post-Traumatic Stress Disorder (PTSD) that had plagued me for many years, and of which dominated my reactions while on the facility which included extreme Startle Reflex was associated with this specific trauma related diagnosis. I was greatly saddened by even the possibility of something going on with me that I could not handle myself or knew of. I had had this extreme reaction many times in my life since leaving the military and now vigilant while on this facility. I always blew it off as normal. I did not know that it was abnormal. However, this symptom was a determining factor by the severity of my reaction itself along with other indicators. Yes, I could remember other times in my life experiencing the phenomena however, I found it insulting, whenever a person observed this reaction and looked at me as if I were crazy after witnessing it.

I was able to complete the program of 60 days in recovery, though barely making it through the required minimum stay and finally promoted to the Women Advance Program on the facility. I carried with me by that point the insult that everyone thought something was wrong with me.

The United States Veterans Initiative (USVETS) is a very structured program with an itinerary of day-to-day activities, meetings, groups, played out by the book along with designated time in the resource center. In the resource center resumes could be perfected and I would receive assistance with the job search, getting a residence, and hopefully regaining my life and my children.

Now in the women's program, with no definitive change to my behavior, after about a month or so of being there one of the staff members began asking me had anything, such as an assault, ever happened to me in the military. She prefaced this saying, "Something must have happened to you seeing how attractive you are." Was I happy about her asking me this question? Absolutely not! They were trying to pry into all areas of my life and extremely personal territory that I felt that was none of their business. I was angered and offended feeling that they too, once again, were yet again, also, trying to label me as crazy or that something was wrong with me now in this program.

On another occasion, the program director of Women's Advance stopped by as I sat watching television in the day room and said, "We just can't believe that nothing ever happened to you." Again, I was anything but happy, and was highly offended with the perception that something was wrong with me and that it was being constantly being thrown in my face and even offended and hurt by it. They were bringing up, out of the clear blue, a situation that had ultimately cost me my marriage due to my ex's malicious verbal abuse concerning the incident, only, and I repeat, only when I wanted a divorce. His verbal abuse resulted in the decision of needing to get as far away from him as possible thereby affecting the decision I made regarding the children, after him portraying me as unfit, which was horrendously difficult for me to cope with afterward when I arrived in Los Angeles in 1998. Frankly I could not cope with the decision at all as I thought. I knew I had to leave him or self-destruct.

As a result of their probing, I was becoming extremely resentful and angry. I did not want to revisit the painful circumstance or the impact it had had on my life apparently overall, or any role in the resulting failed marriage or the fact that I no longer had my children with me. It was all connected.

I was emotionally worn and distraught when I finally arrived in California having been taken through the wringer living with his negative comments nearing 13 years of marriage and my wanting out. His specific comment maliciously about the incident, hurt deeply, I learned in therapy, and very likely, contributed to my overwhelming reaction, self-destruction, drinking, and great depression of which I did not know how to process. It had definitely ultimately led to my decision to divorce him.

I had always been a truthful, honorable woman throughout the marriage and in my life. Never could anyone declare me anything different or less, nor would the investigators ever find anyone to say differently later, with the exception it now appeared of using a vindictive ex-husband seeking to create doubt. Trust me, if they could find someone, to counter or justify their heinous covert actions around me and especially, to counter this book, now also, they would surely have.

This self-serving group using street tactics and advanced technology hoped to strategically used malicious verbal abuse to weaken and influence me to break. This was along with hoping to elicit guilt or even implant guilt through their perceived technological advantage using this brilliant technology. However, I remain unmoved. Funny how I had always been held in high regard by my ex-husband. This was until I began mentioning divorce.

The cops around me were nothing more than individuals of little real integrity now cowardly angry at book exposure, possible embarrassment, and determined to get their way with 20 to 1. There had been no satisfaction for their narrow-minded egos, as I stood, against their arrogance of which they just could not cope with and resulted in the escalated effort around me using horrific covert psycho-physical torture now destroying tissue and organs in my body.

What they did not get is that they held absolutely no power except as bullies proven now by their own desperation for any resemblance of fear in me. I still to this day, cannot believe that these psycho cops felt that I should be afraid of them, report nice things about them, and be afraid to call it as I see it. This showed me how desperate they really are in hoping to preserve a false perception. At the end of the day, along with extreme torture, the best they could come up with were weak minded name calling while hiding out at a computer terminal at the workstation, or at times adjacent locations never having the ability to come forth honorably.

I could state my case, they could only watch me do so in publication and they were murderously angry about it and wanting blood. I would continue my efforts to expose them, their unethical use of the highly advanced technology, Psy Op tactics, and strategies, of what was happening to not only me but numerous and thousands of others in America today and globally. They resorted to calling malicious names and appeared to be gaining pleasure out of substandard, petty behavior. These poor lost souls just could not accept that I was not scared. This is apparently unusual for them use to intimidating everyone into submission.

My ex had asked me to marry him after the incident marrying six months later. It is completely illogical to any intelligent minded person to think that any man would ask a woman to be his wife if he perceived her as having done something wrong. My ex knew I was then, and always have been a lady. However, he could not make the same claim of fidelity due to a specific incident in Germany that nearly shattered the marriage four years after marriage. Right after we had the second daughter in 1987, he had a one-night stand with someone. After my badgering him, sensing it, he tearfully apologized for cheating and told me he would never do it again. I thought I could forgive him. However, I was not mature enough to accept this hurtful violation of trust and it came up in arguments often my trust diminished. Also impacting the trust issue was the fact that he would never revealed who the person was when I asked him. This eventually tore away at the marriage combined with drinking to relax together on the weekends after the kids were asleep. It left an open wound of doubt, insecurity, guessing and suspicion.

After the continued questioning by staff after returning to the women's program about any history of assault, I decided that I was not going to divulge anything nor open this wound. A short while later, however, added to the list of mandatory meetings and groups, was now mandatory attendance at post-traumatic stress groups. I was not happy about this at all. I felt that I was being forced or pressured. I was so upset by the overall situation, and the repeated prying, that I went back over to the Veterans Village Recovery Center area and talked with a nursing staff member there that I trusted. I told her that it seemed as if everyone were zeroing in specifically on me asking me had anything ever happened to me feeling that I was again being singled out.

Because I was having extreme anger issues, I was required to also attend a mandatory anger management classes in addition to my regular meetings and groups. It was ultimately in the anger management class that I began to open up about the incident, and the aftermath, to a Veteran's hospital psychologist about the despair I had held inside for years. When I did open up, it was due only to a desperate need for relief from the intensity of the severe emotional and psychological affect as a whole which I did not know, again, how to cope with effectively and apparently never had.

As with most, I needed help after a shatter marriage. However, the verbal abuse which arose associated with the incident in the military had played a major role in the demise of the marriage and most importantly also my psyche. The Long Beach VA hospital staff psychologist, who ran the anger management class, told me that it was not my fault when I questioned her why my ex had verbally abused me about the assault many years later. Her response was that my ex blamed me for something going on inside him that he directed at me as malicious insults as part of his personal and his very own ego driven psyche.

Why did these women continually ask me "Had any incident ever happen to me?" Why me? Were there definitive signs and traits that I displayed that they recognized? Why was it mandatory for all women in the program to attend the PTSD group afterwards? It was not until 2008, when I returned to the facility at the same Long Beach, California Veteran Village Recovery Center and the USVETS location that I understood why. This time I was back to participate in the Renew Program now firmly in place for a few years after the year and a half I spent weekly in therapy myself.

The Renew Program is a 12-week program designed to lay a foundation of positive coping and adjustment in dealing with PTSD issues for women. It was, in 2008 that I learned of the establishment of Renew in the mid-2000s. I left the facility moving to Anaheim, California in 2002 and stayed for 4 years. It was established a few years afterwards. The Renew Program is a coordinated effort between my Long Beach VA hospital therapist, a PTSD expert, and the director of the Women's Advanced Program for USVETS.

Could the goal of establishing this program be the reason for the repeated questioning of whether I had ever had or the other women ever had any types of incident in this area from staff during my stay on the facility before, I now wondered? Now in the Renew Program, I now understood possibly why the outreach coordinator had also called me specifically about a year after I left the facility asking me if I could return to the facility as a representative for the program and speak with a local Congresswoman visiting the site. Apparently, they sought a grant, and support for establishing this specific program. Why me? I believe it was because of my appearance and how I carry myself. Sadly, most of the female veterans, of all races, in the women's program had had very difficult adjustment issues after leaving the military and some had been homeless for quite some time and suffering. Female veterans are also considered a high-risk group and underrepresented in the VA system.

There was not a single thing illegal or unethical occurring by these dedicated caring professional staff members seeking to address issues specific to female veterans, nor were staff members, again, incompetent, easily manipulated or naive. And, in my case, again it was staff that associated my behavior traits, in both the VVRC and Women's Advance Program with other issues and not me!

When I found a place and employment, the issues I had been having for years, continually plagued me and continued to create dysfunction. I was unable to maintain employment by history spanning over many, many years. My inability to maintain employment had also had an impact on the marriage, depression, and contributed to low self-esteem.

In 2004, I was given full benefits by the VA retroactive to 2002. This was also during the timeframe that I was isolated and alone, and sought companionship around a woman, I had known as a youth who would also ultimately make her contribution, through sheer old fashion jealousy, to the unjust situation hovering over my head.

Was there supposed to be happiness for me afterwards the diagnosis, benefits and knowing? No, in fact it was even more shattering. I still had a difficult time accepting that something had factually been going with me all those years as subtle influences and had contributed to my many failures. My reactions confused even me in life. The failures in my life throughout the years had been a bitter pill to swallow and left a deep emotional scar as inadequate in some way.

CHAPTER TEN

"Fortitude is the marshal of thought, the armor of the will, and the fort of reason."

— Francis Bacon

The Drug Enforcement Agency appeared to be the law enforcement agency initially spearheading the High Intensity Drug Trafficking Area (HIDTA) program in participation with other federal, state and local authorities, such as LAPD, connected by government fusion centers focused on Los Angeles County. In my case, I was done abusing my life, numb to the emotional pain, and wanted to live by September of 2007 after hitting the imaginary brick wall of consciousness and waking up to the fact that I must survive and I had a lot to live for.

Six months after realizing that I was not going to drop dead from the broken-heart attack I sought, I was only left with a feeling that something had to change and immediately as my only reality. This was when moving to Scottsdale, a place I knew nothing about or anyone came to mind.

As I did the final packing that day in March 2006 in the apartment in Anaheim, preparing to drive to Arizona the next morning, the fact that the door knob was unscrewed and hanging very loose when I came home early that morning from a friend's house stood out in my mind but made little sense to me. As I packed, I tried to think of any way that the screws could have unscrewed themselves but could not come up with a logical explanation. As I continued cleaning up the last of my belonging, there appeared to be commotion outside and around the complex. Something was amidst. It was even more obvious because it was a weekday and usually very quiet at that time in the morning around 9:00 a.m. I left the door open for the fresh air as I did the final packing.

What drew me to the front door the first time was the sound that a tow truck makes when it is loading a vehicle, the beeping noise. I stepped out onto the balcony and went to the edge to look over to see what was happening. I saw the neighbor across the street below talking with the driver of the tow truck. I distinctly heard him ask her why there were so many federal agents around the facility. She then nodded in my direction and said, "Drugs." "What did she just say? Did I just hear her say drugs?" I thought. After hearing the neighbor's remark, I walked back into my apartment to digest what I had definitely heard. I then decided to go back to where I was standing to see if she would say anything else. This time when I did, I glanced down the street and their stood an official, professional looking, clean cut older white male. He was dressed in dress pants, dress shirt, no tie or jacket. When I glanced in his direction, what struck me was that he immediately turned his head to avoid eye contact with me and he had something in his hand appearing to be a two-way radio. Feeling that he may have been actually watching me but unsure, I turned and walked back into my apartment still trying to digest what was happening and again was said by the neighbor leaving the door open. She had gone inside her residence. Could she had actually nodded in my direction? This time with my mind racing, I then returned to the open door to get a better look at him. In a matter of minutes, the man had disappeared.

In spite of what I had heard the neighbor say, somehow my mind could not register that someone was actually really after me and ready to bust into my apartment. It seemed like something out of a movie. I did not think that the situation was real at first. The realization began to sink in, as the possibility rang loudly in my head, that it was a possible that they were factually after me. And they wanted to catch me before I left the state. It was difficult for me to believe because I was never involved heavily in drugs although apparently someone in law enforcement, very possibly the DEA or Federal Bureau of Investigation, or Veterans Administration, or the Los Angeles Police Department or all of the above felt that I was. And I could not deny that I had factually seen with my own two eyes the neighbor nod also in my direction after responding to the tow truck driver's question. However, since I was not doing anything and had five months of sobriety under by belt, I felt no cause for alarm as reality evaded me.

My mind did not grasp, at that time, the magnitude of the beginning stages of what began slowly brewing around me in March of 2006. I then headed to the kitchen to finish cleaning up the scattered unwanted items left on the counter and floor. Everything useful had been transferred to my daughter's new place or the trash bin of that which could be carried or I did not want. I had begun working in the bedroom when I first arrived home and now decided to start in the kitchen.

One of the very first things I notice was that a partially smoked marijuana bud, from the old life and extremely small, was now intentionally wet and stuck to my kitchen wall just over the sink. Whoever had tried to stick it there had tried several times before it stuck leaving finger print marks in the area around where they had tried and tried before successful. It did not take much imagination to think after that, that someone had entered my residence, or to understand that someone had also probably gone through the entire apartment, most likely with the Canine Division to find it. They would have had to because it was less about 1/8th of an inch in size.

For the past three days I had been staying with a dear friend. This person was the one whom had first gotten me involved with AA. Later I would realize that weird unexplainable things had also been happening for the three days that I slept on his couch before returning home to pack when the television while watching it began acting very strangely so much to the point that I turned it off. Most people are unaware but experts on reverse technology say that any television set manufacture after 1995, some say as far back as 1992, have the capability not only to receive a broadcast signal, but to also send one.

And today, microchips are added to newer models during manufacturing to include of course computers and phones. That's correct, any television manufactured during these times has a built-in feature enabling sending a broadcast signal from your living room of live images of what's happening in your home even if turned off and still plugged in! I began to recall that I had also noticed, before that morning, strange men, appearing around the very secluded property whom appeared to intentionally avoid eye contact with me it seemed though I did not think much of this previously.

There was always peacefulness at my old friend's home. His home was buried deep within a canyon in the hills of Los Angeles on spiraling four acres of fruit trees and nature. A court order for me to complete a program for a DUI ultimately snapped me back to reality which would turn into a warrant and trouble for me if I did not fulfill the order. I was drained and tired of putting problems on top of problems and couldn't take it any longer. If I had been followed, and it appeared so, during my six months of insanity, one thing I knew for sure was that I was not crazy enough to put myself in a position of my own making with a warrant out for my arrest if I could prevent it.

Five months before, I was curled up in the fetal position, alone, on the floor, crying gut wrenching tears begging God to help me and remove all burden from me isolated and alone. I plead for divine intervention. My world had gotten so dark spiritually and wrapped in the intensity of the unbearable pain and disappointment of my life that nothing provided even short-term relief and never had. It was severe depression that prompted me to drink to begin with. Although the pain I felt was psychological and emotional, I could feel it vibrating through every cell in my body as a physical reaction as well. It was powerful and is memorable, easily recalled to this day as great sadness. Nothing could sooth it. I had hit rock bottom, and the only direction for me was either up or the actual death I thought was the cure. Death does not have to be a physical occurrence, I would later understand. It can also be death of a way of life, thinking, or experience, brought by the passage of time in the healing process. All things eventually run its course and must do so by Universal and Divine Order.

I was spent, emotionally, physically, mentally, and there was nothing left for me to give to the pain or feed to it. I was all cried out, had acted out anger, and hoped to die, but miraculously, was still alive and the fog began to lift as a spark of light deep within began to flicker and grow. It started similar to the small flicker under my vehicle, after the car accident before the flame spread and engulfed the entire vehicle. It was this loving light's nudging that had brought me home in a trance of hopefulness.

However, there it was, a tiny enticement creatively stuck to my kitchen wall as a message from someone along with their finger prints marks as proof that they had been there. And of course, again, there was the issue of the door knob being loose when I came in which I tightened with a screw driver. They could have at least tightened it when they left. Or, was it left that way intentionally for me to notice it? When I saw the tiny marijuana joint, which was laced with cocaine, obviously placed where it was, I freaked. There was absolutely no disputing that it was purposely put there to make sure that I saw it or even perhaps as temptation. Could someone believe that I would dry it off and smoke it while they watched me ready to break the door down?

In the place of any urge for self-medication was now determination to never revisit the depth of the emotional despair that had been my nemesis. But who would do such a thing? My first thought had been that possibly my daughter had found it and stuck it there. A cardinal rule was that I never had drugs around them in any form. My history with substance abuse use was brief and sporadic at best. However, the constant arguments with my older daughter, the incident involving the youngest daughter, and the so-called friend, along with everything, divorce, issues surrounding the divorce, etc., and complete dysfunction had effectively pushed me over the edge.

Immediately after remarrying, my ex-husband evicted the oldest from his new home in Colorado sending her to me. The oldest daughter was at the age when girls began to naturally, in some cases dislike their mothers and she could not stand his new wife and kept trying to break them up. However, in her case, she had good reason to dislike both me and her father.

The middle girl had been allowed back into his home, with the youngest, in Denver, but the oldest was still not welcome. She was fifteen after he lied to have them taken from me during divorce proceedings that again, had me arrested, which as stated devastated me. I had given her good reason to be angry with me as she watched me torture myself with my inability to cope with life on life's terms. So, I at first thought that she may have found it and stuck it there to embarrass me.

When I saw it, I realized it was an invitation. My instincts, for unknown reasons immediately sent me racing to my closet or perhaps it was by an intentional subliminal suggestion, I would later considered. I just knew to look where I used to hide my stash which was inside of an old coat pocket in the back of my closet. I reached into the coat pocket, which I had cleaned out after deciding I was done and nearly passed out when to my surprise I felt something definitely inside the pocket. This could not be what I think it is, I thought to myself.

What I pulled out of the coat pocket that day, which I had thoroughly cleaned out a few months prior sent shock waves through my body. It was a small piece of cocaine of about $10 worth. Had it been anymore, it would have been even more questionable. $10 was all that I would ever purchase or even less mostly. I stood there shocked, mortified, horrified, stunned and yes with the front door still wide open. I just could not believe my eyes. I search my mind searching every corner of it trying to remember if I had possibly left something behind in the coat pocket five months earlier when I cleaned it out turning the pocket inside out to insure it empty at that time. Had I missed this? And if so how? The answer was a resounding NO. I had absolutely not left anything in there. I had thoroughly cleaned the pocket.

When I declared myself done and wanting to try to resurrect my life and create some degree of happiness for myself, the first place I cleaned was of course the place where I would stash stuff. In the addiction of substance abuse, most people don't save anything or leave anything for a rainy day. Still not believing that it was real, I popped it into my mouth, hoping that I was wrong. However, when my tongue immediately froze, I knew that it was the real thing and it was obvious high grade. I did not care. This great evil was not stronger than the will of God within me.

Had someone been watching me all along inside my home and observed me hiding drugs in the pocket? Or had the canine division been directed to the coat by residue? Was it intentionally put there like the small marijuana joint stuck to the wall in the kitchen?

The only explanation obviously was that someone had to know that I hid things specifically inside the old coat pocket. How they knew it, I did not know or even care at that moment. If this was factual, and it appeared so, by the evidence in my hand, and feeling in my mouth, then the fact that I had been probably watched inside my home for a while could be a reality. After reality flooded my mind, I returned to the real world. I raced back to the front door. I looked outside. The entire apartment complex was eerily quiet. I did not even hear a bird chirping it seemed. I shut the door, then raced back to the kitchen, turned on the garbage disposal, and dropped both items down the drain as the disposal did its job by grinding the two items into oblivion. I then went back to the door, opened it again, and looked out. It appeared that all was clear, and quiet. I now even saw a neighbor milling about and yes, I could even hear the bird's chirping again.

I quickly finished what I was doing, all the while very, very, very thankful to God and emotionally flooded with gratitude. I was grateful and thankful that I had found what had been placed in my coat pocket to entrap me. While I continued cleaning, with the realization of the blessing, I was even more determined to begin anew. Nobody said the road would be easy in life and I had learned a powerful lesson on coping, endurance, trusting and faith, life and experience the best teachers.

My mind began to make other connections. I began to play back scenes such as shopping one day at the 99 Cents Only Store a few weeks prior. I remembered that day I had seen a similar looking, older white professional man following me as I walked through the store. At that time, there was also an older, white female also in the team of about three or four undercover federal looking people. I realized that they might be after me when one of these men worked his way up close enough to me to watch me intently when I bent over and picked up an item on a bottom display shelf. Although I was on my cell phone, his zeroing in on the area when I put the item back surveying it did not escape me as I continued shopping. And there also was the incident at the car wash also. Another man, similarly dressed walked by me saying,

"God is watching you."

Hey, wasn't this just what I had told three teenagers who came up to my car and asked me for money when I pulled into the 7 Eleven earlier? Still a bit shaken by the odd remark, at the car wash that day, I took my seat as my SUV was washed, picked up the newspaper as a distraction while tossing over repeatedly in my mind what he had said to me to intimidate me obviously. I decided to just ignore it and ignore him too.

It would be for these reasons, that when I first heard the scratching noise of something type of device moving across the concrete ceiling, on the patio above me in 2008, that I first began calling the Drug Enforcement Agency first off.

About two weeks after getting settled into my new apartment in moving in on July 1, 2008 in Signal Hill, California, I was sitting quietly reading a book and relaxing when I heard a scratching noise move across the ceiling. It sounded like someone was trying to position something directly overhead of where I was sitting. The first thing I did was to get up and walk outside to see if anyone was working on the patio above which was my roof. There was no sign of anyone sitting out sunbathing typical of some days by upstairs neighbors. The day was quiet around 2:30 p.m., in the cool breeze of the summer afternoon. So, I went back inside and took my seat and again opened the book I was reading. When I had gotten comfortable, the noise started again. When it stopped, giving the appearance that whatever it was had achieved its goal of better positioning, just overhead, I sat thinking for a moment what it could be. If someone lived in an apartment above me, it would be explained as what I now knew as portable see through wall technology that I first experienced in Scottsdale, Arizona in 2006. However, my roof was the extended concrete patio, as stated, for the upstairs apartments housing only patio furniture.

In Arizona, when I first heard the neighbor seeming to follow me around in 2006, I would move around intentionally hoping to confirm that I was factually being followed below as I moved around from above by some type of x-ray device. I wondered what would happen if I did it this time with no one living over me. I got up and moved to the couch. When I did this, the scratching noise followed me step by step scratching its way along the same path I had taken, once I settled, it settled, and then appeared to move around to again regain focus a second time. I then decided to move to my bed, sitting on the edge. The same thing happened. The noise followed me then stopped directly overhead. I then left the room and walked into the kitchen. It did the same. I moved to the bathroom, the same. It was at that point that I realized that something big was going on of which had again followed me back across state line returning back to California, in June of 2007 after a life-threatening car accident demolishing my SUV. However, I would later learn that these situations are not out of the question as most would think. Due to the military spy satellites already in place and orbiting our planet real time satellite or remote viewing data and imagery is cost free to a requesting agency.

In most cases, you cannot hear the satellite radar laser when it penetrates some types of surfaces, and moves around. However, the concrete patio seemed to be the exception and as it turned out a blessing in awareness for me. Apparently, some agency decided to stop by to see what I was doing each day and to make sure I was really sober at that and nearing 10 years later continued. Most people felt that a target had to be a big-time heavy weigh person of interest, as did I at first, however, this is simply not true today. "You are not that important" or, "Why you" were frequently said in response to my telling people about the surveillance and this was constantly said as a form of ridicule or that you are crazy.

I would learn of the program funded by the Office of National Drug Policy, called the High Intensity Drug Trafficking Area (HIDTA) under the President's drug czar originating in the Executive Office of the president. Resources provided to the HIDTA Program have grown from $25 million in Fiscal Year 1990 to $192 million in FY 2000 and I can only imagine the funding by 2012 resources and technological advancement availability.

The Los Angeles, HIDTA website address is: (https://www.ncjrs.gov/ondcppubs/publications/enforce/hidta2001/la-fs.html)

The website documents a physical location of advanced technology called the "War Room" that are located in the centers of operations. Operations are non-stop and twenty-four hours a day with personnel in working shifts. This program is national.

The Los Angeles HIDTA mission statement:

It is the mission of the LA-HIDTA to measurably reduce drug trafficking; thereby reducing the impact of illicit drugs in this and other areas of the country. This mission is accomplished through the use of multi-jurisdictional (federal, state, and local), collocated, and commingled law enforcement initiatives designed to attack, disrupt, and dismantle major drug trafficking and money laundering organizations that are operating in and through the LA-HIDTA region...

Another example is the mission statement of the Washington D.C. / Baltimore HIDTA:

To enhance and coordinate America's drug-control efforts among federal, state and local agencies in order to eliminate or reduce drug trafficking (including the production, manufacture, transportation, distribution and chronic use of illegal drugs and money laundering) and its harmful consequences...

The technology being used around me after reading the Los Angeles HIDTA's website could very easily be available in this huge government financed initiative as also shown by specific operations in the excerpts highlighted below:

1. Los Angeles County Criminal Information Clearinghouse (LACRCIC)—the mission of the Los Angeles County Regional Criminal Information Clearinghouse (LACRCIC) is to produce and provide intelligence products, enhanced information sharing, and advanced systems technology to federal, state and local law enforcement agencies in order to ensure officer safety and enhance operational efficiency and effectiveness. This is done by real time surveillance directing their colleagues (more than likely by technological telepathy also) from the operation center.

2. War Room / Information Unit Activity—The War Room provides "real time" operational and tactical intelligence support by tracking, around-the-clock, all federal, state and local law enforcement undercover operations within the four-county region known as the LA-HIDTA. On-site Intelligence Analysts are available to immediately research various law enforcement intelligence databases thus enabling officers to conduct enhanced narcotic investigations.

3. Special Operations Center—The LACRCIC has established a Special Operations Center that is designed to support major law enforcement operations–in particular, electronic surveillance (wiretap). The center employs state-of-the-art automated information management systems (SINS) and electronic surveillance equipment and is configured to house and support an on-site staff of investigators and analysts for the duration of any special investigation/ operation.

4. Intelligence Support System—The Intelligence Support System (ISS), which is comprised of the LACRCIC, LAJDIG, and INCH, is aligned through a cooperative partnership identified though an approved matrix of responsibilities and associated Memorandum of Agreement. Unique in the entire country, a memorandum of understanding amongst these intelligence initiatives identifies definitive lines of responsibility, enhances lines of communication and affords an enhanced level of service to the LA-HIDTA law enforcement community. Components within the LA-HIDTA ISS provide responsive 24/7-day DE conflication, pointer index, case support, post seizure analysis, target profiles, organizational identification, intelligence fusion, special support services (electronic surveillance), and training.

The program initiatives, on the Washington D.C. / Baltimore website list the definite involvement by agenda of a civilian community effort.

For example, the Washington/Baltimore HIDTA website states:

"HIDTA will employ enhanced intelligence processes in high-crime neighborhoods that are centers for drug abuse and distribution. The Information Center is comprised of two key elements—Watch Center and the Community Policing Prevention Program Initiative."

All along, it was obvious that I was being targeted by oversight that included a ground effort originating from a state-of-the-art operation center.

In my opinion, specific, detailed, patented advanced technology availability, such as non-lethal directed energy weapons, synthetic telepathy, mind and thought deciphering, brain wave analyzing and human biometric mapping software, dream manipulation, or portable microwave subliminal message carrying technology, are available in these technologically advanced programs and centers of operations. Fusion center operations also coexist with military installations.

I had no doubt in my mind that it was satellite entering my residence each day. What else could it be? Had not the letter from the judge spoke of a federal spying program in 2006.

The Warrantless Spy Program, approved during the Bush-Chaney administration also approved law enforcement entering a home without a warrant.

USA Patriot Act–section 213

Section 213 is the first statute ever enacted in the history of American criminal procedure to specifically authorize an entirely new form of search warrant-what legal scholars call the sneak and peek warrant (also dubbed the covert entry warrant or the surreptitious entry warrant). A sneak and peek search warrant authorize police to effect physical entry into private premises without the owner's or the occupant's permission or knowledge to conduct a search; generally, such entry requires a breaking and entering. - Donald E. Wilkes, Flagpole Magazine Sept 2002.

Later, in 2008, I began to hear noises coming from the storage room next door in the Signal Hill apartment sounding as if someone was positioning something portable against the wall there also. One day, I woke early opened my front door and sat waiting for the person to leave. I noticed twice that whoever it was left around 6:30 a.m. as if his shift had come to an end and it very may have been penis cop. However, on this morning, whomever it was would not get home on time except through the manager's distraction, intervention and my finally deciding to close the door to shower.

The Federal Intelligence Surveillance Act (FISA). Signals intelligence collection of targeted individuals within the United States as detailed earlier, is governed by the Foreign Intelligence Surveillance Act (FISA.) The Foreign Intelligence Surveillance Act of 1978 ("FISA" Public Law 95-511, 92 Stat. 1783, enacted October 25, 1978, 50 U.S.C. ch.36, S. 1566) is an Act of Congress which prescribes procedures for the physical and electronic surveillance and collection of "foreign intelligence information" between "foreign powers" and "agents of foreign powers" (which may include American citizens and permanent residents suspected of being engaged in espionage and violating U.S. law on territory under United States control) and domestically the Electronic Communication Privacy Act (ECPA.) Violating U.S. law on territory under U.S. control is where a bogus charge of narcotic trafficking could fit as justification.

A bogus narcotic trafficking charge may have been manipulated under the guise of "violating US law on territory" used as the foundation for my targeting. Fusion centers and a joint intelligence sharing initiative were inspired by these laws resulting in heinous effort to legally take and destroy lives by immoral men sitting at the technologies helm.

During the years of the so-called "War on Drugs" which preceded the "War on Terrorism," letters written by involuntary U.S. citizens used as human test subjects of which many reported regularly vanished from the mail or mailed responses back to them were never received. There appeared to be a conspiracy of silence surrounding a testing program some say which many felt even involved the United States Post Offices across our country I learned while doing research. It appeared that an involuntary guinea pig testing operation was in place to test advanced technology on those falling victim to a so-called inability to stop the flow of drugs into the United States. If anything, this reality appeared to be a conspiracy within itself. With thousands of satellites in place for many reasons, dating back many years that can zero in on and read even a letter in a person's hand the inability to stop the influx of drugs seems suspect and some would argue by intent.

The term "War on Drugs" was first used by President Richard Nixon in 1971. Today drug control issues within the United States fall under the funding source for the High Intensity Drug Trafficking Area program or HIDTA. HIDTA is the initiative of the Office of National Drug Control Policy ONDCP under the President's drug czar originating in the Executive Office of the President. And, yes, every piece of technology that I mention, specifically real-time surveillance is available to these huge operations in these centers which have a large budget provided to enforce the program. This may be also be, I suspected the funding source which also supports money for technology, etc., provided to civilian agents in Community Policing / harassment groups. Resources provided to the HIDTA Program have grown from $25 million in Fiscal Year 1990 to $192 million in FY 2000 and I can only imagine the funding and advanced technology of today.

I arrived in Los Angeles, California in 1996. During this time, a local Congresswoman was in the news daily in open protest of drugs being openly sold on every block, saying that drugs were intentionally, purposely, put into the African American community to finance Iran/Contra.

Iran / Contra came to light in November of 1986 as a political scandal. During the Reagan administration, Reagan administration officials secretly made it possible to sale arms to Iran that was under an arms embargo. The hope was that the sales would secure the release of hostages and allow intelligence agencies with the U.S. to fund the Nicaraguan Contras. The Boland Amendment prohibited funding by our government of this cause.

A series of articles in the San Jose Mercury News on August 18-20, 1996 alleged that the CIA was involved with Nicaraguan Contra rebels who raised money for weapons by selling cocaine to Los Angeles area street gangs:

a. (Gary Webb, "America's 'crack' plague has roots in Nicaragua war," San Jose Mercury News, August 18, 1996, p. A1

b. Gary Webb, "Shadowy Origins of 'crack' epidemic," San Jose Mercury News, August 19, 1996, p. A1

c. Gary Webb, "War on drugs has unequal impact on black Americans," San Jose Mercury News, Au-gust 20,1996, p. A1

d. Tony Perry and Jesse Katz, "As Drug Debate Rages, Dealer to Be Sentenced," Los Angeles Times (Washington Edition), August 23, 1996, p. B1

e. Gary Webb, "The Crack Masters," New Times (Los Angeles), September 12-18, 1996, Vol. 1, Num. 4.

The environment when I arrived in Los Angeles, California, at that time was far from the well-manicured lawns and two and three car garage homes where my children played oblivious to the harsher realities of this world, and my ex-husband and I called home. The onus reality by contrast saddened me beyond belief in the already haze of despair, loss, will carrying a boatload of heavy-duty psychological baggage and the intense emotional pain I brought with me.

Note: Gary Webb supposedly committed suicide. However later, some would allege he was assassinated as revealed in the documentary in the following link:

http://www.prisonplanet.com/articles/december2004/141204webbmurdered.htm.

One thing is sure. An epidemic was in full force, preying on the psychologically vulnerable in an already depressed community of lost hope and unfulfilled dreams. One thing is also certain, intentional infiltration of drugs into specific communities continues to be one of the greatest forms of mind control of individuals, groups, and large populations. This includes both illegal and legal drugs and the fact is that drugs played a very important role in mind control studies within the United States during the 20-year testing period of famed MKULTRA.

CHAPTER ELEVEN

"The fortitude to fight on through to the very end. This strength is not only the basis of happiness; it is also the force by which social wrongs can be righted."

— **Daisaku Ikeda**

I amusingly remember an old lady telling me once that I had never been to this planet by incarnation before. I laughed when she also said that I was sent here due to being a warrior of many lifetimes. It was known, she said, that if something was wrong or unjust; "You would fight not only for yourself but also for others" she told me. This was amusing to me at the time. Factually, it had been life's painful abuses, which had pushed me into taking action, fighting, and a stand.

As their fruitlessness appeared too waned, due to my understanding of the techniques of the program, their procedure changed. Ironically, it was the technology itself that allowed me into the dark recesses of the inner workings of the minds of those working these operations. Technological telepathy works as not only a transmitter of your thoughts but also as a receiver of their voices in the operation center of the comments of those targeting you, as well as others sitting nearby observing and commenting.

It saddened me what I found when I got an in depth look into the mentality of these groups. The disappointment was in the revelation of extreme, distorted thinking held by people in positions of public trust, who will justify anything to include covert technological murder as long as it is unknown to the public. They are also heinously ego driven by a false sense of power, misused authority and superiority, and a belief they can do whatever they want.

If they doubted my courage at this stage in their Psy Op games then they were truly in the wrong profession and out of touch with reality. There was nothing on the planet that would stop me knowing I was being wronged or even if, amusingly, I were called to take action by Divine Order or purpose as the old woman had said. I was going to see this through; I had to, no matter what and I meant it.

Many targeted individuals suffered from loss of employment, home, and family the result of being deemed unstable after revealing the targeting. The long arm of military and law enforcement's reach now even more extreme through satellite surveillance, and black bag technology, along with manipulated and inspired covert harassment groups and disinformation which impacts employment and leaves the target's life in ruins.

In my case, they could not affect my livelihood the way they would have liked too. I could not be fired nor ever did I have an inability to not to pay my rent. For this, I was eternally grateful realizing that this too allowed me the ability and opportunity to take a stand and fight and help with the exposure effort of thousands today targeted by this monstrous program. Even if I had to change residences, I still always had the means to pay for food and shelter. Yes, they could make my living environment a living hell, uncomfortable, destroy relationships, isolate me from family and friends, torture me to near death draining by tissue and organ of vital fluids by microwave cooking, but I would still have physical shelter.

Our country is at war. The result is that anyone could become a person of interest for a number of reasons and even for speaking out against the war over a phone line. A comment could be made then picked up by ECHELON. ECHELON is a name used in global media to describe the signal intelligence (SIGINT) collection and analysis network operated on behalf of the five signatory states to the United Kingdom and United States of America Security Agreement. The

United Kingdom and United States along with Australia, Canada and New Zealand are known as AUSCANNZUKUS or the Five Eyes.

The highly perfected technology in use today and its capabilities has put fear in many who know of the horror which can be created. These books ultimately are about my strong belief that unawareness of its full power no matter what status in life by profession or position is the most harmful evil of its kind today. This would be confirmed later to me by someone in the legal field when I sought help reinstating how knowledgeable yet fearful many are.

They pulled out their entire bag of technological tricks around me. Because my apartment was secluded in the back of the building in Signal Hill, I myself was stunned at the full capability of many of these technologies. I would frequently hear someone scratching someone against the wall trying to obviously focus on what I was doing from next door. One night I heard someone moving around in the storage apartment next door and it woke me around 2:00 a.m. When I woke, there before me was a hologram of a small hideous looking creature. What had I just seen? I asked myself in disbelief as I lay there in the dark? Was it a nightmare? I then heard a man's voice calling out my name who was the undercover person whom had kept pestering me in the shiny black truck aka "Is this big enough for you." And calling out my name was timed precisely after the image disappeared, poof, into mid-air. It was not a nightmare because I was fully awake, for sure when I saw it standing next to my bed for about 10 seconds. It was I would learn a hologram.

Are visual holograms possible? A website titled "Project Blue Beam: High-Tech "Religion" (Holograms of UFOs, religious figures tested in Arizona) Forbidden Knowledge TV states:

Project Blue Beam: High-Tech "Religion"

Two scientists with high level security clearances describe the ground-based and satellite technologies which can beam holographic images of religious figures and UFOs over a region, such as a battlefield, to influence enemy to surrender -- or maybe to cause U.S. Citizens to comply with their own government?

Who knows? The scientists are not allowed to discuss the details but one admits that "American technology needs to be tested on Americans -- and American Citizens have already been damaged by the testing" of what some researchers call "Project Blue Beam."

This technology was being tested at the Army base at Fort Huachuca, Arizona in the 1990s at the time of this interview.

Today, with much of the U.S. news media functioning like the "politburo" mouthpiece of a failing state, it may be best to be mindful of what could really be behind the recent spate of UFO reports and how these may have been used to divert attention away from other events or reports that are more vital to people's everyday interests...

In April of 2012, the music industry's rap elite successfully used a visual hologram to bring to life Tupac Shakur for a performance during the Coachella concert, and later Michael Jackson, stunning the audience with mix feelings after reviving the dead. One of the first visual holograms was done in music industry with Natalie Cole singing with her father, Nat King Cole in the duet Unforgettable in 1991.

Psychological Electronic technology once termed mind control technology today is highly perfected through the scientific advancements of prolific inventors such as Nikola Tesla. And, the ongoing non-consensual testing that it took to get these advancements to their current state of perfection was not pretty and left great destruction in its path to its current state of being.

Of all the great inventions and discoveries of Nikola Tesla, nothing stood out as holding potential to be of great benefit to humanity than his discovery of Radiant Energy in 1889. The series of observations that led to the discovery of Tesla's Radiant energy grew out of experiments that Tesla conducted attempting to duplicate the results of Heinrich Hertz of Germany. Hertz clarified and expanded the electromagnetic theory of light that had been put forth by Maxwell.

James Clerk Maxwell was an English scientist who developed a scientific theory to explain electromagnetic waves. He noticed that electrical fields and magnetic fields couple together to form electromagnetic waves. Neither an electrical field (like the static which forms when you rub your feet on a carpet), nor a magnetic field (like the one that holds a magnet onto your refrigerator) will go anywhere by themselves. But, Maxwell discovered that a changing magnetic field will induce a changing electric field and vice-versa.

Originally electricity and magnetism were thought of as two separate forces. Hertz was the first to demonstrate the existence of electromagnetic waves by building an apparatus to produce and detect VHF and UHF radio waves affirming the existence of electromagnetic waves. Hertz announced the discovery in 1887.

Tesla's had well over 700 patents attributed to his name. This included his work with radio transmission, lasers, radar, and Tesla Coils that would eventually evolved into the High Frequency Active Auroral Research Project. A Tesla Coil is a type of resonant transformer circuit invented around 1891. Tesla used these coils to conduct innovative experiments using electrical energy transmission, electrotherapy, lighting, phosphorescence, x-ray generation without wires. These early works laid the foundation for the electromagnetic weaponry of today.

Dr. Stefan Possony was an expert on electrical warfare and revolution in the beginning of his writing "In Scientific Advances Hold Dramatic Prospects for Psy-Strategy," by Dr. Stefan Possony, 1983 July, Defense and Foreign Affairs, Page 34, Dr. Possony states: "The history of psy-ops technology is about 200 years old and it will continue to progress."

And Dr. Possony was right, in the 1700s; some of the first testing began as man began to make the connection between electricity and the human brain and mind. In the history of "Electrical Excitation," Drs. Chaffee and Light in, "Electrical Stimulation of the Nervous System, 1934" wrote of the first awareness of a connection of electromagnetism and the human body saying, "The history of neurophysiology has been decided in large part by the development of electric-recording instruments on the one hand, and by the increasingly effective use of electric currents for stimulating on the other. The early developments of these two sciences went forward hand in hand.

Since many of the discoveries in electricity were due to the tell-tale sensations and spasms caused by the passage of a current; in the absence of precise instruments for measuring electrical currents, the unique susceptibility of the neuromuscular system to electrical excitation made it an indispensable detector."

Excerpts below touch on the history and the scientific advancement and early beginnings from Drs. Chaffee and Light:

1746 - A group of scientists in Leyden encountered unexpectedly the "capacity" of an electrified glass of water, because of the sudden shock which accompanied its discharge medicine, in its traditional weakness, promptly embraced the new spark phenomenon as a therapeutic agent, and applied it with little hesitancy to human ailments.

It was logical that electric sparks should one day be applied to exposed nerves and muscles, and to Galvani and his coworkers belong the credit for this crucial experiment, which resulted in the discovery of the electrical excitability of nerves (1780-83). "Thus, paving the way for Galvani's second great contribution, the discovery of chemically generated electric current (1789).

Luigi Alyisio Galvani Italian physician and physicist, in 1791, discovered that the muscles of dead frog's legs twitched when struck by a spark, sparking curiosity into bioelectricity, and the signal and electrical patterns of the nervous system.

Oersted (1820) in linking the two forces of galvanism and magnetism provided a basis for the detection of a current by its magnetic effect. The instrument constructed on this principle was called "galvanometer," and the appellation is proper not only for its descriptive force, but because the device marked the first advance over Galvani's other "meter," the animal electrometer.

French physiologist, François Magendie pioneered experimental physiology. Magendie (1822), while utilizing the galvanic current to supplement his studies of the spinal roots, demonstrated that stimulation of the anterior roots causes muscular contraction and that of posterior roots sensation.

German physician and physiologist, Emil du Bois-Reymond, in 1845 began to apply the methods for generating alternating currents recently uncovered by Faraday (inventor of Faraday Cage which is the only known protection today) to the uses of physiology. His device, an induction coil with a magnetically driven breaker in the primary circuit, produced a series of closely spaced stimuli- as the current went through its cycles.

As a German neurologist and neuro-psychiatrist he was experienced in human and brain electricity as a gunshot wound to the head operating physician in the Prussian Army. He counterpart Gustav Fritsch was an Anatomist. For many years, attempts had been made to elicit responses from the application of currents directly to the surface of the brain, but these resulted in failure until Fritsch and Hitzig in 1870, announced that electrical excitation of certain small areas of the cerebral cortex of the dog would give rise to muscular movements in the opposite side of the body. The studies have not been confined to animals alone, however, for as early as 1909. Cushing pointed to the results of electrical stimulation of the post-central gyrus during the course of surgical removal of intracranial tumors. Harvey Cushing played a pivotal role in modern neurosurgery.

In 1915, Keeton and Becht, during an experimental study of the pituitary body in dogs, implanted iron filings directly into the gland. 1920 John Hopkins Medical, "The Autonomic Control of the Pituitary Gland, R.W. Keeton, and F.C. Becht, F. C: The stimulation of the hypophysis in dogs.

Walter Rudolph Hess using fine electrodes to stimulate or destroy specific areas of the brain in cats and dogs, Hess mapped the control centers for each function to such a degree that he could bring about the physical behavior pattern of a cat confronted by a dog simply by stimulating the proper points on the cat's hypothalamus. In Zurich, Hess developed a technique for bringing conducting wires out through the skin to form a direct electrical circuit, and his patience and thoroughness in handling this difficult method are an inspiration to those who would visit his laboratory. In this country Mussen, Bradford Cannon, and others have adopted similar mean.

Professor Chaffee designed a circuit which would be simple, effective, durable and which would incorporate the precision methods of electro physics, so that subsequent physiological analyses might rest on ground as secure as possible.

In summary, a method is presented for the study of excitable regions in the nervous system during the normal life of an animal.

1933, a medium-sized dog was operated on under Nembutal anesthesia and the right hypoglossal nerve was exposed and stimulated for identification with the ordinary close-coupled inductor. A small secondary coil was inserted into a recess in the subcutaneous tissue and the platinum electrode was brought to rest just within the nerve sheath. The indifferent electrode consisted of a silver plate Y2 inch square.

1933 and 1934 testing continued on dogs and monkeys.

In operations from the 1930s until the early 1970s, experiments within the United States delved into everything from drugs, to hypnosis, to electronic shock treatment and even lobotomy. There were classified experimental programs such as: MK-Ultra, Bluebird, Arti-Choke, Chatter, Casti-gate, MK-Delta, MK-Naomi, Third Chance, MK-Search, MK-Often, naming only a few. The experiments and testing centered on controlling the human mind through technology and drugs. These were secret programs involving many prominent members of institutions in the medical and scientific communities who were used to investigate and, in some cases, legitimize various forms of behavior modification using remote control or remote neural monitoring on human subjects.

The U.S. government is said to have conducted three types of mind-control experiments to including MKULTRA:

1. Real life experiences, such as those used on Little Augie and the LSD experiments in the safe houses of San Francisco and Greenwich Village.

2. Experiments on prisoners, such as in the California Medical Facility at Vacaville.

3. Experiments conducted in both mental hospitals and Veterans Administration hospitals

There were three scientists who pioneered work using an electromagnetic field to control human behavior in the United although the Soviets had experimented in this area many years before. The three scientists were Dr. Jose Delgado, psychology professor at Yale University; Dr. W. Ross Adey, a physiologist at the Brain Research Institute at UCLA, and later the Loma Linda VA Hospital; and Dr. Wilder Penfield, a Canadian.

In 1965, a project in the U.S. called Project Pandora was undertaken in which chimpanzees were exposed to microwave radiation. In Project Pandora, these three scientists would later document different brain signals and specific actions, emotions and pathological states of human minds recording the findings. Research in this area verified that when microwaves were used to fire specific signals at victims' brains, they experienced the moods, behavior and the pathological states, carried by the signals. This meant that by mimicking natural brain frequencies, the human brain could be controlled remotely by use of extremely low frequency broadcast carried by pulse modulated microwave beams (ELF pulse modulated microwave remote mind control technology,) Microwave and Control by Tim Rifat.

The CIA-funded Dr. Ross Adey to investigate mind-controlling and hormonal-effecting uses of pulse and amplitude-modulated microwave and radio frequency. Ross Adey experimented with 450MHz, which in the UK system is microwave, as the British take 400MHz to 400GHz as microwave. His associate, Dr. Blackmore, experimented with RF frequencies at around 150MHz. This was developed by the British Army, the Secret Police, into a variety of pulse-modulated, or amplitude modulated, radio frequency or microwave transmitters, which focused on the target ELF which had bioactive effects which could be used to kill or mind control their targets. The amplitude or pulse modulation of the carrier wave allows the British Army/Secret Police (MI5) operatives to induce ELF frequencies on the victim, even though the carrier wave is in the RF or microwave range."

The U-2 spy plane was the brainchild of the Central Intelligence Agency, and it was a sophisticated technological marvel. Traveling at altitudes of up to 70,000 feet, the aircraft was equipped with state-of-the-art photography equipment that could, take high-resolution pictures of headlines in Russian newspapers as it flew overhead. Flights over the Soviet Union began in mid-1956. The CIA assured President Eisenhower that the Soviets did not possess anti-aircraft weapons sophisticated enough to shoot down the high-altitude planes.

The early Eisenhower years (1953 to 1960) saw the initiation of two different systems for conducting overhead spying or reconnaissance. The U-2, high flying airplane and Agena satellite system, paved the way for today's current space system programs.

The Agena, a rocket powered platform was designed to launch and support military payloads and had a variety of functions including spying and surveillance. Both the U-2 and the Agena have played very significant roles in U.S. security affairs for quite a few decades. In the early 1960's and afterwards they provided data on Soviet plans and deployment and laid the foundation for U.S. strategic response to Soviet efforts.

Historically, it was initially the military satellite program which led the way for the eventual United States space programs during the 1960s and 1970s. By New Year's 1961 two U.S. spy satellite programs verged on brilliant success. Thanks to the energetic advocacy of Richard M. Bissell, Jr., of the CIA. The International

Telecommunications Convention of 1973, which possesses treaty status, regulated the use of comsats (Communication Satellites) and radio frequencies.

The space program's beginning was in the formation of several agencies, government, industries, the military industrial complex, universities and non-profit institutions and the result of fear of either a possible technological surprise or attack by the Soviets. Aerial strategic intelligence and surveillance and warfare was not considered in depth until that time and resulted in the production of the major technologies in current use which were principally involved in the arms race during the Cold War and resulting technology currently orbiting our planet.

A number of programs played a role in the ideation of influence technology through testing, research and development. One major program is the Law Enforcement Assistance Administration (LEAA).

LEAA was founded as an arm of the Department of Justice as a concept endorsed by President Richard Nixon. Under the Nixon Administration, LEAA sought to compile scientific data on youth and criminal activity hoping to curtail possible criminal acts lessening crime in society.

The initial LEAA objective was to run a series of test on youngsters as early as age six to determine if there was any predisposition to possible future activity. If after failing this series of test, the youngster was to be relocated to a type of boot camp / concentration camp for reprogramming.

This program, though heavily invested with over 5 billion dollars never was fully implemented. By theory, the program showed possibility, however, the program failed.

In 1970 after a meeting with Nixon himself, and top aides in the Nixon administration such as John Mitchell - Attorney General, and Nixon's Chief of Staff, Harry Halderman, a pact was forged between the LEAA, sponsored by the Department of Justice, and the National

Institute of Mental Health. The National Institute of Mental Health was connected with the Heath, Education and Welfare Department. The goal was behavior research programs.

Over 350 behavior modification programs were implemented involving medical and surgical procedures along with personality altering drug modification. Though the importance of LEAA waned, the National Institute of Mental Health stepped to the forefront spearheading continued research in behavior modification. Other players heavily involved were the Department of Veterans Affairs, who later apologized for its role, admitting that- surgical and other medical applications were a part of the Veterans Administration functions. The fact is the DOD VA hospital continues to be a site for testing and also training hospital for students.

There were other government agencies active in this endeavor to psychologically manipulate and control the human mind of not only youth but also adults. They were the Department of Defense, the Department of Labor, and the National Science Foundation with each having a very significant number or active programs.

As a direct result, the courts in the 60s were inundated by lawsuits from victims claiming to have been used in these experiments as human guinea pigs. Some of the most horrific abuses occurred in mental institution and prisons outside of the public eye due to the very nature of the perception of what these two institutions inhabitants stand for.

Fifty psychosurgeries were performed during this timeframe at the Atmore State Prison in Alabama leaving the recipient as little more than zombies. African American inmates suffered the most and were deemed the perfect candidates for testing in a continued prevalent racial ignorance and prejudice that continued to relegate African Americans to a place of inferior non- entities in the world and as a result deemed the perfect guinea pigs.

As the lawsuits continued to pile up, they eventually caught the attention and consciousness of Samuel James "Sam" Ervin Jr., who was a Democratic Senator from North Carolina. Senator Ervin began questioning the funding, humanity, and ethics of these programs. A Senate Subcommittee headed by Senator Ervin began to investigate the numerous behavior modification programs and the complaints and disfigurement of its alleged victims. During the height of the endeavor, LEAA was involved aversive techniques and psychosurgery which involved brain surgery on normal brain tissue for personality / behavior modification.

These programs, performed by the specific government agencies above totaled well over 500 projects, combined, with LEAA alone having 537, as one of the largest scientific endeavors in history which ran rampant in behavior modification. The results, of these specific programs would later become the foundation for the CIAs supreme behavior modification program to date called MK Ultra.

Again, of the few, the Veterans' Administration (VA) openly admitted that psychosurgery was a standard procedure for treatment and not used just in experiments. The VA Hospitals in Durham, Long Beach, New York, Syracuse and Minneapolis were known to employ these products on a regular basis. And the VA clients could typically be subject to these behavior alteration procedures against their will. The Ervin subcommittee concluded that the rights of VA clients had been violated.

Not only were studies taking place in the United States including institutions of higher learning regarding influence technology, but similar studies were also being conducted in Great Britain. In the Washington Associated Press, May 22, 1988, Barton Reppert, Associated Press, Writer, "Looking at the Moscow Signal the Zapping of an Embassy 35 years later The Mystery Lingers." Reppert stated "Since the early 1980s, however, federal government support for non-ionizing radiation bio effects has declined markedly. W. Ross Adey, at that time was a leading researcher based at the Veterans Administration Medical Center in Loma Linda, California, told a House Subcommittee that current levels of government funding now about $7 million a year are disastrously low" seeking more funding. In the 1980s Dr. Adey performed some crucial experiments using microwave carrier-waves modulated with ELF waves to modify brain tissue responses and global research in these areas beginning all over the world.

The TETRA System: Mass UK Mind Control Technology and the Zombification of Britain's Police is now a Reality by Tim Rifat, excerpts below reports:

"The TETRA system pulses at 17.6 Hz broadcast at 400 MHz are essentially the Pandora Project funded by the CIA in the late 1960s and early 1970s. Dr. Ross Adey, the chief researcher on the Pandora Project released a video to leading United Kingdom researchers which proved that not only does the TETRA system cause ELF zombification by massive release of calcium ions into the cerebral cortex and the nervous system, but the activated calcium ions also cause massive hormonal disturbances which lead to frenzied imbalances, emotional and physical states.

Use of the TETRA system on or by the police will eventually lead to psychotronically controlled police officers who may be totally controlled in any situation and are very useful for states of economic or social chaos where extreme and violent behavior is needed without any conscious or moral compunction resulting in so-called police robots.

High level research connects Operation Pandora to joint CIA/MI6 Operations since the 1960s, Operation Woodpecker USSR 1976 (Russian version of High Frequency Active Auroral Project or HAARP.) Operation HAARP is still running in USA working along with the Ground Wave Energy Network. GWEN Towers are said to be able to define specific pulse frequencies to cause specific brain malfunctions or illnesses. For instance: cause illness, depression/suicide, manic behavior, and anger, blindness if aimed at the head or heart attack if aimed at the chest.

Other consequences of frequencies used but not listed here are hysteria, trauma, lust, murder and cancer, and may all be induced. (From the Confidential Report, TETRA for the Police of England and

Wales by B. Trower) More information can be found in "Update on Murder and Mind Control: The Secret Uses of ELF Modulated Microwave and radio frequency (RF) by the British Army" regarding Great Britain.

Typically, Mr. Rifat has been labeled, delusional and self-serving, for his exposure efforts, by those seeking to discredit him in Britain, it the controlled media there as are many strategically today globally.

Before reading this, I had no idea how accurate I was when feeling that those operating around me in "the program" had to be effectively mind controlled before most. As a result, when I stumbled on the tetra system research, I was not surprised by a scientific ideation resulting in a definite desire to render those enforcing these programs for big brother as mind-controlled puppets. To some degree, admittedly it makes perfect sense. This information could be used to explain the horrific heinous behavior around me, and the pacifying understanding that others could treat so many so inhumanely and as if valueless.

CHAPTER TWELVE

"Democracy has proved only that the best way to gain power over people is to assure the people that they are ruling themselves. Once they believe that, they make wonderfully submissive slaves."

— **Joseph Sobran, The Myth of "Limited Government"**

The International Telecommunications Convention of 1973, which possesses treaty status, regulated the use of comsats (Communication Satellites) and radio frequencies. By 1963 the government supplied 88 percent of the entire Caltech budget, 66 percent of MIT's 59 and 56 percent of the University of Chicago's and Princeton's and a 25 percent chunk of Harvard's and Stanford's. Over the years and today, Universities have played a role in research, continued testing and development.

Verbal concern, officially regarding influence technology capable of subliminal delivery took shape in the early 60s with the United States believing the Soviets had surpassed them scientifically in this area. Technology that had quietly flourished over many years in classified testing and research programs inevitably would later become a force to be reckoned with globally and intentionally unpublicized. The first advanced subliminal manipulation technology that began to surface did so in the early 60s is said to be the Silent Sound Spread Spectrum or (SSSS).

During his farewell address in January of 1961, President Eisenhower, a dedicated, deeply patriotic, public servant broke tradition in an aberrant speech appearing to caution the American citizens regarding the Military Industrial Complex.

The Subliminal Carrier, or again, Silent Sound Spread Spectrum," is said to be essentially mind control through dissemination of silent sounds and connected to the digital delivery system. Some believe this technology is the sole motivation for the mandatory switch from analog to digital television on June 12, 2009 in the United States. It is believed the switch was necessary to free up analog frequencies to make room for scanners to read implantable Radio Frequency Identification, microchips implants and to track people and products throughout the world. This technology is also called the S-Quad or "Squad" in military jargon. It was developed for military use by Dr. Oliver Lowery of Norcross, Georgia, and is described in United States Patent #5,159,703 "Silent Subliminal Presentation System" for commercial use in 1992. The abstract reads:

A silent communications system in which non-aural carriers, in the very low (ELF), or very high audio-frequency (VHF) range or in the adjacent ultrasonic frequency spectrum, are amplitude-or frequency-modulated with the desired intelligence and propagated acoustically or vibration ally, for inducement into the brain typically through the use of loudspeakers, earphones, or piezoelectric transducers. The modulated carriers may be transmitted directly in real time or may be conveniently recorded and stored on mechanical, magnetic, or optical media for delayed or repeated transmission to the listener.

This system, or "sound of silence," is said to allow for the unwarranted implantation of specific thoughts, emotions, and even prescribed, physical actions and reactions subliminally. In short, it supposedly has the very real ability to turn human beings into manipulated puppets in the hands of certain handlers or controllers or puppet-masters pulling the strings of this advanced technology.

Today, laws such as USCA, Title 18, Chapter 119 or Executive Order 12333 now would allow government, through the authorization of a cognizant court, to utilize multiple avenues towards the assurance of an effective demonstration of these technologies now delivered by satellite radar or laser in the United States and globally?

Who would have guessed that as a result of the deployment of commercial communications satellites around the globe beginning in the late 50s and heavily in the 1970's, that microwave technology could emanate from space for testing could be conducted by a government legally against its citizens or the unsuspecting as a possibility?

Electronic Surveillance

Electronic Surveillance is the imposed observation of a person's belongings, person or surroundings through the use of electronic listening devices, video recording or transmitting devices, spectral imaging through heat or infrared, sound or other radiation sources, and any other means of observing a person's actions, possessions or routines to include satellite radar, optical eye.

Surveillance Abuse

Surveillance abuse is the use of surveillance methods or technology to monitor the activity of an individual or group of individuals in a way that violates the social norms or laws of society. Mass surveillance by the state may constitute surveillance abuse if not appropriately regulated outside the scope of lawful interception. It is illegal because it violates a once held sacred right to privacy.

Bullying

"Bullying is abusive treatment, the use of force or coercion to affect others particularly when habitual and involving an imbalance of power. Bullying may involve harassment, physical assault or coercion and may be directed persistently towards particular victims, perhaps on grounds of race, religion, sex or ability. The "imbalance of power" may be social power and/or physical power. The victim of bullying is sometimes referred to as a "target." Bullying consists of three types of abuse, emotional, verbal, and physical. It typically involves subtle methods of coercion such as intimidation. Bullying can be defined in many different ways. Bullying ranges from simple one on one bullying to more complex bullying in which the bully may have one or more 'lieutenants' who may seem to be willing to assist the primary bully in his bullying activities."

Mind Control

Mind control (also known as brainwashing, coercive persuasion, mind abuse, thought control, or thought reform) refers to a process in which a group or individual "systematically uses unethically manipulative methods to persuade others to conform to the wishes of the manipulator(s), often to the detriment of the person being manipulated."

Iridium Satellite System

The Iridium Satellite System is one of 66 low-earth orbiting (LEO) satellites that comprise this system. The original company went bankrupt so the US Department of Defense assisted in making sure the system stayed in operation. This system is currently maintained by the Boeing Company. Iridium multiple spot beams (cells) blanket the total earth surface. The original design uses 77 satellites. This system has transmitting and receiving coverage of the entire planet. Each circle is a coverage sector.

Directed-Energy-Weapon

A directed-energy weapon (DEW) emits energy in an aimed direction without the means of a projectile. It transfers energy to a target for a desired effect. Intended effects may be non-lethal or lethal. Some such weapons are real, and are under active research and development.

The energy can come in various forms: Electromagnetic radiation, in laser, masers, or heat; particles with mass, in particle beam weapons; sound in sonic weapons.

High Power Microwave devices use microwave radiation, which has a shorter wavelength than radio than directed energy weapons. This equipment, based on microwave, infrasound, neuron-science, biofeedback, and other technology, has the capability to administer a variety of effects when remotely directed at the victim either while inside their homes or away from their homes such as headaches, laser-like burns, rashes, sharp pains that feel like electrical shocks, mood alteration, and neurological trauma. Used against humans, generally is considered 'non-lethal.

However, the use today, reported by thousands is that it is being used relentlessly from state-of-the-art operation centers as a means and method of covert physical torture for various and many reasons. And as stated, due to it being undetectable as radio frequency radio waves, human organs and tissue are being destroyed from relentless attacks directed at targeted individuals.

However, electromagnetic weaponry, by capability, 'does' pose health threats to humans. In fact, "non-lethal" weapons can be deadly." Some common bio-effects of electromagnetic or other non-lethal weapons include effects to the human central nervous system resulting in physical pain, difficulty breathing, vertigo, nausea, disorientation, or other systemic discomfort, as weapons not directly considered lethal can indeed cause cumulative damage to the human body. These weapons come in the form of vibrations, which can be used to target a specific organ in the body causing scar tissue to form leading to the death of that organ. These weapons can cause heart attacks and strokes. There are approximately 100 plus vibrations that attack the heart. There are vibrations that cause panic attacks and sleep deprivation. There are frequency vibrations that can cause a targeted person to go mad and/or crazy, as well as many other capabilities. All that would show up in an autopsy is that the person died from natural causes.

Northrop Grumman has available a high-energy solid-state laser-weapon system that they call Fire Strike. The system is modular, using 15 kW modules that can be combined to provide various levels of power.

Yes, short-term exposure to the intense radiation can cause a wide range of physical disorders. And the weapons are capable of a silent, covert war against the target or specific individual(s) and are used to terrorize a targeted person over a period of time.

Artificial Telepathy 101
Except from MindTech Sweden.com below:

The experience of "Artificial Telepathy" is really not that extraordinary. It's as simple as receiving a cell-phone call in one's head.

Indeed, most of the technology involved is exactly identical to that of cell-phone technology. Satellites link the sender and the receiver. A computer "multiplexer" routes the voice signal of the sender through microwave towers to a very specifically defined location or cell. The "receiver" is located and tracked with pinpoint accuracy, to within a few feet of actual location. But the receiver is not a cell phone. It's a human brain.

Out of nowhere, a voice suddenly blooms in the mind of the target. The human skull as no "firewall" and therefore cannot shut the voice out. The receiver can hear the sender's verbal thoughts. The sender, in turn, can hear all of the target's thoughts exactly as if the target's verbal thoughts had been spoken or broadcast. For this reason, the experience could be called "hearing voices" but is more properly described as "artificial telepathy…"

Programming through Mass Media

Mass media are media forms designed to reach the largest audience possible. They include television, movies, radio, newspapers, magazines, books, records, video games and the Internet. Many studies have been conducted in the past century to measure the effects of mass media on the population in order to discover the best techniques to influence it. From these studies emerged the science of Communications, which is used in marketing, public relations and politics. Mass communication is a necessary tool to insure the functionality of a large democracy; it is also a necessary tool for a dictatorship. It all depends on its usage.

In the 1958 preface for A Brave New World, Aldous Huxley paints a rather grim portrait of society. He believes it is controlled by an "impersonal force" a ruling elite, which manipulates the population using various methods. His bleak outlook is not a simple hypothesis or a paranoid delusion. It is a documented fact, present in the world's most important studies on mass media... The Vigilant Citizen – "Symbols Rule the Word, Not Words nor Law"

MindTechSweden.com recommended movies associated with mind control and nanotechnology.

Nanotechnology was first publicized in 1980 by K Eric Drexler. He was referenced the term when he spoke of building machines on the scale of molecules, a few nanometers wide such as motors, robot arms, and even whole computers, technology far smaller than a cell. Much of the work being done today that carries the name 'nanotechnology' is not nanotechnology in the original meaning of the word. Nanotechnology, in its traditional sense, means building things from the bottom up, with atomic precision. Physicist Richard Feynman in 1959 envisioned this theoretical capability.

For detailed information, on the movies below, along with movie clips and an explanation, of Direct-to-Speech, paralleling (mind control) and suggest-to-conscious, and association with highly advanced influencing technology, check out: www.mindcontol.se, subtitle Mind Control – What is happening - remote control of every single synapse on this website. The following are messages in movies by those who feel obligated to openly inform humanity of an agenda it appears.

- The Matrix (1999)
- Office Space (1999)
- Bandits (2001)
- The Matrix Reloaded (2003)
- Toxic Skies (2008)
- The Happening (2008)
- Gamer (2009)
- Metropia (2009)
- Surrogates (2009)
- The Box (2009)
- A Serious Man (2009)
- Telephone (2010
- The Crazies (2010)
- The Greenberg (2010)
- Shutter Island (2010)
- Family Guy – season 10, episode 5 (2010)
- Family Guy – It's a Trap (2010)
- The Adjustment Bureau (2011)
- Hanna (2011)
- Transformer 3 (2011)
- Lindsey Williams (2012)
- Ultrasonic (2012)

The MindTech Sweden website also gives video clip examples of Direct to Speech showing several news reporters and television personalities who began to speak gibberish which cannot be control or explain by the individuals. One of these examples is a United States television personality named Judge Judith Sheindlin as reported below:

On March 30, 2011, Judge Sheindlin was rushed to a Los Angeles hospital Wednesday morning after she suddenly started saying things that didn't make sense, a studio insider revealed. "She was just sitting on the stand during taping and she started saying things that didn't make any sense," a source close to the situation told RadarOnline.com, exclusively.

"She said, 'I need to stop, I'm not feeling well.'"

The 68-year-old judge was only two cases deep into her taping when her bizarre behavior prompted her to stop and have a crew member call 911.

"She said couple of sentences that didn't have anything to do with the case and then she stopped speaking and said she wasn't feeling well," the source said.

"The stage manager called the paramedics and they came and took her away."

The Los Angeles City Fire Department confirmed to that a paramedic ambulance was dispatched to the KTLA Studios in Hollywood, where Judge Judy tapes her show, at 9:12 a.m. today. Sheindlin's rep, Gary Rosen, confirmed that the judge is in the hospital and will be staying overnight for observation.

"The judge was feeling nauseous and had some intestinal discomfort and decided to go to the hospital to get it checked out," Rosen said.

"They are keeping her overnight for tests."

Another movie depiction of the Direct to Speech dynamic can be seen in Bruce Almighty (2003)

Below Are Various Historical Online Excerpts in No Specific Order:

After the war the demand for technology, research and advancement necessitated and resulted in Operation Paperclip and ODESSA where some of the first mind control experiments began. Operation Paperclip was the initiative to relocate top German scientist to the United States following World War II, 1939 – 1945, and it was during these times that actual testing began in depth in the actual endeavor of physical and psychological manipulation of the human brain for, let's say other than health reasons.

***

The Soviets reportedly began to delve into the actual biological effect of microwaves as early as 1953 as noted earlier. A number of laboratories were set up across the Soviet Union and in the Eastern Europe, including one at the Institute of Hygiene and Occupational Diseases Academy of Medical Sciences. Although the Soviets reported on their experiments in the open literature, the parameters they defined were insufficient for duplicating the experiments, and some scientists in the United States questioned whether the whole matter was disinformation. It was not. The Russian experiments in the control of a person's mind, factually, through hypnosis and radio waves were conducted in the 1930s.

***

The history of science, the military, corporations and government involvement from the 1940s up to today says that classified military research was used to fight The Cold War. For this reason, it can be seen how secret, highly classified technology could have been developed outside the public eye and with the "Top Secret" support of top government officials. Teams of elite scientists were used to tackle military problems resulting from World War II.

The Cybernetics Group, Brain Research Institute, the Institute for Defense Analysis and their JASON Group and also the Golden Fleece Group are a few examples. Prominent scientists were given military funding generated by the race to surpass the Russians during The Cold War (1946 to 1991) immediately following World War II.

***

The plans to create a mind-controlled workers society ideation has been in place for a long time. The desire and current technology grew out of experiments that the Nazis started before World War II and intensified in Nazi concentration camps. And what is not publicized that Operation Paperclip transferred these scientists to the United States to continue their ongoing studies.

***

The Soviets had long understood the powerful biological impacts of radio frequency (RF) and microwave (MW) technologies. In the early 1950's they were becoming increasingly aware of the non-thermal bio effects from microwaves from years of research prior to. Historically the Soviet Union has invested huge sums of money and time investigating microwave remote manipulation of the brain and their effects and programs in energetics and psycho-energetics technology, known to the West as psychotronics.

The bulk of the initial work on the science underpinning this technology had been done in the West and smuggled to the Soviet Union. This included some of Tesla findings which also evolved in the Hitler regime's research programs. For decades, the scientific community of the West had ignored the work of people like Moray Abrams, Hieronymous, Tesla, De la Warr, Down and Reich, giving the Soviets at least a 30-year head start to build to consolidate their position in psychotronic weaponry. When Brezhnev suggested at the 1978 SALT negotiations banning weapons "more frightful than the mind of man has ever conceived," President Carter had no idea what he really was suggesting.

***

Mind control experiments have been part of California for decades and permeate mental institutions and prisons as exampled by LEAA. But, it is not just in the penal society that mind control measures have been used. Minority children were subjected to experimentation at abandoned Nike Missile Sites along with Veterans who fought for American freedom was also subjected to the programs. Funding and experimentations of mind control as stated earlier have been part of not only the U.S. Health, Education and Welfare Department, the Department of Veterans Affairs, the Central Intelligence Agency through MK Ultra, and the Phoenix Program, the Department of Defense, the Department of Labor, the National Institute of Mental

Health, the Law Enforcement Assistance Administration, and the National Science Foundation but also the Stanford Research Institute, and the Agency for International Development,

***

Robert G. Heath joined Tulane's faculty in 1949 after participating in Columbia University's Greystone Project, a study of the use of topectomy (the removal of small portions of the brain's frontal cortex) as an alternative to the more radical procedures of prefrontal or transorbital lobotomy.

In the 1950's, the now Tulane psychiatrist and coworkers engaged in studies of the human brain that were sponsored by U.S. government agencies and included black prisoners among its experimental subjects. Psychiatric "treatment" of African Americans has included some of the most barbaric experiments ever carried out in the name of "scientific" research and not very long ago.

In the 1950s in New Orleans, black prisoners were used for psychosurgery experiments that involved electrodes being implanted into the brain.

The experiments were conducted by psychiatrist Dr. Heath and also an Australian psychiatrist. Dr. Harry Bailey, who boasted in a lecture to nurses 20 years later that the two psychiatrists had used blacks because it was "cheaper to use Niggers than cats because they were everywhere and cheap experimental animals."

Neurosurgeons at Tulane, Yale and Harvard did extensive investigations into brain electrode implants with intelligence funding, and combined brain implants with large numbers of drugs including hallucinogens.

Sadly, the African American community has always been a primary testing ground for various types of nonconsensual human guinea testing as a whole, being the difference, along with various other segments of other communities within our society.

Beginning in 1950, Heath and his colleagues performed surgical operations upon a number of mental patients in order to implant electrodes and small tubes into the brain's emotional core. Dr. Robert G. Heath, of Tulane University, had implanted as many as 125 electrodes in a human being's brain during that time. In his experiments, he discovered that he could control his patients' memories, sexual arousal, fear, pleasure, and cause hallucinations. Subsequent EEG recordings made during electrical or chemical stimulation of the selected subcortical areas provided a clearer picture of the specific circuitry and the neurochemical processes involved in schizophrenia and other psychotic conditions. However, noteworthy, classified technology mimicking Schizophrenia was fully secretly being tested and developed. Heath and his fellow scientists were working at or very near the outer limits of existing neurophysiological knowledge, a fact that was not lost upon U.S. military and civilian intelligence agency officials, who were already engaged in highly secret efforts to develop psychochemical weapons, as well as interrogation and mind control techniques that could be used against Cold War adversaries.

Andrija Puharich, MD, original name is Henry K. Puharich (February 19, 1918 - January 3, 1995) was an Army officer in the early 1950s. During that time, he made frequent visits Edgewood Arsenal Research Laboratories and Camp Detrick, meeting with various high-ranking officers and officials, primarily from the Pentagon, CIA, and Naval Intelligence. The Edgewood Arsenal is currently officially called the Edgewood Area of Aberdeen Proving Ground. Puharich was a medical and parapsychological researcher, medical inventor and author, who are perhaps best known as the person who brought Israeli Uri Geller and Peter Hurkos, to the United States for parapsychology investigation. Uri Geller was an Israeli born, self-proclaimed psychic living in England known for his trademark television performances of spoon bending and other supposed psychic effects. Peter Hurkos, was a Dutch psychic and he also investigated Mexican psychic surgeon Pachita.

Dr. Andrija Puharich (in the 1950 & 60s), found that a clairvoyant's brainwaves turned to 8 Hz when their psychic powers were operative. In 1956, he observed an Indian Yogi controlling his brainwaves, deliberately shifting his consciousness from one level to another. Puharich trained people via bio-feedback to do this consciously, that is, creating 8 Hz waves with the technique of bio-feedback. A psychic healer generated 8 Hz waves through a hands-on healing process, actually alleviating that patients heart trouble; the healer's brain emitting 8 Hz.

One person, emitting a certain frequency, can make another also resonate to the same frequency. Our brains are extremely vulnerable to any technology that sends out ELF waves, because they immediately start resonating to the outside signal by a kind of tuning-fork effect.

Puharich further experimented, discovering that, 7.83 Hz (earth's pulse rate) made a person "feel good," producing an altered-state 10.80 Hz causes riotous behavior 6.6 Hz causes depression.

Puharich made ELF waves change RNA and DNA in the body, breaking hydrogen bonds to make a person resonate at a higher vibratory rate. He really wanted to go beyond the psychic 8 Hz brainwave and attract psi phenomena.

James Hurtak, who once worked for Puharich, also wrote in his book, "The Keys of Enoch" that ultra-violet caused hydrogen bonds to break and this raised the vibratory rate.

Puharich presented the mental effects of ELF waves to military leaders, but they would not believe him. He then gave this information to certain dignitaries of other Western nations. The United States Government burned down his home in New York to shut him up, whereas he then fled to Mexico.

In Mexico, Puharich continued to monitor the Russian ELF wave signal and the higher harmonics (5.340 MHz) in the MHz range. He was somehow induced to work for the CIA and he and Dr. Robert

Becker designed equipment to measure these waves and their effect on the human brain. Puharich started his work by putting dogs to sleep.

By 1948/49, he had graduated to monkeys, deliberately destroying their eardrums to enable them to pick up sounds without the eardrum intact. He discovered a nerve from the tongue could be used to facilitate hearing. He created the tooth implant that mind-control victims are now claiming was put in by their dentist, unbeknownst to them, and causing them to hear voices in their head. These were placed under caps or lodged in the jaw as the technology continued it agenda by various nations for political control of the human mind.

***

From the late 1940s onward, close ties existed between the army's Edgewood Arsenal, where chemical warfare research and experimentation were conducted, and the CIA and various military intelligence services. By 1951 the sometimes cooperative, sometimes competitive military-CIA nexus had given rise to a coordinated army-navy-air force-CIA endeavor called Project Artichoke which would be one of the forerunners for MK-ULTRA.

In 1953, Project Artichoke grew into to a larger and more ambitious undertaking later known as Project MK-ULTRA. Astronaut Gordon Cooper, one of the original seven Mercury astronauts, confirmed the existence of a mind control program administered by NASA in the 1950's and 1960's involving gifted American school children.

***

At the conclusion of World War II, American investigators learned that Nazi doctors at the Dachau concentration camp in Germany had been conducting mind control experiments on inmates. They experimented with hypnosis and with the drug mescaline. Mescaline is a quasi-synthetic extract of the peyote cactus, and is very similar to LSD in the hallucinations that it produces. Though they did not achieve the degree of success they had desired, the SS interrogators in conjunction with the Dachau doctors were able to extract the most intimate secrets from the prisoners when the inmates were given very high doses of mescaline. Dr. Joseph Mengele of Auschwitz notoriety was the principle developer of the trauma-based Monarch Project and the CIA's MK-ULTRA mind control programs. Mengele and approximately 5, 000 other high-ranking Nazis were secretly moved into the United States and South America in the aftermath of World War II in Operation Paperclip. The Nazis continued their work in developing mind control and rocketry technologies in secret underground military bases.

***

Richard Helms was the director of the CIA from 1966 to 1973. He was the only director to have been convicted of lying to the U.S. Congress over CIA undercover activities. In 1977, he was sentenced to the maximum fine and received a suspended two-year prison sentence. Richard Helms is the father of the MK-ULTRA project. The MK-ULTRA program was originally run by a small number of people within the CIA known as the Technical Services Staff (TSS). Another CIA department, the Office of Security, also began its own testing program. Friction arose and then in-fighting broke out when the Office of Security commenced to spy on TSS people after it was learned that LSD was being tested on unwitting Americans.

To understand the full scope of the problem, it is important to study its origins. The Kennedy subcommittee learned about the CIA Operation MK-ULTRA through the testimony of Dr. Sidney Gottlieb, CIA Agent and one of the primary players. The purpose of the program, according to his testimony, was to "investigate whether and how it was possible to modify an individual's behavior by covert means." Claiming the protection of the National Security Act, Dr. Gottlieb was unwilling to tell the Senate subcommittee what had been learned or gained by these experiments.

He did state, however, that the program was initially engendered by a concern that the Soviets and other enemies of the United States would get ahead of the U.S. in this field. Through the Freedom of Information Act, researchers are now able to obtain documents detailing the MK-ULTRA program and other CIA behavior modification projects in a special reading room located on the bottom floor of the Hyatt Regency in Rosslyn, Veterans Administration.

The most daring phase of the MK-ULTRA program involved slipping unwitting American citizens LSD in real life situations. The idea for the series of experiments originated in November 1941, when William Donovan, founder and director of the Office of Strategic Services (OSS), the forerunner of the CIA during World War II. At that time, the intelligence agency invested $5000 for the "truth drug" program. Experiments with scopolamine and morphine proved both unfruitful and very dangerous. The program tested scores of other drugs, including mescaline, barbiturates, Benzedrine, cannabis indica, to name a few. The CIA experiments infringed upon the much-honored Nuremberg Code concerning medical ethics. Dr. Cameron was one of the members of the Nuremberg.

***

Dr. Jose Delgado was hired by the CIA to do experimentation with miniaturized electronic implants. In a speech recorded in the February 24, 1974 edition of the CONGRESSIONAL RECORD No. 26, Vol. 118, Dr. Delgado had this to say: "We need a program of psychosurgery for political control of our society.

The purpose is physical control of the mind. Everyone who deviates from the given norm can be surgically mutilated. "The individual may think that the most important reality is his own existence, but this is only his personal point of view. This lacks historical perspective. "Man does not have the right to develop his own mind. This kind of liberal orientation has great appeal. We must electrically control the brain. Someday, armies and generals will be controlled by electric stimulation of the brain".

Dr. Delgado was a pioneer of the technology of Electrical Stimulation of the Brain (ESB). While giving a lecture on the Brain in 1965, Dr. Delgado said, "Science has developed a new methodology for the study and control of cerebral function in animals and humans."

Brain transmitters, also called electrodes, stimoceivers, and endoradiosondes, can control the brain and transmit data. They can be used to influence people to conform to a political system. They can be applied to remotely monitor and control human beings to serve as agents. The technology exists and is being utilized. The devices usually remain in a person's head for life.

***

Origins and Techniques of Monarch Mind Control

Monarch Programming is a method of mind control used by numerous organizations for covert purposes. It is a continuation of project MK-ULTRA, a mind-control program tested on the military and civilians. The methods are astonishingly sadistic (its entire purpose is to traumatize the victim) and the expected results are horrifying: The creation of a mind-controlled slave who can be triggered at any time to perform any action required by the handler. While mass media ignores this issue, over 2 million Americans have gone through the horrors of this program. The article below looks at the origins of Monarch programming and some of its methods and symbolism… Secret Arcana – Uncovering the hidden forces shaping our world.

***

Electronic Surveillance by definition, Title 50, Chapter 36, Subchapter 1, § 1801 excerpt defining Electronic surveillance by law:

(f) "Electronic surveillance" means—

the acquisition by an electronic, mechanical, or other surveillance device of the contents of any wire or radio communication sent by or intended to be received by a particular, known United States person who is in the United States, if the contents are acquired by intentionally targeting that United States person, under circumstances in which a person has a reasonable expectation of privacy and a warrant would be required for law enforcement purposes:

the acquisition by an electronic, mechanical, or other surveillance device of the contents of any wire communication to or from a person in the United States, without the consent of any party thereto, if such acquisition occurs in the United States, but does not include the acquisition of those communications of computer trespassers that would be permissible under section 2511(2) (i) of title 18; the intentional acquisition by an electronic, mechanical, or other surveillance device of the contents of any radio communication, under circumstances in which a person has a reasonable expectation of privacy and a warrant would be required for law enforcement purposes, and if both the sender and all intended recipients are located within the United States; or, the installation or use of an electronic, mechanical, or other surveillance device in the United States for monitoring to acquire information, other than from a wire or radio communication, under circumstances in which a person has a reasonable expectation of privacy and a warrant would be required for law enforcement purposes.

The active role of health care professionals cannot be denied, whether knowingly or unknowingly in efforts to deny the existence of mind control efforts. This is specifically relevant in the field psychiatry and psychology. Some would argue that there appears to be a joint conspiracy to discredit people speaking up regarding, factual personal experiences regarding the various advanced influence technologies. These highly educated individuals cannot be that naïve as some would have you believe. The diagnosis of those speaking up across the board coincides with a quick diagnosis of delusional or psychosis disorders without investigations or in fairness to some health care professionals, the inability to investigate if what the patient is saying is factual.

***

In 2008, Dr. Ralph Hoffman, a psychiatric professor at Yale who studies delusions documented his belief that numerous individuals experiencing surveillance and psychotronic technology, globally, was related to little more than the results of numerous websites of numerous victims, activist, whistleblowers, including those used in factual testing programs or as guinea pigs speaking up. What continually amazed me is the inability to accept even the remotest possibility by some, that the technology exists, thus denying laws, and patents advanced from historic inventors.

***

Igor Viktorovich Smirnov was a scientist born in Russia was best known for his prominent role in Soviet-era research into mind control as well as the human behavior study he called "psycho-ecology." Smirnov transitioned from military research to the treatment of patients with drug addiction and mental problems after the dissolution of the Soviet Union, December 25, 1991, forming the Peoples' Friendship University of Russia. The studies focused on "psycho-correction." This is a term used to define subliminal messages to alter a subject's will or modify a person's personality without the person's knowledge. Smirnov would later gain brief fame in the U.S. in 1993 when the Federal Bureau of Investigation consulted with him for advice on ending the Waco Siege. Smirnov proposed blasting scrambled sound over loudspeakers to persuade the dissidents to surrender, however the FBI declined the plan. Smirnov died in November 5th 2004, leaving his wife to run the Institute.

In May 2009, the U.S. announced plans of the Department of Homeland Security to award a contract for testing of an airport screening system based partly on Smirnov's concepts in association with a Canadian company, Northam Psycho-technologies, acting as distributor for the Psycho-technology Research Institute. The concept is called ManTech SRS Technologies.

Dr. Igor Smirnov, of the Institute of Psycho-correction in Moscow, says in regard to this technology: "It is easily conceivable that some Russian 'Satan', or let's say Iranian (or any other 'Satan'), as long as he owns the appropriate means and finances, can inject himself (intrude) into every conceivable computer network, into every conceivable radio or television broadcast, with relative technological ease, even without disconnecting cables. You can intercept the (radio) waves in the ether and then (subliminally) modulate every conceivable suggestion into it.

If this transpires over a long enough time period, it accumulates in the heads of people. And eventually they can be artificially manipulated with other additional measurements, to do that which this perpetrator wants them to do. This is why such technology is rightfully feared."

***

Corporation involved in the satellite business, includes not only Lockheed, but General Dynamics, RCA, General Electric, Westinghouse, Comstat, Boeing, Hughes Aircraft, Rockwell International, Northrup Grumman Corp., CAE Electronics, Trimble Navigation and TRW in a long, long, long list. Their areas of expertise are in Intelligence Analysis, data and imagery, building technology, maintaining it, and also 'Top Secret' psychological operation to include Internet and social network involvement.

***

All across the military, there is interest in translating thoughts into computer code, and vice-versa. Today, DARPA funded researchers have taught monkeys how to control robotic limbs with their thoughts. Defense contractor, such as Northrup Grumman, is building binoculars that tap the unconscious mind. Honeywell has built a system that monitors pre-conscious neural firings, to help pick out targets in satellite imagery. The JASON's, the Pentagon's premiere scientific advisory board, has warned of the dangers of enemies implanted with brain-computer interfaces. And the Defense Intelligence Agency released a report, saying the military needs to spend more on neuroscience – up to and including "making the enemy obey our commands.

***

Science has decoded the brain signals so that direct communication with the brain is possible. Today, the brain's electromagnetic signals can be remotely detected SQUIDs (superconducting quantum interference devices) have military applications in magnetometers used to detect submarines and mines. SQUIDs can detect the most tenuous magnetic fields, even those generated by brain cells. They exploit the properties of a Josephson junction, which is constructed from two superconductors separated by a non-superconducting layer. Lockheed has built an HTSC SQUID. The extreme sensitivity of SQUIDs makes them ideal for studies in biology.

Magneto encephalography or MEG for example uses measurements from an array of SQUIDs to make inferences determining neural activity inside the brain. SQUID has the capability of gaging the target's emotional state using –neurological feedback from the central nervous system via satellite radar. If a target's emotional state is accurately assessed, then those tracking the individual can use various tactics in a full protocol in a highly advanced subliminal manipulative effort along with other forms of influence / mind control technology.

***

The John F. Kennedy, Jr. speech, April 27, 1961, on Secret Societies said:

"We are opposed around the world by a monolithic and ruthless conspiracy that relies primarily on covert means for expanding its sphere of influence--on infiltration instead of invasion, on subversion instead of elections, on intimidation instead of free choice, on guerrillas by night instead of armies by day. It is a system which has conscripted vast human and material resources into the building of a tightly knit, highly efficient machine that combines military, diplomatic, intelligence, economic, scientific and political operations."

And for this cause, God shall send them strong delusion, that they should believe a lie. That they all might be damned who believed not the truth, but had pleasure in unrighteousness.

2 Thessalonians 2:11-12 - King James Version

In Thessalonians 2, the apostle Paul sets out to allay the anxieties of 1st Century believers that they have been "left behind." The Spirit that inspired the Apostle seems to have had an additional agenda, to convey an additional message for today's generation. Perhaps, inadvertently, or perhaps as a result of his surpassing great revelations, the Apostle thereby ended up writing about the culmination of a diabolical mischief which in the future would be the equivalent of those elements of society already present in the days of the Roman Empire whom he described as the "the secret power of the lawless," would perpetrate.

Eventually these elements would usher in the short-lived hegemony of a future anti-Christ who would be the worst anti-Christ ever. Paul's dire predictions could not have been fulfilled in his own day. The required technology did not begin to exist until the late 20th century. It is stated that the artificial simulation of quasi-supernatural effects, precisely the effect of Voice to Skull/Synthetic or Artificial Telepathy, mood altering technology and microwave weapon is crucial to the plot which the Apostle describes, and this counterfeiting of the miraculous significant and wonderful has only become technologically feasible in recent times. The 1st Century believers were reassured by the Apostle that this entire calamitous turn of events would be delayed until such time as a future generation of mankind lived in such complete indifference to what was true and what wasn't true (regardless of the effect of that choice upon their eternal destiny) that it would become just for God to allow this calamity to befall them.

Some of the technologies documented in John McMurtrey's scientific papers, and perhaps other technologies even more advanced, are predicted to be abused in order to procure worldwide belief in a huge lie that will enable mankind to be subjected to, and perhaps actively to choose at least at first, the dreadful future autocratic government it will by then thoroughly deserve, headed up by a blasphemous leader who will disallow freedom of religion, insisting that he alone should be worshipped…

Excerpt from Christians against Mental Slavery, Bible Study prepared by John Allman Courtesy of John McMurtrey:

While delusional thinking does exist, the common assessment that if a person believes themselves targeted, that they must be mentally ill is highly questionable in light of the capabilities of these brilliant patented advancements now highly perfected. Study after study has proven definite microwave bio-effect congruence with Schizophrenia and John McMurtrey is one of the leading scholars in this area.

Sadly, the heinous, manipulative, technological activity around a targeting is so traumatizing that many otherwise "mentally healthy" individuals can easily develop mental health issues as a result of the stalking by satellite and portable surveillance, and the complete effort overall by use of the "black bag" technologies combined with an intense organized stalking effort. The individuals manning the technology vindictively seem to go to great lengths seeking results and data and are willing to do or say anything right or wrong in programs that if they were to come forth would expose themselves and these covert operations.

These types of surveillances are the result of a spiritual disease and moral decay that is unsurpassed in the history of humanity today. In my opinion, never has Ephesians 6:12 - For we wrestle not against flesh and blood, but against principalities, against powers, against the rulers of the darkness of this world, against spiritual wickedness in high places - held a more profound meaning. It does not get any higher than what is orbiting our planet today. Targeting's are result oriented situations whether for testing purposes to provide data, for law enforcement, revenge, manipulation, or to silence a whistleblower or even a political opponent. As a result, mental illness is not an indicator of whether or not the activity is actually taking place.

Whenever George Orwell's 1984 is mentioned, although it is fiction, and I have intentionally never read it, I consider the great possibility that Orwell may have been privy to classified information more than what he let on in his fictional accounts of a powerful unseen "shadow government." 1984 is transposed 1948. This government, Orwell called, Big Brother had to sole agenda of complete control of the human mind and totalitarian agenda. His account was written in 1948, published in 1949 and some argue mirrors what is happening today in a highly advanced technological totalitarian agenda. In fact, 1984 mirrors a political party seeking control of the world right down to dynamic of "thought police" as a futuristic, 'Policed Stated' portraying them as the guerillas for Big Brother's agenda. One of the terroristic methods used by those manning this brilliant technology from their place of operation, using the thought deciphering, patented technology, is the perpetual repetitive playback back to the target of their every thought as a form of continued terrorism.

Take away the words "mind control" and think of someone being manipulated by suggestions or told that what they know is not the truth, that it is their imagination and not by voices beamed directly into their head, then it is easy to see that 1984 is alive and well in 2011. It is understandable, that the use of the term "mind control" would make the public think of people in a stupor. However, the fact still remained that some recognize what is happening to them and are able to spread the word though at a cost. True also, yes, there are people in today's society that believe in aliens and being abducted by aliens, but they do not belong to the group of people that are passionately trying to alert the public to the abuses escalating on citizens via these covert, subliminal, manipulative weapons.

In my case, time is on my side.

The website raven1.net, by Eleanor White, one of several women activists in the Targeted Individuals community in Canada says that Electronic Mind Control (e-weapons) victims are of four basic types:

1. Guinea pigs
2. Corporate whistle blowers and workers' compensation claimants or those whose claims expose corporate misdeeds
3. Pleasure objects for surveillance and e-weapon holders who are sexual perverts
4. Unlucky slobs who inadvertently pissed off the wrong person at the wrong time

Sadly, there is also the widespread unrestrained use by individuals who are imperfect, entrusted with the public's trust who desecrate, once held Constitutional Rights having the covert means to do so.

Man's curiosity into manipulating the greatest organ of the human body, the human brain through research dates back many, many years as documented in many research programs.

***

Below is an actual job description and job requirements for working in the operation / fusion center in Los Angeles County in Norwalk, California where the Joint Resource Intelligent Center (JRIC) is located. Civilian's working in various capacities work alongside federal, state and local personnel:

Intelligence Analyst (Records Examiner) in Norwalk City Norwalk Agency Federal Bureau of Investigation Position Schedule Full Time Salary 27.04-27.04

Requisition Code 640504-0112

Job Description

Forfeiture Support Associates (FSA), a government contractor in support of the US Departments of Justice and Homeland Security has an opening for an Intelligence Analyst located at the Joint Regional Intelligence Center (JRIC) located in Norwalk, CA.

The accepted candidate will be processed for a Top-Secret Security Clearance. Candidate must be able to qualify for and maintain a Top-Secret Clearance.

In support of JRIC, an Intelligence Analyst executes the following duties:

- Provide analytical support to Federal and local law enforcement agencies
- Establish, organize, analyze, and manage case files
- Run database checks, research and compile target lists
- Review and analyze raw intelligence reports, crime reports, and assessments
- Analyze targets telephone tolls and cell tower records
- Create analytical charts and graphs to include a timeline of events and known associates
- Create biographical profiles to include identifying information (e.g. addresses, phone numbers)
- Assist lead analyst or official in obtaining/collecting and analyzing all documents/information to complete case file
- Create, distribute and receive documents, intelligence products, bulletins, etc.

- Provide administrative information and assistance concerning case to other investigative agencies, local law enforcement agencies, US Attorney, and other DOJ processing units, and higher headquarters
- Extract data from agency database for management and program reports
- Perform word processing relevant to case documentation
- Perform data entry relevant to case An Intelligence Analyst must meet the following qualifications:
- A four-year undergraduate degree is preferred
- Must have one year's experience in a field related to law enforcement or related analytical field
- Attention to detail and the ability to read and follow directions is very important
- Computer skills are a must
- Good oral and written communications skills are necessary

Must possess a demonstrated ability to analyze documents to extract information.

This position requires US Citizenship. A 10-year minimum background investigation will be performed on candidate to secure a Top-Secret Security Clearance. FSA offers a comprehensive benefits package. For a full list of available benefits, visit us on the web…

***

I had tried in August of 2009, while in Arizona, to get justice for myself with filing of the unsuccessful civil complaint in the Arizona district court:

Mitchell v. National Security Agency et al, Case Number: 2:2009cv01659, August 12, 2009 and by 2015 four other hopes for judicial intervention as my life was slowly being taken were filed.

Give me an 'A' for effort for at least trying in Arizona against the odds, and inexperience. Below are cases of many others who too have sought justice through the legal system from covert harassment and electromagnetic assault, abuse and victimization, and in cases detailing gang stalking, mind control, Neurophone, Voice to Skull (V2K) now called Synthetic or Artificial Telepathy and energy weapon assaults and other influence technologies:

1. Norm Rabin

United States District Court/Eastern District of New York –CASE NO: CV-93-3681, CASE NO: APPEAL NO: 936370, CASE NO: CV 984435

Brief Synopsis–this case is regarding electromagnetic assaults, gang Stalking, mind control, etc.

2. David Larson

United States District Court/Central District of California–Case No: CV-09-01296

Brief Synopsis–this case is regarding implants and residue left in His body from implants.

3. James Walbert

District Court of Sedgwick County, Kansas–Case NO: 08-DM8647

Brief Synopsis–this case is regarding electromagnetic assaults and gang stalking

4. Jesus Mendoza

Case NO: (S.D. Tex) M03-38, US S. CT. CASE NO: 04-9908, US Court of Appeal for the Fifth Circuit Case NO: 04-40095, CASE NO: 06-0155, US Court of Appeals for the District of Columbia Circuit Case NO: 06-5108

Brief Synopsis–this case is regarding electromagnetic assaults and gang stalking, including assaulting his children

5. Connie Marshall

US Court of Federal Claims Case NO: 09-733C

Brief Synopsis–this case is regarding electromagnetic assaults, gang stalking, destruction of property (car engine and radiator, washer, dryer, electric igniter switch on heater in home, destruction of treadmill, computers, fax machines, business and job, intercepting mail (even registered and certified), attacking my pets, intercepting e-mail and tele., changing my birth certificate, manipulating social security records, increasing debt, constant torture, torment and harassment, etc.

NOTE: Ms. Marshall now has several pending cases regarding related conspiracy in that the Commonwealth of Kentucky is participating and creating the infrastructure to allow these crimes to be committed against her. Ms. Marshall has signed certified receipts and/or taped the Officials on every level in Kentucky stating, "We have been told not to assist you," and Danny Lawless, Police Officer stated, "No one is going to assist you, because you are Redlined."

6. John St Clair Akwei

Civil Action 92-0449

Brief Synopsis: This lawsuit reveals a frightening array of technologies and programs designed to keep tabs on individuals.

7. Stan J. Caterbone

US District Court Case NO: 05-2288

8. Donald M. Friedman

Case NO: 06-CV-2125

United States District Court for the District of Columbia, Federal District Brief Synopsis–this case is regarding directed energy and microwave weapons

9. John Finch

REF: OTP-CR-70/07 & EM_T01_OTP-CR-00122_07 &

EM_Ack_OTP-CR-742_09 the International Criminal Court (ICC)

Brief Synopsis–Electromagnetic Torture and Abuse

10. Lambros vs. Faulkner, Et Al

Civil Case # 98-1621 (dsd/jmm) United States District Court of Minnesota Brief Synopsis: Torture, Forced Implantation and Transmitters in head. Swedish doctors familiar with treating victims that have been implanted stated that foreign bodies do exist in Mr. Lambros and that they are most likely transmitters.

(www.lambros.name/ricosuit4/rico24.html)

11. Geral W. Sosbee Ex FBI Agent

Writ of Certiorari # 01-182

Supreme Court of the United States

Brief Synopsis: Electromagnetic Torture

12. Brian Wronge

Eastern District Court # (?)

Brief Synopsis: A doctor confirmed that he had metallic or paramagnetic foreign body in the region of the anterior left axilla. An Anatomist stated: 'When I pass the microphone over his body it picks up vibration and white noise sound waves that would be emitted by computer. When we had been doing this for a minute or so the sound dropped as though someone had turned down the frequency somewhere. This happened in the area under his arm, near his forehead and in some places along the vertebral column." It was also stated that these chips are probably operated by some transmitter that the body sends sound waves out to such as Gwen Towers.

http://www.lambros.name/pdf/citysunarticle_wronge.pdf

13. The International Committee on Microwave Weapons (ICOMW) – Harlan Girard US District

Court for the District of Columbia

Brief Synopsis: Class Action Lawsuit regarding Offensive Microwave Weapons

14. Jones vs. Ault

Cite 67 F.R.D. 124 (1974) CASE NO. CV474 – 279 AND CASE 474 -293

US District Court for the South District of Georgia, Savannah District

Brief Synopsis: Brain controlled and monitored by Electric or Parabolic Sound. Surveillance System tuned to brain want only monitors and combs body picking up sound and voices.

15. Huang Si Ming, Hong Kong Professor Sues the US for Mind Control (FILED IN 1996)

Brief Synopsis: Huang claims that one of the devices in his teeth can read his thoughts and talk to his mind while he is sleeping.

16. Soleil Mavis, http://www.peacepink.ning.com

> A. Soleil Mavis has filed several lawsuits regarding, "Remote Mind Control Abuses and Torture." A. International Criminal Court, Reference No. EM_T01_ OTP-CR-00122_07
>
> B. United Nations Petitions Team–Results–No Reply, No Reference Number (Filed Lawsuit 2007)
>
> C. The Registrar European Court of Human Rights–Counsel of Europe (Sent by Letter Dec. 2009) Results: No Reply Yet, No Case Number D. Curia – To: The Registry–Rue Du Fort Niedergrunewald–L-2925 Luxembourg (Sent by Letter Dec. 2009) Case Ref: No: T-507109AJ

17. James Gee

Reference NO: EM_ACK_OTP-CR-742_09 International Criminal Court Head of the Information and Evidence Unit Office of the Prosecutor–P.O. Box 19519 2500 CM the Hague, the Netherlands

Some lawsuits not listed but can be located on the Internet are the cases of: Diana Napolis, John Mecca, John Allman, and the ACLU and mine. My case was dismissed for lack of subject matter jurisdiction with prejudice leaving me very few options.

"We are all playing our individuals roles, working together as part of a larger spiritual team to advance humanity and the world to a more loving and conscious place. To do so, the old ways must be challenged and weakened."

On a spiritual note, everyone played a role in this book's completion no matter what their appearance. It was their prompting, that kept me writing and fighting. Love my foundation, apparent egotism theirs. However, balance is achieved by the meshing of both the negative and positive. It was they who educated me completely on how these operations work and they did a very good job of doing so. The fact that they did not leave and sat watching their efforts becoming reality refusing to accept that the technological advantage they thought they had had failed them spoke volumes.

Gone are the days that if an official police investigation began on or around an individual that person had to be legally notified. In fact, during decades of nonconsensual mind control testing it is not unheard of a person to be set up to use prior to a full targeting as a person watches in surreal fashion their life destroyed.

With today's advanced, patented technology in hand, law enforcement can interrogate a person secretively by their voices beamed directly into a target's brain terrorizing the target and hope to break the target down physically, psychologically and emotionally. This is even more poignant when the targeted individual is unaware of what is factually available today, the technology itself, or law's authorizing usage.

The end result for those monitoring a target can be the unethical creation of the manipulated outcome in which they seek in what are also called Remote Neural Monitoring programs. If successful in a covert or even overt psychological manipulation campaign using the advancements written about in this book, backed up by using others, and the creation of many levels of technological harassments and illusion techniques, street theatre, it appears that what was once an unethical, unofficial targeting or even a human testing program, can become official, but, this is only after creating fear through death threats also. The human brain has no firewall of protection against the powerful, unseen, technological invasion by the highly perfected capability of advanced influence, mind invasive technology, or by what was once termed mind control, today, again, psycho-physical / psychological electronic or "psychotronic."

These programs encompass a full agenda of tactics, strategies, protocol and operate as a full covert machination of great propensity backed up by deployment of intense physical and psychological crippling using undetectable technology making it extremely difficult for it to be proven. It is unseen to the human eye.

In my case, perhaps the greatest sadness and source of my rightful anger overall, lay in the fact that those targeting me never had a valid case unless they managed to scare me or convince me of wrongdoing and even more so immoral is the fact that after they failed, would even take my life. My life meant nothing to those sitting at their computer terminals, or guiding those living around me. When weighed against the capability afforded by the covert technological use and the games and devaluing of a human life for what appeared to be their egotistical amusement, they tried and tried and tried to break me. I bravely managed to turn the table to some degree unafraid to tell my story. Again, life is not perfect folks and it appears that it is not supposed to be. We all will stumble and fall and get back up. Life is full of hills and valleys, pain and sorrow and joy.

Later, I would suffer the full brunt of their effort in what appeared to be a then turned cowardly crucifixion, the result and base of the exposure through publication and the denial of what were once ethical constitutional rights. Towards the finalization of this publication, two things became a reality. Those working in these programs today have the ability to covertly target a person until the day they die, and do and also the realization they could and would likely continue trying to brainwash, manipulate and influence me long after they should have departed after fruitlessness as the indicator of this being a technology testing program while banking on useful public disbelief of a technological reality. The belief that they had a technological advantage, which they felt would eventually win, kept them lingering and maliciously abusing me along with obvious repetitive subliminal threats of my demise and the frustration of the reality and repeating "she's not scared at all!" Again, it has always been my hope for them at my door and my situation before the justice system? However, we live in a climate where state secret laws, passed by the bush administration, national security orders and media gag orders prevent revelation to humanity of the monstrosity happening today as a great sadness.

CONCLUSION

April 26, 2012
Operation Center
Technological Sexual Exploitation

"It looks like we have a book" one of these men said working the 10:30 p.m. to 6:30 p.m. shift from their vantage point in my ceiling as I wrapped it up. This said as they watched me edit the last chapter of this manuscript before going to bed last night. However, without a doubt, they had continued efforts to misspell words, misconstrue sentences, and insert I noticed each time I did a review that simply were not there. I have to hope that the message is clear, and the information valuable, in spite of ongoing tampering.

This morning I woke with a sexual suggestion whispered as soon as I opened my eyes. One of these creatures said "dick." A few days ago, first "pussy" then "rape" was said also in the one-word games. This is not the first time they have said just a word. A few years back another favorite was "crazy," "suicide" and "dead."

I would later realize why while watching television they were heading down the road of these specific sexual terms and suggestions. When a typical sex scene played out in a movie I was watching began, so did the satellite delivered, beamed sexual stimulation. I felt an instant throbbing sensation in my vagina. This is fruitless with me because I knew where it was coming and it disgusted me. For one, I am not controlled psychologically by sex urges or through the lower part of my body or lower realm of consciousness. My satisfaction in life does not come from physical or sexual pleasure. I left the animal kingdom in another lifetime.

When all else has failed, it appears these sick individuals still feel that they can still control me or control this situation by placing me in a position to desire sex. More than likely based on the ongoing compliment games they are playing now, maybe one of them thinks he could show up to provide a remedy after the manipulated stimulation.

After they watched me immediately document this heinous act and violation of me, here immediately, and my distaste for it, the degrading name followed then a radar laser energy weapon attack to the left leg bone that they have been working on for months now as an isolated targeted area.

That's right folks. This group of pathetic retards technologically raping me has the audacity to call me names after they realized that I don't want to play with them.

After the microwave pain beam attack the ridicule of "You can't prove it" then followed as I shifted the protective covering to lessen the assault hopefully.

Sexual terrorism is the order of the day and a new form of legalized terrorism now in the hands of law enforcement in many forms as documented below, it is nothing new in the excerpt below including technologically:

On April 2nd, 2012, the US Supreme Court ruled that jails do not violate privacy rights by routinely strip-searching everyone, even those arrested on minor traffic offences. This decision is part of a disturbing trend in US law enforcement practices: The addition of a sexual humiliation component to them – a component that was found in the most oppressive police states in History. Due to its powerful psychological effect on people, sexual humiliation is currently used in places where physical and psychological torture is tolerated such as Guantanamo Bay and now, this technique is becoming increasingly tolerated on civilians…The Vigilante Citizen – "Symbols Rule the World, Not Words nor Law"

The next morning while using the restroom, after pulling down my panties,

"She's clean" was said for the umpteen times as they surveyed my undies. I guess I should be grateful. I can only imagine how a woman would suffer if she did not meet their standards, but I am not. I don't need them to like me nor do I need their approval.

March 2, 2012
11:00 p.m.
Occupy Psychiatry

"Okay, that's it! I have got to do something to push this situation into the open or it appears they will covertly kill me or make me gravely ill" trying to stop book publication as the energy weapon attacks continue to escalate. The fact is they can torture me this way covertly for the rest of my life. And it appears that that is just the plan as they become less verbal. As I prepared for bed my bedroom was immediately irradiated with microwaves. I need court involvement immediately or else it appears.

The microwave pain beam is now coming so heavily from the three adjoining apartments, next door, downstairs below and downstairs next door, and also from the operation center that I can literally smell the heavy metals densely in every room of my apartment. I have got to do some to push the letter and hopefully get the situation before the judicial system.

Earlier my daughter phoned asking me if she could store her belonging at my residence having to move from her apartment in the morning. She later called back asking if she could just come over and spend the night instead of me picking her up early in the morning.

Having reached my peak, I hatched a hopeful plan to get arrested. I got out of bed and first told my daughter, what I was planning. Before heading downstairs to confront the neighbor below me where the radiation was coming from the heaviest, I gave her my bankcard with instruction on how to bail me out of jail. I packed up this book, and my camera showing the extensive protective material lining my walls and bed. My plan was to disturb the peace just enough to get arrested thereby hopefully getting the two things these covert operations do not want, exposure and court involvement. This has got to stop. I must try something.

I first went to the window on the side of the six-unit apartment building where I live. This is the neighbor's bedroom directly below. I could see the wall unit possibly used through the open window curtain in the dimly lit room. It appeared someone quickly, surprised, or possibly forewarned via satellite had just in the nick of time slipped out of view. I then returned to the front door and began pounding on his door very loudly yelling,

"Turn that microwave off right now" over and over again at the top of my lungs

"The book is done! Turn it off! I will not stand for it a moment longer!"

Over and over, I pounded. The only response was the light in the living room turned off and the place became completely dark and quiet.

He was inside, now playing possum as I continued banging and yelling. While he did not come out, the neighbor next door to him, adjacent to me below did. I had already had a run in with him. It was right before the apartment that I now banged was rented and I caught him coming from inside the then empty apartment one night with keys. I had gotten suspicious that someone was going in their when I kept feeling radiation coming from the then vacant apartment and would limp downstairs as quickly as possible hoping for a sighting. However, in the dark, with no curtains, there were still places where I could not see if someone were hiding to include the closet. This situation worked in conjunction with operation center monitoring. For example, if a cop is sent to a location, the operation center can report to them where a person is hiding inside a residence and if they are armed in advance.

"You better get yourself back inside" the other neighbor demanded harshly as he now stood on his porch with still no response from the door I pounded.

I ignored him at first and continued banging. A relative briefly staying with me one day asked me what this particular man did all day. He appeared to sit in the apartment with no television or radio on. I knew what he did all day when I felt the radiation rays come from the angle of his apartment as positioned to mine. Also, his familiar voice rang out inside my apartment with threats and name calling through the likely telepathic ray gun use. The Panasonic "Tough Book" real time viewing laptop software enables a person to expertly guide the energy weapon beam with accuracy for up close attacks inside my home.

I remembered the night I caught this neighbor sneaking around the vacant apartment. At that time, he had also demanded aggressively that I return to my apartment or else. When I refused, he got in my face, telling me that he was a member of a street gang called the Bloods and that I was 'disrespecting' him in a life-threatening manner.

Logically those participating in these covert harassment groups do not want attention drawn to them at all. They want to do their dirty work in the dark, quietly and if they can get you believing that you have no help, support, and that no one will ever believe you, then it is green light to step up the games of harassment and painful microwave torture to excessive levels as coercion. The object is to push you over the edge into their hands by breaking the law in some way. The argument ended that night with him with a draw. He returned to his apartment and I returned to mine.

However, tonight when I would not budge ignoring him and continued banging on the other door, this man then jumped off his porch and once again got extremely close in my face with his face twisted up so that he looked demented. I told him I was not going anywhere and if he put his hands on me then he would surely be jailed. He continued to yell, "GET IN THE HOUSE, GET IN THE HOUSE, GET IN THE HOUSE!" This was said over and over again. When he realized that he was not going to bully me with his demand, getting nowhere and failing a second time, he then playing the fear game to the hilt said, "I've got something for you" and rushed into his home indicating he had a possible weapon. I did not budge but stood waiting to see what he had for me and even moved closer to his door. He returned with nothing except the same threat yelled at the top of his lungs for me to get inside and a physical gesture designed to see if I would flinch or whether I was fearful if he lunged at me. I looked at him and made the same flinching gesture back at him to see if he would jump himself. Another neighbor had lunged at me also when we met up in the parking garage after threats. "You'll see, what's going to happen" was his threat. This one had the nerve to push me slightly. I pushed him back as he headed to his vehicle and I headed to mine.

During this time, my oldest daughter stood on my porch taking in the whole scene. Shocked and unbelievably to my ears she then began telling the now fully assembled group from all of the apartments around me sending the toxic rays into my apartment, "She's ill." When I heard this, I realized that this child was not trying to help me and was not on my team of one, of just me, and that if anyone could hurt me, and it could be her. I slapped her hard across her face hurt, and told her to get back inside. She complied, but did not go upstairs instead stood in the shadow of the doorway.

The yelling for me to get back inside continued over and over. My refusal to comply resulted in two officers of the Los Angeles Police Department showing up. As I stood talking with one of them explaining the situation, especially regarding the electronic weapon torture I have been enduring, night after night, all of the neighbors, including the one whom had demanded that I get back inside quietly slipped back into their apartments. My daughter had now returned upstairs.

One officer stood talking with me outside, downstairs, while the other went upstairs to speak with her. The one talking to me did not seem very surprised when I told him about the technology or the covert harassment, and kept asking how they could help me. When the second officer returned, from talking with my daughter, I guess they realized how they could help me and possibly themselves also. Instead of going to jail, I would be transported to the psyche war of a local hospital. But first, one of them explained, they needed to have their sergeant come out and review the situation before doing so.

They then set me in the squad car parked outback, one officer stayed with me, and the other interview the neighbors. When the sergeant arrived, he spoke with the two officers then came over to the car to speak with me where I sat handcuffed in the backseat. I told him what was happening and that I had written a book about it and told him I just finished the final proof, and that I had an initial proof as evidence in my purse. He pulled the book out, looked through it briefly then told me that they were going to take me to the hospital to be checked out.

During the drive to the hospital, both officers were surprised when I mentioned that the LAPD factually has a real time surveillance division (RACR) telling them it is mention in this book. "How did you know that?" The officer driving said in surprised. When they first arrived, I was given the impression they were there to help me. As I mentioned, "How can we help you" was repeatedly said by one of the arresting officers after I told them what was and had been transpiring for months. Plain and simply the neighbor(s) were trying to intimidate and bully me into silence as an extension to the group targeting me and it appeared to be a well-planned strategic effort with law enforcement's approval and the providing of the neighbors with portable technology to do so.

I would be placed on a 72 hour hold for observation at the hospital. When I returned home 5 days later, this same neighbor, his voice carried into my apartment laughed saying, "You went to jail." When he said this, I realized that he was part of the law enforcement sponsored covert harassment group under the guise of the vigilante Neighborhood Watch / Community Policing. Why? Because law enforcement would have known that I was taken to the hospital and not to jail.

When we arrived at the psychiatric emergency room that night and staff learned that I was a veteran a transfer to a VA hospital would go into works immediately for the next day. It was late, now nearing 11:00 p.m. and I would have to stay the night in the waiting area on the unit. Just before closing time at 5:00 p.m. the next day a transport ambulance arrived ready to take me to the Long Beach VA. I had hoped to be taken to the West Los Angeles, VA hospital but there were no beds available there.

When I heard that I would be transported to the Long Beach VA, I knew that I was being placed in yet another precarious situation and an ominous feeling engulfed me. This feeling was a knowing of what to possibly expect in advance one there. Had not this VA specifically been the first, in late October 2010, after moving into the apartment in Long Beach, California and suffering similar technology attacks, after returning from Arizona, officially document me as delusional? This had been the result after I complained of the exact same persecution from the neighboring apartment upstairs at that time. At times, my continued effort to get some type of documentation about my plight was consistently being used against me. As described earlier on, I later move out of this apartment in just 15 days in November of 2010 becoming homeless at the Salvation Army homeless shelter on the West Los Angeles VA facility.

I arrived Friday evening, March 3, 2012 at the Long Beach VA and met with the staff psychiatrist briefly just after 6:00 p.m., just as her shift ended for the evening. She told that I would be able to speak in more detail with the on-call weekend psychiatrist early Saturday morning. When she told me the name of the psychiatrist, I was floored.

Seemingly as an act of fate, I would see the exact same psychiatrist who had played a major role in me getting my VA compensation ten years earlier whom I had not seen for ten years. In the book, I carried in my belongings, were also three paragraphs dedicated to the interaction with him in this book. I was now elated that I had the book with me. I was optimistic. This I felt would convince those targeting me there had been no wrongdoing on my part as they surely continued the surveillance of me. In reality, it is not about this at it. It is about technology testing and the need for test subjects.

The next morning, I woke earlier in eager anticipation.

Without a doubt, the biometric real tracking of my life had been ceaseless occurring around the clock as Big Brother's puppet's eyes and ears watched and listened and made comments insuring I knew they were there as usual. They had read the book, reading along as I wrote every single word from the operation center. Yet they refused to accept the fact of no validity, and depart choosing to continue using, abusing, victimizing, and toying with me covertly.

Early Saturday morning, one of the nurses found me telling me that the Veteran Village Recovery Center (VVRC) director wanted to meet with me. This is procedure for new patients on the ward. With book in hand I was ready for the meeting having highlighting the section regarding his involvement. At first, he did not remember me. It had been ten years. However, when I jolted his memory, first explaining what had happened during our last encounter, my agitation, and why an investigation was now centering on me ten years later, regarding my VA compensation. He remembered the situation. I then read the paragraphs written about his involvement in 2002 that jarred his memory.

Early Sunday morning, I was again called to his office. He told me that he had decided to release me as of 2:00 a.m. Monday morning that would be 72 official hours taking me out of 51/50 status or involuntary hold, and switching me to voluntary. As we finished our meeting, he then said,

"I am aware that microwave is being used today. However, it is only used for terrorist."

This is a common belief today I told him. The laws today allow this type of targeting by electronic / real time surveillance included also for other reasons, narcotic trafficking or even warrantless suspicious behavior. I reiterated my belief that this bogus charge may have been levied against me, by this operation wanting to target me and literally wanting to get inside my head and approved by misleading the court. I was never a heavy drug user. Once inside my head, they found nothing they could use unless they could have convinced me of wrongdoing by radio frequency influencing or threats and a hope to scare me. They failed and were now trying to stop my book exposure I told him by around the clock torture.

I went to bed hopeful Sunday night after he left. It was a good thing that I had gotten a full night's rest. I would surely need it Monday morning. When the Attending psychiatrist for the Long Beach VA inpatient psyche ward came to work, along with the Residents and I was called in for an interview. My first question was, "Am I still going to be discharged today day?" He told me no worries that I would. He then asked me to explain what happened, and how and why I felt myself being persecuted by microwave technology. To my surprise, after I told him what I had been enduring and telling everyone else, he then told me that he changed his mind after hearing my story. I was now being placed on an involuntary 14-day hold for evaluation and that they were going to force me to take anti-psychotic medication.

In most states, before a person can be held against their will, the court must intervene guaranteeing the protection of the rights of the individual. In my case, there was no exception. Two days later, I sat with an assigned court advocate from the Los Angeles Superior Court. Also present was a Mental Health Referee from the Los Angeles

Superior Court ready to hear why the 14-day hold should be upheld, or whether I should be release.

To my chagrin, just when I felt the situation hopeful, I learned that my daughter had phoned the doctor telling him that I was a danger to myself and others, that she was frightened of me, and that I was gravely mentally ill. My daughter was with me that night, due to a third eviction officially, with two unofficial evictions during a five-year period. She also held no credible employment for a couple of years. I later learned from my middle-born daughter that this daughter, her sister, had called her while I was in the hospital. It appeared that she was trying to pull her into an apparent scheme to have me committed, indefinitely and possibly have herself designated as my Conservator. Well that would solve her money, transportation and housing problems.

The hearing with the court referee was set for March 7, 2012 at 3:00 p.m., five days after I had been first taken to the hospital then transferred to the VA. Both sides were required to state their justification. After hearing both sides, I speaking for myself, I was released immediately. I was not, nor have ever been a danger to myself or others. I am well groomed, and articulate, my bills are paid on time, and I am social. I presented the facts that I manage my life effectively, a very clean home, buying groceries and even more so, had in hand, a well research book documenting my situation in a clear concise and legible manner showing an organized mind and thinking process. As far as my daughter was concerned, she was being used without a doubt.

"Why is it that whenever a person comes to the VA for help, they always leave with a diagnosis?" This was asked by another veteran as I stood talking with a staff member after the hearing while the paperwork for my immediate release was being prepared. Again, it a documented fact that a VA hospital doctor, Don R. Justesen, in Kansas was one of the first to test the Voice to Skull/Synthetic Telepathy in 1975 as I said earlier.

A lot of people, in law enforcement or connected to the court system, already know what is happening and the technology in use today. The referee's curiosity about any signs which reveal microwave is being directed at a target stood out in my mind. During the five days that I spent in the VA hospital, my eyes had stopped draining fluid, as a direct result of the microwave beam, my blurred vision cleared up, and the specific area on my body they targeted began to heal and I began to walk better.

I returned to my room, relieved and grateful for God's work through others after the hearing and for a quiet moment to express my gratitude. The Advocate sought me out just before leaving. I was only slightly surprised when she told me that a lot of people know about the microwave technology being used today. She suggested that I consider taking something if for no other reason but to help me continue to cope with the full technological physical and psychological assault coming from many directions and by different means. I told her I would consider it. She then looked at me intensely and said those books are going to help a lot of people. I then replied this is what it is all about. She then left.

What cushioned the blow and the disappointment with my daughter was the realization of the likelihood that this group was factually using her and anyone else they could. This I observed firsthand many times. Family members can play a pivotal role in declaring a person incompetent strategically especially when those in power want you discredited at all cost.

This, and also the fact, that I love her.

Dear Journal
March 20 2012
Occupy - Fusion Centers, Covert Harassment Groups / Neighborhood Watch / Community Policing, Mobbing/Gang and Organized Stalking

"In Utah, on AM radio there was a "Homeland Security" announcement by the Sheriff's Department in recruiting effort for citizens to become part of the "Neighborhood Watch" and "Community Patrol Programs" The announcement said they were looking for citizens to join what was called the "Technical Division" which involved using computers for secret assignments. The request and public service announcement also said that THOUSANDS of citizens are already involved."

***

March 21, 2012
Dear Journal
Occupy Supreme, District and Superior Court

When I arrived home the Galley final proofs I had ordered the night before I was taken to the hospital were waiting for me after release on March 7th. Today, I decided to send some the proofs out to as many judges as I can. What did I have lose?

April 11, 2012
Dear Journal
Occupy Operation / Fusion Centers

Abraham Lincoln once said:

"Nearly all men can stand adversity, but if you want to test a man's character, give him power."

***

During the last days toward book's publication, the heavy-duty arsenal of black bag technology came out in full force. This included dream manipulation technology believe it or not. Although I can attest to only twice, the patents below show that images can be transferred subliminally, through pre-recorder video scenery. In late 2011, I remember a specific incident where dream manipulation technology was used. As I think back, another specific occurrence was also in 2008. As mentioned, most if not all of the technology directed at a target coincides with the necessity to gaging any resulting emotional reaction of fear to determine effectiveness.

Dream manipulation technology, used to manipulate my dreams usually had a sexual theme. For example, an undistinguishable blurred facial image of a woman being assaulted. The following patent below appears to have the ability gage emotions and visual subliminal dissemination:

US Patent # 6,292,688 (September 18, 2001) Method and Apparatus for Analyzing Neurological Response to Emotion-Inducing Stimuli, Patton, Richard Abstract - A method of determining the extent of the emotional response of a test subject to stimuli having a time-varying visual content, for example, an advertising presentation. The test subject is positioned to observe the presentation for a given duration, and a path of communication is established between the subject and a brain wave detector analyzer. The intensity component of each of at least two different brain wave frequencies is measured during the exposure, and each frequency is associated with a particular emotion. While the subject views the presentation, periodic variations in the intensity component of the brain waves of each of the particular frequencies selected is measured. The change rates in the intensity at regular periods during the duration are also measured. The intensity change rates are then used to construct a graph of plural coordinate points, and these coordinate points graphically establish the composite emotional reaction of the subject as the presentation continues.

When this technology was applied to me, I remember waking with my heart racing and my heartbeat pounding in my ears. I am not sure if this specific technology is capable of delivery through the satellite system, as with the others, but more than likely it is. Based on my personal experience, it is 100% deliverable by projection from adjoining apartments.

By November 2011, they were desperate for any result they would give them leverage. As a result, they forced dreams of mild pornography on me which usually were inappropriate scenes between the faceless women, usually always with her back turned to me in the scene and participating in deviant sexual acts voluntarily. The men in these dreams were sometimes clearly seen and appeared in the role as supporting cast. The faceless woman obviously was playing the role of possibly me. Documented below are four patented technology that today have this capability:

1. **United States Patent # 5,134,484 (July 28, 1992)**
   Superimposing Method & Apparatus Useful for Subliminal Messages

Wilson, Joseph - Abstract—Data to be displayed is combined with a composite video signal. The data is stored in a memory in digital form. Each byte of the data is read out in sequential fashion to determine: the recurrence display rate of the data according to the frame sync pulses of the video signal; the location of the data within the video image according to the line sync pulses of the video signal; and the location of the data display within the video image according to the position information. Synchronization of the data with the video image is derived from the sync pulses of the composite video signal.

A similar technique is employed to combine sound data with an audio signal. Data to be displayed may be presented as a subliminal message or may persist for a given time interval. The data may be derived from a variety of sources including a prerecorded or live video signal. The message may be a reminder message displayed upon a television screen to remind the viewer of an appointment. The data may be stored in a variety of different memory devices capable of high-speed data retrieval. The data may be generated locally on-line or off-line and transferred to memory which stores the data necessary to create the message.

2. **United States Patent # 5,128,765 (July 7, 1992) System for Implementing the Synchronized Superimposition of Subliminal Signals**

Dingwall, Robert - Abstract–An apparatus and system for the controlled delivery of a subliminal video and/or audio message on to a source signal from a video tape player or similar. The source signal is divided into audio and video portions. A video processor reads the synchronization information from the source signal. A controller transmits a stored subliminal image at designated times to a mixer amplifier fully synchronized with the source signal. Concurrently, an audio subliminal message is applied to the source audio at a volume level regulated at some fraction to the source audio. The combined signals are transmitted to a monitor for undistracted viewing.

3. **United States Patent # 5,123,899 (June 23, 1992) Method & System for Altering Consciousness**

Gall, James - Abstract–A system for altering the states of human consciousness involves the simultaneous application of multiple stimuli, preferable sounds, having differing frequencies and wave forms. The relationship between the frequencies of the several stimuli is exhibited by the equation g = s.sup.n/4 .multidot.f where: f = frequency of one stimulus; g = frequency of the other stimuli of stimulus; and n=a positive or negative integer which is different for each other stimulus.

4. **United States Patent 5,052,401 (October 1, 1991) Product Detector for a Steady Visual Evoked Potential Stimulator and Product Detector**

Sherwin, Gary - Abstract–An automated visual testing system is disclosed which presents an alternating steady state visual stimulus to a patient through an optical system that modifies the stimulus image. As the image changes, the patient produces evoked potentials that change. The evoked potentials are detected by a product detector which produces the amplitude of the evoked potentials. The product detector includes filters which isolate the patient's evoked potentials, a modulator which detects the response using the stimulus source frequency and a demodulator that determines the amplitude of the response. The product detector detects the level of the steady state evoked potential signals even in the presence of substantial background noise and extraneous electroencephalograph signals. These detectors can be used to monitor the evoked potential produced by visual, aural or somatic steady state stimuli. The components described above can be used to produce a system that can determine to which of several different displays an observer is paying attention by providing images that blink at different frequencies and product detectors for each of the stimulus frequencies. The product detector producing the highest output indicates the display upon which the observer is focused.

***

May 23, 2012
Dear Journal

No one is going to believe you, you are crazy was said this morning. Of the many games in "The Program" this they believe is their ace in the hole. They bank on disbelief by others and as a result manipulate and destroy many lives.

As they continued to monitor my editing, and the realization of exposure etches closer, "We can get her through that girl" is said. Yea, right not my daughter, and if I have my way, no one's daughter either!

May 24, 2012

Dear Journal

To: Naysayers and skeptics I challenge, "What if?"

***

"We now have the ability to terminate you covertly and quietly, without leaving a trace or even leaving the building and it is unseen and detectable and again, "You can't prove a thing!" We told you not to publish that book! As they reveal this, the new targeted position is the organ located in the middle portion of my back, right side.

September 14, 2012
Dear Journal

I had a left hip replacement yesterday. When I woke after the surgery, the nursing staff tried to move me to transport me to my room for recovery and I was in excruciating pain. The problem is that the intensity of the pain did not radiate from the surgical site but instead 80% was centered in the entire front portion of both legs radiating from my ankles upward to the front of both thighs. As my mind registered, what obviously must have happened while in surgery, I knew, from experience that I had been obviously attacked by the "so called" non-lethal Directed Energy Weapon during surgery ruthlessly.

Those targeting me 24 hours a day, 7 days a week and privy to every aspect of my life watched the procedure, seeking to benefit from my weakened state. My suspicions were later immediately confirmed when "You need to confess" was said as I cringed in pain unable to move my right leg even an inch. Apparently, this monstrous group, sitting comfortably at their computer terminals in the operation center and deploying effortlessly the energy weapon lay in wait, choosing to painfully impact, the healing process strategically after the surgery.

One thing they appear to have enjoyed immensely while targeting me overall is the crippling affect this technology has on the human body and their repeating "She can't walk" while contributing extra pain to both legs combined with an already painfully deteriorating left hip. If anything at all, the right leg should have been totally, unequivocally, pain free but it actually was in even more pain when I woke than the left.

As soon as I was transported to my hospital bed for recovery, I knew I needed to act fast. I looked up and found the telephone phone number in Washington, D.C. of the highest-ranking leader at the Department of Veterans, who is the Secretary of the Department of Veterans Affairs, his Chief of Staff, and Patient Advocate. I called them and detailed everything. I detailed the extreme including the continued verbal abuse. I now wonder if they have decided that they would be satisfied, in light of failure, that trying to push me into suicide as a form of victory if nothing at all, due to the consistent verbal taunting will suffice. Even more heinous is the continued intense psychological effort to influence me of wrongdoing, combined with the extremely painful physical attacks as coercion escalating. I also mentioned this book as reference, hopefully to my sanity, and provided information on where to take peek inside my painful story of struggles and the how, when, where and why of my targeting.

Typically, while at the hospital, as many other times, I noticed that staff in every location I was taken apparently already had been informed of my status in advance by the police giving the impression that I am supposed to be a criminal and some actually appeared to be ready to go into action typical of the use of others in organized stalking campaigns motivated by disinformation. When I was able to get up one day I approached the nurse's station in a wheelchair. The nurses did not see me because of the chair sitting low as I approached. I decided to go out and personally talk to them after first buzzing them at my bedside. As approached, and before they noticed me, I factually heard one nurse tell another, "You know the police are after her" then the other responded, "I heard" then they both laughed. Boy oh boy what I would give to have any of the many and numerous people they have used as pawns in my targeting a court of law and sworn under oath to verify what police are telling people in the ongoing intimidation effort.

Thank God, for the strength to write this book through it all. Bringing this book to the hospital, after realizing what they were doing from many previous experiences has helped to level the playing field for me, tremendously, and by the time I made it home from the hospital, I had sold six copies.

The question now is. Will the Director of the Department of Veterans Affairs or his staff deem me worthy of relief from the fruitless pain I suffer day in and day out in the now 7-year non-ionizing radiation deployed to my body, by those appearing to be motivated on behalf of the Department of Veterans Affairs?

This cold-blooded, ruthless, inhumane group appears to be willing to use horrendous abuse to stop the exposure, and cover up these heinous acts while hiding cowardly and anonymously? I cannot believe one of them said, "She made us look bad." No, they made themselves look bad. The only power they have always had is an ethical ability to assess the situation, and morally move on.

They chose not to, due to the covert ability to secretively do these things to many, and the ever-present knowledge that no one ever believes the technology exists or that it is being widely used in nonconsensual situation on the unsuspecting. They appear instead to have chosen to instead maliciously attack while requesting of me to stop my efforts or suffer the consequences. One thing I know for sure these unscrupulous individuals don't want you to even see their faces.

Close to my release after my two weeks stay, I noticed yet another incident of the likely deployment of the technological ability to be cast over an environment and used to influence folks who haven't a clue. As I entered the hospital cafeteria, I saw the hospital security officer talking with a woman who had been very kind to me but changed abruptly and became very cold. As I passed them, saying "Hi" with no response back from either, the woman said, "She probably did do what they say." I then heard the security guard sounding extremely surprised that they both had the exact same thought at the exact same time say, "I was just thinking the same thing" flabbergasted. This is no surprise to me.

As I learned, as they follow me around by satellite, I have witnessed this happening time and time again. A thought materializes in someone's head and that person thinks it originated as their very own thought but factually is a thought beamed into their head by those overseeing everything from their operation center, manipulating as stated, an entire environment with the objective to create chaos. Believe it or not!

September 30, 2012
Dear Journal

It appears that the Department of Veterans Affairs may have come through. The attacks to my body have subsided somewhat and as each shift comes in fully loaded to begin the harassment, I have heard one say, "The VA said to leave her alone," several times.

However, how many times have they said someone told them to leave me alone after I phoned a government official such as the U.S. Attorney, and then increased the merciless torture in this game of emotional highs and lows of PSYOPS.

What happens when undisciplined men are given the ability to watch a woman they perceive attractive, or find interesting, or who is now a threat to them given the ability to simply type a name into a computer system and locate a targeted individual at anytime, anywhere on the planet? Answer - you get egotistical men, who can't believe that by God, through it all I am still standing, and an apparent motivation and determination, in this disbelief that they have to break me down. You get a group of morons still trying to antagonize me no matter what anyone requests apparently.

Today as they watched me getting dressed, a typical tactic has been to repeat everything sub-vocal thought letting me know of their presence "Look at that bra" when I put on a new bra I purchased, or "She's not that fat" or, "She looks good," and of course "She's gone" followed later by "B" we're going to kill you!" This technology is a schizophrenic diagnosis best friend.

Last night I sat outside Starbuck (Wi-Fi at home kept malfunctioning) updating what has transpired recently to this book on my laptop. A sheriff pulled up right beside me in the parking lot and just sat there while those in the operation center assessed my reaction for any sign of fear. I then heard them report, "She's not scared at all" for the umpteen times sounding disappointed. I do not fear them, and never have had a reason to. When he saw that I could care less and kept working on my computer, ignoring him, he pulled off Starbuck had closed over an hour ago, and it was just he and I sitting there.

They just can't grasp that I WANT THEM AT MY DOOR.

I want my situation brought into the JUSTICE system by any means possible. After the sheriff left, I then heard one of them say "Disable her car," then another replied, "We can't, why, because she still has it running." It was around 10:45 p.m., and they wanted me stranded outside the now closed Starbucks.

Sometimes, from out of the blue, I've noticed a great sadness encompasses me. From experience, I have come to recognize this is likely during times that they switch from technological telepathy to the subliminal repetition and delivery of extreme verbal abuse and threats.

Perhaps what is more saddening than anything is the fact that many are being remotely targeted in this manner up until the day that they die? This is the result of no checks or balances of those operating freely in The Program and the fact that "You cannot prove a thing" they tell me repeatedly. Everything that happens essentially is played out, remarkably inside a target's head.

Ethical Use laws need to be in place, yesterday, and are urgently needed for technological advancements that are here to stay. How can targets prove what is happening? It will be an uphill battle.

October 4, 2012
Dear Journal

I had my first follow up appointment with Ortho today. On the drive to the hospital, I could feel the radar laser attacking various parts of my body, such as oddly both shoulders, and seeming to alternate between both knees. When I met with the Nurse Practitioner, determined to get documentation, I asked her to put into my medical file, whether she believed me or not, my concerns and new pain originating in these specific areas. She did. On the way home, the game plan changed I guess after this request. Already knowing of mild arthritis in my right hip with relatively no pain, I guess these monsters decided the right hip would be a better location to target because it would be even more difficult to prove as opposed to two healthy knees. Yes, there is a method and protocol to the painful madness. As a result, I suffered severe attacks for the rest of the day and long into the night that were so powerful to my right hip groin area, similar to how the pain started in the left hip, that was unbearable leaving my right leg extremely painful and my hope to begin to walk normally gone. Let's see how long before I need a hip replacement in the right hip as the sadistic, systematic organ damage effort continues as they use their technological advantage to hurt me as leverage.

I would later come to realize, that I had likely been placed into some type of human guinea testing technology testing program, dating much further back than I could have ever imagined. This awareness was based on my review of specific coinciding experiences during my life, as if they were being manipulated at a certain time and with my understanding today of "The Program" as I began to connect the dots shockingly!

One must understand also that drugs have always played a vital role in mind control studies, such as LSD, etc., which was covertly given to unsuspecting civilians, for example, which is a documented fact as being part of MKULTRA and that there has been, unquestionable intentional infiltration of drugs into specific communities as a form of ongoing testing of not only illegal drugs but also legal drugs designed to assist in controlling individuals, groups, and large populations.

Today, no one is exempt as a useful human test subject, as efforts towards mass population control continue, globally, as a very effective and useful tool in ongoing efforts to advance a long idolized global agenda or NWO!

The End

REFERENCES

Courtesy of Mr. Paul Baird – Satellite and Human Experimentation

TV References

Discovery Channel 19 Science Mysteries: Beyond the Truth: The Real Men in Black, Dandelion / Transmedia Corporation, 1998. Executive Producers Bruce Burgess and Danny Fenton, U.K.

Content – Mind Control Experiments (e.g. MKULTRA) and Manchurian candidates (programmed killers). Experiment examples include brainwashing, hypnosis, implants, Neurophone voices and more.

Beyond Treason

- www.truthemergency.us/pages/dcworkshops.html Content–A 90 min. video highlighting government experiments on the military and civilian populations.

Others include cryptic reference to mind control or 'voices' in fictional programs e.g. "The 4400', "Heroes', "Herman's Head" etc.

Book References

Non-Lethal Weapons, Dick Russell, Prevailing Winds, Premiere Issue. (March 1995)

Armageddon: Killing Them Softly, Russell Short, GQ. (March 1995)

Damage Control and Human Radiation Experiments - Glenn Alcalay, - Covert Action Quarterly (Spring 1995)

Electromagnetic Interaction with Biological Systems, Professor James C. Lin, Plenum Press, N.Y. 1989

Angels Don't Play This HAARP - Dr. Nick Begich and Jeanne Manning, Earth Pulse Press, (Anchorage 1995). (Includes numerous patents)

Earth Rising the Revolution - Dr. Nick Belgich, James Roderick by Earth Pulse Press Inc. 1999.

Towards a new alchemy–The Millennium Science - Dr. Nick Begich - Earth Pulse Press (Anchorage Alaska 95)

A Nation Betrayed, Carol Rutz.

See www.wanttoknow.info/nationbetrayed10pg

Bluebird, Dr. Colin Ross. See www.wanttoknow.info/ bluebird10pg

Remote Control, The Battle for Your Mind", Steve Lynch, 2006, Vertex Publications

Satellite Tyranny – P. Baird, 2009. EarthLink Publishing Copies of 'Satellite Tyranny' by Paul Baird, a compilation of the articles on this site, can be obtained from Diane Frola, Earthlink Publishing, E-mail: auforn@bigpond.com

1996–Gloria Naylor - Third World Press Inc.

Torture, Killing Me Softly, 2009 - Tek Nath Rizal.

A New Breed – Satellite Terrorism in America, Dr. John Hall, AEG Publishing.

Soul Catcher, Vol. 2, Dry. Robert Duncan", Amazon, JH..

Articles

The Media Mafia, Paul Baird, "Hard Evidence" magazine, Vol. 1, May-June 2001, pp34-35 (See "Surveillance Results")

Microwave Mind Control: Modern torture and control mechanisms eliminating human rights and privacy, Dr. Rauni, Leena Kilde, M.D, Spekula, Sept 25, '99 (Dr. Kilde was the chief medical officer for Finland)

Microchip Implants, Mind Control and Cybernetics, Dr. Rauni Kilde M.D, Spekula, 3rd quarter, October 23, '94

"Non-consensual brainwave and personality studies by the U.S government", Cheryl Welsh, Web Site Proof of Anti-Personnel Technologies–Illegal experimentation on humans - Paul Baird, Exposure, pp. 34-35, vol. 5, no. 4, 1998. (See "technologies")

High Tech Civilian Control Studies, Warren Hough, The Spotlight, Washington, page 1, vol. 21, no. 31. (July 31st, 1995)

"Schneidas Hears Voices", Brad Clifton, the Daily Telegraph, Sydney. (Feb 25th, 1997) ... discrediting article

Jana's Fanatic, Naomi Toy, the Daily Telegraph, Sydney. (May 20th, 1997) page 1, discrediting article

"Secret Weaponry–Past Present and Future", Jerry W. Decker, (Director of Vanguard Sciences, Exposure, vol.4, no.1, 1997 (pp29-32)

Newsfront–Wonder Weapons, Douglas Pasternak, Melbourne, Sunday Herald Sun, (July 20th, 1997) pg. 56-57. US news and world report.

Nazis of the New World Order, Big Brother in the 21st Century - Paul Baird, Exposure, pp32-34, Vol. 7, No 2, 2000 (See "Surveillance")

Mind Wars–Big Brother is out to get you, Tim Rifat, Enigma Magazine, UK ISSUE 6, 1998, pp13-16 (Contact Tel: 44 161 624 0414, FAX 44 161 628 4655).

The Great Conspiracy, The News Monitor, no. 25, vol. 6/5, Part 1.

Aerial Mind Control–The threat to Civil Liberties, Judy Wall (Editor "Resonance"), NEXUS, Oct-Nov '99

U.S Military use of mind control weapons confirmed, Judy Wall, Editor Resonance (Includes countless patents on subliminal mind control technologies).

Review of patents relating to synthetic telepathy - Judy Wall, Ed Resonance.

The Military use of electromagnetic, microwave and mind control technology - Armen Victorian, Lobster #34, Hull, UK. Social Engineering-Crimes against humanity - P. Baird "Hard Evidence" pp. 25-32, Vol. 2, No 1, Jan-Feb 2001. (See "Surveillance")

Synthetic Telepathy – Dr. Richard Alan Miller

Crimes of the Ruling Class – P. Baird "Hard Evidence" Vol. 2, No 4, June 2002 p 30-39 (see 'Surveillance Results section).

The Sons of Satan – P. Baird "Hard Evidence" Vol. 4 No. 1 Jan-Feb 2004 pages 18-25 (see the Technologies section) Brainwashing and its Consequences, P. Baird, HARD EVIDENCE, pp. 20-31, Vol. 4, No 5, Sept-Oct, 2004.

Remote Behavioral Influence Technology Evidence - John J McMurtrey, M.S. (© 2003, 23/12/2003)

Electromagnetic and Informational Weapons: The Remote Manipulation of the Human Brain - Mojmir Babacek, "New Dawn", Mar-Apr 2005 pp. 51-56

The Ultimate Blasphemy : Mind Reading Technologies etc., Paul Baird, May 2005 (see "Using Surveillance Results" page) "Hard Evidence", Vol. 5, No 3, 4,5 and 6 July–Sept 2005

Minority Rules, Paul Baird. Hard Evidence - Vol. 6, No 4, pg. 29-33, 2006.

Computer State, Paul Baird. Hard Evidence - Vol. 6, No 5, pp. 44-51 (see "Using Surveillance Results" page)

Censoring the Truth (RIP Democracy), Paul Baird. Hard Evidence - Vol. 7, No 4, July 2007 pp. 46-55 (see "Surveillance" page)

Spies–Villians not Heroes, Paul Baird. Hard Evidence - Vol. 9, No 2, March 09 pp. 38-42 (see "Technologies" page)

Conspiracies of Silence, Paul Baird. Hard Evidence (see "Using Surveillance Results" page), Vol. 10, No 2, Mar/Apr'10, pg. 46-51.

The Shocking Menace of Satellite Surveillance - Hard Evidence - Vol. 9 No 3, May-June 09, pg. 22-26.

Truth and Opinion (see "Using Surveillance Results" page)

NOTE: Whilst articles on the available technology can be located, accounts relating to actual political targets are rare. The media cannot (or will not) run sympathetic items. They only publish stories discrediting those who react badly (or foolishly) to the harassment. In short, certain sections of the media are both knowledgeable AND complicit. Others are apparently powerless to stop them.

MAINSTREAM MEDIA / ENTERTAINMENT

NOTE: References are subtle and ambiguous as the industry is criminally controlled with many actively participating in harassment & cover ups.

Many writers source information from military and agency contacts then cover themselves by using it only for 'inspiration'; altering the facts/context. So, for example, the true capabilities of military/spy/mafia technologies may be attributed to 'psychic aliens'. Equally the true mistreatment of innocent targets is also hidden. This complies with government secrecy provisions and makes writers and entertainments partially to blame for the suppression/brainwashing that allows for innocents to be destroyed without a public outcry.

Movies

"Minority Report"–Mind reading and thought policing (Cover: the story refers to psychics in a futuristic setting).

"The Matrix"–Computer / Human interfacing (Cover: A futuristic / fantasy tale).

"Conspiracy Theory"– Covert Victimization of innocent people.

"Enemy of the State"–NRO & NSA Satellite Surveillance.

"A Beautiful Mind"–Neurophone Harassment / Setup (Cover: Based on a true story where schizophrenia was the explanation).

"The Hothman Prophecies"–Neurophone & Brain Scanning Experiments (Cover: Based on a true story labeled as a psychic phenomenon).

"The sixth day"–mind reading and cloning (Cover: Sci-Fi)

"Replicant"–mind reading, programming/experimentation, cloning (Cover: Sci-Fi)

"Vanilla Sky"–Computer / Human interfacing (Cover: Sci-Fi)

"Independence Day"– Neurophones and government conspiracy (Cover: psychic 'alien invasion' story)

"Spiderman 1"–Neurophone used on killers (Cover: a schizophrenic comic book villain)

"Star Wars" (various)–Nonverbal communication (Cover: psychic aliens)

"The Truman Show"–Personal surveillance

"Stranger than Fiction"– Neurophone / voices

"Inception", 2010 – Refers to the input and extraction of ideas during sleep.

Music

"I Don't Like Mondays" ...esp. "Silicon chip inside her head is switched to overload..." (Cover: Based on a true story of a young murderer.)

"Feel" esp. "I sit and talk to God but he just laughs at my plans. My head speaks a language I can't understand."

"Goodbye Norma Jean / English Rose" ...esp. "...And they whispered into your brain, they put you on a treadmill..." (Cover: Based on the true stories of murdered celebrities Marilyn Monroe & Lady Di).

"The Voice Within"–Christina Aguilera

"Gloria" esp.....or "the voices in your head" (Cover: the colloquial use of that phrase)

"Little Voice (Inside My Head)" Hillary Duff

"Hotel California" esp. "and those voices from far away keep calling me… wake you up in the middle of the night just to hear them say..."

Others making cryptic references include: "If you could read my mind "," Every breath you take (I'll be watching you)", "Can't get you out of my head "etc. Any of these can also be used to harass monitored listeners / Viewers through corrupt DJs.

"The Climb", Miley Cyrus (esp. "...there's a voice inside my head says you'll never make it").

"17", Jet, esp. "...there's a voice in my head, it won't leave me alone

Related Websites

Citizens against the Covert use of Bio Neural Telemetry Weapons - Dr. Rauni Kilde

Cheryl Welsh–Citizens against Human Rights Abuse Cheryl Welsh – Mind Control Forum

Periscope

Mind Control: Neurophone Illegal Human Experimenting

Spy zone

Ace–Advocacy Committee for Human Experimentation Survivors

The Centre for Democracy and Technology

The Seed: UK Alternative Information

Freedom

International Committee of the Red Cross

Steve Bratcher Former CIA

Earth Pulse Press Inc.

Mind Control Forums

MKZINE (mind control magazine)

Carol Rutz (author of "A nation betrayed: Secret cold war experiments performed on our children and other innocent people")

MKULTRA CIA mind control

MKULTRA Continues

War on Activists

Military Human Experimentation Protocol

Media Filter

Looking Behind The (Alien) Military Abduction Agenda in Propaganda Evidence of Military Kidnapping of Alleged UFO Abductees Conspire.Com "Voices in Your Head" Towards A Psycho–Civilized Society CIA Psych–Ops political corrections www.us-government-torture.com CAMS, John Allman http://www.slavery.org.uk

Dr. John Hall monarch – The new Phoenix Program–Marshall Thomas Advice and support can be obtained through the following

Organizations/People:

Mind Justice News Group – Contact – Allen Barker alb@datafilter.com

Mind Justice Formally Cahra (Citizens Against Human Rights Abuse)

Contact – Cheryl Welsh welsh@dcn.davis.ca.us OR welsh@mindjustice.org Note: They also run victims' stories on the internet – see mind control forum (www.mk.net/~mcf/victim-hm.htm)

The International Red Cross, Geneva. They Are Fighting The "Concentration Camp" Situation Re: Political Targets Who Are Oppressed Covertly. Committee D. Coye 022 734 6001

The UN in Particular Unidir (The UN Institute for Disarmament)

Research Unidir@Unog.Ch) which now officially recognizes non-lethal/mind control weapons and recommending their removal. (The Human Rights Committee should also help but are slow to react).

The European Parliament, which passed a resolution (called "resolution on the environment, security and foreign policy") a 4-0005/99, Jan 28th 99 which called for a worldwide convention to ban these weapons for human manipulation.

US Rep Dennis Kucinich (D-Ohio) - He introduced a bill to ban weapons in space. It was called "The Space Preservation Act Of 2001" (HR 2977)

(SEE http://www.dcn.davis.ca.us/~welsh1-02-3.htm) – info@ Kucinich.us The US Congressional records show that "mind control", "psychotronic weapons" and "mood management" were referred to in HR 2977; evidence that the technology exists. Unfortunately, the bill had to be reintroduced as HR3616, which was watered down and excluded the terms that worried those responsible for the evil technology in question.

Michigan governor (www.senate.michigan.gov) Public Acts 256 and 257 (28/12/03) outlaw using EM weapons on anyone (Penalty – 15yrs to life)

The Church of Scientology – CAPP (Campaign against Political Psychiatry)

CCHR – Kim Cullen and Ashleigh McEwan (02) 9211 4787

CAMS – Christians against Mental Slavery - Contact: John Allman (John_W_Allman@hotmail.com) also info@slavery.org.uk

Amnesty International

Judy Wall, Ed "Resonance" Magazine 684 CR 535 Summerville Florida 33585 USA Dr. Rauni Kilde (Ex-Chief Medical Officer, Finland) Kilde, MD@ aol.com or via Eleanor White – eleanor@Raven1.net

The Mind Control Forum – www.mk.net/~mcf/victm-hm.htm

(Hundreds of victim's stories)

Di Harrison, Editor "Exposure", ausorn@hypermax.net.au

Mind Control Magazine –contact: Ron Patton endure_to_the_end@yahoo.com

UN Human Rights Committee registry@ohchr.org

Lynn Surgalla, Peace &H.R Activist, Former Vice President – US Psychotronics Association

Deborah Dupre, Activist, gdeborahdupre@yahoo.com

ICESH (International Coalition Campaign)

US Rep Jim Guest - Jim.Guest@house.mo.gov

The Worldwide Campaign against Torture and Abuse Using Directed Energy and Neurological Weapons – John Finch johnfinchti@excite.com or MCmailtcam@gmail.com

The Federation Against Mind Control - Europe – http://www.mindcontrol-victims.eu/, MCmailteam@gmail.com, monika.stoces@gmail.com, danny.bonte@gmail.com

Freedom from Covert Harassment and Surveillance (FFCHS) http://freedomfchs.com/, info@freedomfchs.com, dblaron67@yahoo.com, derrickrobinson@gmail.com

Paolo Dorigo, www.associazionevittimearmielettroniche-mentali.org, basmau@libero.it paola.marzianl@libero.it, antanarivo@libero.it

Mikrowellenterror.De http://www.mikrowelienterror.de/, info@mikrowellenterror.de

The Moscow Housing Ecology Committee and the St. Petersbourgh Society of Person's Subject to Remote controlled

Bioenergetic Terror http://www.moscomeco.narod.ru/, pealle@mail.ru, moscomeco@mail.ru, moskomekologia@narod.ru

Soleil Mavis – Peacepink http://soleilmavis.googlepages.com/ soleilmavis@yahoo.com

Takahiro Go to: http://www5f.biglobe.ne.jp%7eterre/index_english.html, http://www.mirall.com/

Mojmir Babacek http://web.lol.cz/mhzzrz/, mbabacek@iol.cz

Swetlana Schunin imitriSchunin@gmx.de">DimitriSchunin@gmx.de, ka4143-896@online.de

Rodin Andria rudyrud2004@yahoo.fr

Moe Hosny – Rule of Law Defenders moe_hosny@yahoo.ca

Jean Verstraeten – Declaration of Alarmed Citizens Verstraeten. jean@belgacom.ne

Eleanor White http://www.raven1.net, ewraven1@sympatico.ca, Eleanor@ravon1.net Eleanor@shoestringradio.net

Dr. Robert Duncan, Mr. Marshall Thomas – The Matrix Deciphered:

http://www.thematixdeciphered.com/, directedenergy@hotmail.com, mindavenger@hotmail.com marsboy683@yahoo.com

Dr. John Hall, Author, info@satweapons.com

Locally, support and information can be obtained through Paul Baird – phone: (02) 9635 0752 (H) OR p.baird@surveillanceissues.com and the website www.surveillanceissues.com

Other

"Secret Societies and Freedom of Speech" – John F. Kennedy, 1961 - Press Conference Address (unreported). To view see: http://www.youtube.com/watch?v=ru4TbL8aweE

"Secret geophysical, directed energy and neurological weapons– Technical and Political/Historical information."–US Congress, European Parl't & UK Parl't–Briefings on secret geophysical weapons and mind control. www.policestateplanning.com/ briefings.html

Below is a list of victim websites in no particular order:

bigbrotherwatchingus.com, Administrator, Renee Pittman

https://youarenotmybigbrother.blog, 100 blogs by Renee Pittman

The mind control forum founded by victim Ed Light contains personal stories from victims. This is probably the first site about mind control...

Peter Grafström's website is written in Swedish and English, talks about possible methods and motives, and his own experiences as a victim.

Cheryl Welsh's Citizens against Human Rights Abuse.

Cheryl Welsh is the founder and president of citizens against human rights abuse, a non-profit organization formed by a group of victims of alleged nonconsensual human experimentation involving electromagnetic and neurological weapon testing programs by the us and other governments.

The group seeks to collect any material on the topic of human experimentation, electromagnetic and neurological technologies, and weapons programs. They network with each other and with other human rights groups. Further objectives of the group are to educate the public about human rights abuse and to prevent it from recurring.

The author of BOYCOTT Brazil, John Gregory Lambros, says his legal pleadings are beginning to work. Please visit his site to read his story.

Project Freedom Network is dedicated toward exposing frequency weapons deployed by the intelligence agencies. This is an excellent site from victim George Farquhar.

From Robert Orin Butner's website Electronic Surveillance Capabilities–Extreme Abuse of Technology:

For other than authorized security purposes, our lives are not to be intruded upon by electronic surveillance technology. However, this subject area is so out of control that access is in the hands of criminal, deranged and stalking personalities. These personalities are not satisfied with surveillance only. They have incorporated other extreme abusive modes of electronic activity, which can destroy our lives while jeopardizing top securities. I am not talking about simple surveillance devices. These are very serious categories of satellite, radio wave, sound wave, electromagnetic, holography and the speculated mind control technologies. Federal guidelines and handling procedures are inept. It is very important to point out that my personal situation is not the typical proclaimed Department of Defense, National Security Agency, other government situation or known case. It is an example of the extent and how (out of control) the technologies abuse is, (into what hands it has fallen) and (how these cases are handled).

James Henry Graf - Angelfire Home

Humanity faces a crisis of law and conscience that few can recognize, still fewer will acknowledge, and none will remedy — a crisis that jeopardizes the very future of human civilization. The essential concepts of human rights and human dignity are under assault as never before. Of particular interest is his Manifesto for the Millennium

The Government Psychiatric Torture Site by Victim Brian Bard

This website features counter-measures to psychiatric warfare, MRI scans allegedly containing foreign objects, MK-ultra, Jose M.R. Delgado, and more.

Canadian victim Eleanor White's site Freedom Isn't Free!

Eleanor White has accumulated a good assortment of references for those wanting more information about neuro-electromagnetic technology in use by our military today. You don't want to miss her site.

Technology of Control from Victim W. Samadhi:

In the United States today, there is a covert war going on. The war involves the use of covert weaponry upon an unprotected civil populace. Psychological operations, directed energy and incredible mind machine interfaces are being used on us citizens, as well as fear. The basic constitutional rights of us citizens are in jeopardy. There is no privacy, no freedom of choice and utter victimization when these technologies are used. Due to corruption in law enforcement and a lack of responsible supervision involving specific surveillance technologies, people no longer have privacy and victims are now a persecuted people. What is the crime? Someone doesn't like the way they think.

International Movement for the Ban of Radiofrequency Weapons Controlling Human Nervous System, - By Czech victim Mojmir Babacek. This is recommended, very well-written.

Norman Rabin's Electromagnetic Signals-Monitoring and Signals-Assault Scandal website states:

The purpose of this site is: to make available to any us citizen my may-august-2000, and other, press release(s) and petition(s), so that people can be informed of this worthy cause, and can consider petitioning our US government from a position of knowledge. Please help petition our US government to stop this crime! The purpose is to inform the public; and, to inform victims of signals monitoring and/or assault.

America's Secret Police by ULTRA 21753 - In this victim's view, his victimization comes from an "ultrasonic" police force that consists of private American citizens who have access to extremely advanced surveillance, harassment, and non-lethal weapons technology. He writes, "This technology is restricted technology and should only be available to special military and special non-secret police divisions but private American citizens have obtained it."

Paul Baird's website—Human Rights, Satellite Surveillance and Experimental Technologies Contains information relating to advanced satellite surveillance and "harassment" technologies which are made available to covert government agencies and organized crime syndicates. Author Paul Baird lists several categories of surveillance and harassment technologies, including audio, visual and data surveillance.

Y2K Millenium Messages from James Whittle.

From another site belonging to James Whittle's Radiation - Rape Is Real:

"This site is dedicated to the spirit of human freedom, dignity, and our basic God-given rights of liberty and the pursuit of happiness. It is intended and will strive to awaken all to the very deceptive, real and present dangers posed by microwave weaponry assault upon human subjects. Unprincipled ambitionists feel driven to control our society, our thoughts, and our very lives with invasive and punishing radiation devices this oppressive system is rightfully called, "The Electronic Concentration Camp."

His site offers a Christian viewpoint on the subject of illegal human experimentation involving electromagnetic weapons. He cites several biblical prophecies that relate to the current situation victims face today.

Allen Barker's website exposes the reality of mind control.

Mind Control: Technology, Techniques, and Politics by Allen Barker: These pages contain documents, links, references, and commentary related to mind control. Mind control is the term in common usage to describe covert behavior modification techniques and the use of neuro-influencing technology. The main focus of these pages is mind control using electromagnetic and acoustic devices, though the use of drugs, hypnosis, and induced trauma also appears. Focusing too closely on one technique can obscure the fact that the methods may be used in concert with each other, and focusing too closely on the technology alone can obscure the tactics which employ the technology. The political aspect of mind control concerns its use in a "free" society: the testing of the technology on nonconsensual subjects, its use in political persuasion and in suppressing dissent, as well as how the very existence of the technology is covered up and concealed.

Finnish victim, Petri Ticklen, provides a website– Against Electronic Mind Control –in both Finnish and English. It contains information about the neuro-radio and neuro-telecommunication, and way to protect you against it.

At Mind-Control Victims Association of Japan, from Terukatsu Ishibashi, the author tells his story of being a victim of neuro-electromagnetic weapons technology.

Martti Koski's website – Mind Control.

Martti Koski, from Finland, has information about illegal human experimentation. On his site you'll find insider stories from people who have experienced electromagnetic mind control as well as a little history of the technology.

Carol Paliwoda, author of A Mind Control Incident in Ohio writes: The following events took place in a suburb of Cleveland (Maple Heights, Ohio) continuously from the year 1973 to the present. It was important to bring this incident to public attention because it reveals a new technology which constitutes a threat to freedom and democracy wherever they exist to an extent which must not be kept secret or ignored. It is in the hands of vicious organized criminal cliques who represent a major threat to the health and safety of everyone on the planet.

Australian victim, Ian Clark, writes about his victimization from 1964 to the present.

Murder by Laser author Mickie Poirier relates her experiences as a victim of electromagnetic weapons testing. Her pages include possible reasons as to the "who" and "why" of the whole thing.

ELECTROMAGNETIC WEAPONS TIMELINE, 1934 to 1993, By Judith Wall, Editor Resonance Newsletter

<u>1934</u> "A method for Remote Control of Electrical Stimulation of the Nervous System", a monograph by Drs. E. L. Chaffee and R. U. Light

<u>1934</u> <u>Experiments in Distant Influence</u>, book by Soviet Professor Leonid L. Vasiliev

Vasiliev also wrote an article, "Critical Evaluation of the Hypo genic Method" concerning the work of Dr. I. F. Tomashevsky on experiments in remote control of the brain.

1945 After World War II, the Allies discovered the Japanese had been developing a "death ray" utilizing very short radio waves focused into a high-power beam. Tests were done on animals. The Japanese denied ever testing it on humans. (From the Strategic Bombing Survey,

Imperial War Museum, London - Cited with photocopies in "Japanese Death Ray", by Peter Lewis, Resonance #11, pg. 5-9)

1950 The French conducted research on infrasonic weapons. (From "The Road from Armageddon", by Peter Lewis, Resonance #13, pg. 9-14)

1953 John C. Lilly, when asked by the director of the National Institute of Mental Health (NIMH) to brief the Central Intelligence Agency (CIA), Federal Bureau of Investigation (FBI), National Security Agency (NSA) and the various military intelligence services on his work using electrodes to stimulate directly the pleasure and pain centers in the brain, refused.

He said, "Dr. Antione Redmond, using our techniques in Paris, has demonstrated that this method of stimulation on the brain can be applied to the human without help of the neurosurgeon ... This means that anybody with the proper apparatus can carry this out covertly, with no external signs that electrodes have been used in that person. I feel that if this technique got into the hands of a secret agency, they would have total control over a human being and be able to change his beliefs extremely quickly, leaving little evidence of what they had done." (From "Mind Control and the American Government", by Martin Cannon in Lobster #23, pg. 2-10. Cannon quits Lilly from his book, The Scientist, Berkeley, Ronin publishers, 1988, also Bantam Books 1981. Research by Peter Lewis.)

After the statement of Dr. Lilly's, how long do you think it would take the agencies, FBI, CIA, NSA, etc. to contact Dr. Redmond in Paris?

<u>1958</u>, <u>1962</u> The U.S. conducts high-altitude Electromagnetic Pulse (EMP) bomb tests over the Pacific. (From "The Road from Armageddon" by Peter Lewis.)

<u>1960</u> Headlines read "Khrushchev Says Soviets Will Cut Forces a Third; Sees 'Fantastic Weapon' ". (From article of same title, by Max Frankel, <u>New York Times</u>, Jan. 15, 1960, pg. 1 as cited in "Tesla's Electromagnetics and Its Soviet Weaponization", paper by T. E. Bearden.)

<u>1965</u> A "Death Ray" weapon was developed by McFarlane Corporation, described as a modulated electron gun X-ray nuclear booster, could be adapted to communications, remote control and guidance systems, EM radiation telemetry and death ray. McFarlane claimed NASA stole the patent in 1965. Reported hearings before the House Subcommittee on Department of Defense Appropriations, chaired by Rep. George Mahon (Dem. - Texas). (From "Hearing Voices" by Alex Constantine, <u>Hustler</u>, Jan. 1994, pg. 102-104, 113, 120, 134. Research by Harlan Girard.)

The man who was in charge of this project said, 'the potential for exerting a degree of control on human behavior by low level microwave radiation seems <u>1965</u> "A project in the U.S. called Project Pandora was undertaken in which chimpanzees were exposed to microwave radiation to exist' and he urged that the effects of microwaves be studied for 'possible weapons applications' ". (From "Electromagnetic Pollution: A Little-Known Health Hazard. A New Means of Control?" by Kim Besley, Great Britain, Pg. 14, Research from Woody Blue.)

<u>1968</u> Dr. Gordon J. F. MacDonald, science advisor to President Lyndon Johnson, wrote, "Perturbation of the environment can produce changes in Behavioral patterns." He was referring to low frequency EM waves in the Ionosphere affecting human brain wave patterns. (From his book, <u>unless Peace comes, a Scientific Forecast of New Weapons</u>, cited in "New World Order ELF Psychotronic Tyranny", a paper by C. B. Baker.)

<u>1970</u> Zbigniew Brzezinski, President Jimmy Carter's National Security Director, said in his book, <u>Between Two Ages</u>, weather control was a new weapon that would be the key element of strategy. "Technology will make available to leaders of major nations a variety of techniques for conducting secret warfare…" He also wrote "Accurately timed, artificially excited electronic strokes could lead to a pattern of oscillations that produce relatively high-power levels over certain regions of the Earth … one could develop a system that would seriously impair the brain performance of a very large population in selected regions over an extended period."(Cited in Baker's "ELF Psychotronic Tyranny" paper.)

<u>1972</u> The Taser, first electrical shock device developed for use by law enforcement, delivers barbed, dart shaped electrodes to a subject's body, and 50,000-volt pulses at two millionths of an amp over 12-14 seconds time. (From "Report on the Attorney General's Conference on Less Than Lethal Weapons", by Sherry Sweetman, 1987, pg. 4, which cites Non-Lethal Weapons for Law Enforcement: Research Needs and Priorities? A Report to the National Science Foundation by the Security Planning Corporation, 1972. Research by Harlan Girard.)

<u>1972</u> "A U.S. Department of Defense document said that the Army has tested a microwave weapon. It was an extremely powerful 'electronic flamethrower'. (From "Electromagnetic Pollution")

<u>1972</u> "A study published by the U.S. Army Mobility Equipment Research and Development Center, titled 'Analysis of Microwaves for Barrier Warfare' examines the plausibility of using radio frequency energy in barrier counter-barrier warfare … The report concludes that (a) it is possible to field a truck-portable microwave barrier system that will completely immobilize personnel in the open with present day technology, (b) there is a strong potential for a microwave system that would be capable of delaying or immobilizing personnel in vehicles, (c) with present technology, no method could be identified for a microwave system to destroy the type of armored material common to tanks." (From "Electromagnetic Pollution" by Kim Besly, p.15, quoting <u>The Zapping of America</u> by Paul Brodeur.)

The report further documents the ability to create third-degree burns on human skin using 3 Gigahertz at 20 watts/square centimeter in two seconds.

1972 Dr. Gordon J. F. MacDonald testified before the House Subcommittee on Oceans and International Environment, concerning low frequency research:

"The basic notion there was to create between the electrically charged Ionosphere in the higher part of the atmosphere and conducting layers of the surface of the Earth this neutral cavity, to create waves, electrical waves that would be tuned to the brainwaves ... about ten cycles per second ... you can produce changes in behavioral patterns or in responses." (From Baker's "ELF Psychotronic Tyranny" paper.)

1973 Sharp and Grove transmit audible words via microwaves [EW: That is, voice to SKULL] (See "Synthetic Telepathy" in this issue of Resonance.

Note: On the website, the relevant paragraphs of Judy's source article are transcribed in: v2succes.htm

1975 - 1977 "Unpublished analyses of microwave bio effects literature were disseminated to the U.S. Congress and to other officials arguing the case for remote control of human behavior by radar." (From the Journal of Microwave Power, 12(4), 1977, pg. 320. Research by Harlan Girard.)

1978 Hungarians presented a state-of-the-art paper on infrasonic weapons to the United Nations, "Working Paper on Infrasound Weapons", United Nations CD/575, 14 Aug 1978. (From "The Road from Armageddon" by Peter Lewis.)

1981 - 1982 "Between 1981 and September 1982, the Navy commissioned me to investigate the potential of developing electromagnetic devices that could be used as non-lethal weapons by the Marine Corp for the purpose of 'riot control', hostage removal, clandestine operations, and so on." Eldon Byrd, Naval Surface

Weapons Center, Silver Spring MD. (From "Electromagnetic Pollution" by Kim Besly, pg. 12.)

1982 Electromagnetic weapons for law enforcement use in Great Britain:

A 10-30 Hz strobe light which can produce seizures, giddiness, nausea, and fainting was developed by Charles Bovill of the now defunct British firm, Allen International. Addition of sound pulses in the 4.0 - 7.5 Hz range increases effectiveness, as utilized in the Valkyrie, a "frequency" weapon advertised in British Defense Equipment Catalogue until 1983.

The squawk box or sound curdler uses two loudspeakers of 350-watt output to emit two slightly different frequencies which combine in the ear to produce a shrill shrieking noise. The U.S. National Science Foundation report says there is "severe risk of permanent impairment of hearing."

(From "Electro pollution" by Kim Besley, citing the Manchester City Council Police Monitoring Unit document.)

1982 Air Force review of biotechnology:

"Currently available data allow the projection that specially generated radio frequency radiation (RFR) fields may pose powerful and revolutionary antipersonnel military threats. Electroshock therapy indicates the ability of induced electric current to completely interrupt mental functioning for short periods of time, to obtain cognition for longer periods and to restructure emotional response over prolonged intervals.

"Impressed electromagnetic fields can be disruptive to purposeful behavior and may be capable of _directing and/or interrogating_ such behavior. Further, the passage of approximately 100 mill amperes through the myocardium can lead to cardiac standstill and death, again pointing to a speed-of-light weapons effect."

"A rapidly scanning RFR system could provide an effective stun or kill capability over a large area."

(From Final Report on Biotechnology Research Requirements for Aeronautical Systems Through the Year 2000. AFOSR-TR-82-0643, Volume 1, and Volume 2, 30 July 1982. See below.)

1986 "The Electromagnetic Spectrum in Low-Intensity Conflict" by Captain Paul Tyler, MC, USN quotes the above passage and further elaborates on the theme. (Published in Low Intensity Conflict and Modern Technology Lt. Col. David J. Dean, USAF, ed., Air University Press, Maxwell AFB, AL. Research by Harlan Girard.)

1983 Nikolai Khokhlov, a Soviet KGB agent who defected to the West in 1976, interviews recently arriving scientists and reports: "The Soviet mind- control program is run by the KGB with unlimited funds." (From: The Spectator, Feb 5, 1983, reported in "New World Order Psychotronic Tyranny" by C. B. Baker.)

1984 "USSR: New Beam Energy Possible?" possibly associated with early Soviet weather engineering efforts over the U.S. (From "Tesla's Electromagnetics and Its Soviet Weaponization" by T. E. Bearden.)

1985 Women in the peace camps at Greenham Common began showing various medical symptoms believed to be caused by EM surveillance weapons beamed at them. (See "Zapping: The New Weapon of the Patriarchy", Resonance #13, pg. 22-24. Research by Woody Blue.)

1986 Attorney General's Conference on Less Than Lethal Weapons. Reviews current weapons available, most date back to 1972: the Taser, the Nova XR-5000 Stun Gun (can interrupt a pacemaker); the Talon, a glove with an electrical pulse generator; the Source, a flashlight with electrodes at the base. These devices are useful only at close range, except for the Taser, and are generally restricted to correctional institutions.

Photic driving strobe lights tested by one conference delegate on 100 subjects, produced discomfort. Closed eyelids to not block the effect.

There is evidence that ELF produces nausea and disorientation. Suggestion to develop fast acting electro sleep inducing EM weapon.

Discusses problem of testing weapons on animals and human "volunteers." (From "Report on the Attorney General's Conference on Less Than Lethal Weapons", by Sherry Sweetman, March 1987, prepared for the National Institute of Justice. (Research by Harlan Girard.)

How many people do you think will volunteer to get zapped by 50,000 volts from this little Taser gun we're testing?

1988 The Pentagon is ordered by courts to cease EMP tests at several locations due to a lawsuit filed by an environmental group. (From: The Washington Post, May 15, 1988, see "US and Soviets Develop Death Ray", Resonance 11, pg. 10. This research was done by Remy Chevalier.)

1992 December. "The U.S. Army's Armament Research, Development and Engineering Center is conducting a one-year study of ACOUSTIC BEAM TECHNOLOGY ... the command awarded the one-year study to Scientific Applications and Research Associates of Huntington Beach CA. Related research is conducted at the Moscow based Andreev Institute." (From "U.S. Explores Russian Mind Control Technology", by Barbara Opal, Defense News, Jan 11-17, 1993. Research by Harlan Girard and others.)

1993 The Russian government is offering to share with the United States in a bilateral Center for Psycho-technologies the Soviet mind-control technology developed during the 1970s. The work was funded by the Department of Psycho-Correction at the Moscow Medical Academy.

"Acoustic psycho-correction involves the transmission of specific commands via static or white noise bands into the human subconscious." The Russian experts, among them former KGB General George Kotov, present in a paper a list of software and hardware available for $80,000. (From Opal article, "U.S. Explores Russian Mind Control Technology.")

A search of a Yahoo search on mind control revealed "A genuine mind control device, $80,000, FOB Singapore, from Gunderson International."

1993 February 28, was the beginning of a 51-day siege on the Branch Davidians at Waco Texas, which ended in the death of more than 80 people. Until this incident, the electromagnetic weapons had kept a very low profile. But in the documentary video, "Waco: The Big Lie Continues", footage from the British Broadcasting (BBC) shows at least three EM weapons used by U.S. government agents. First, the noise generators used against the Davidians. Secondly, a powerful strobe light, shown during a nighttime sequence. And the third was the Russian psychoacoustic weapon, considered, but agents deny use of this weapon against the Waco people. FBI agents met with Dr.

Igor Smirnov in Arlington, VA to discuss the possibility of using the weapons against the Davidians. (From "A Subliminal Dr. Strangelove", by Dorinda Elliot and John Barry, Newsweek, Aug 22, 1994.

"You must not lose faith in humanity. Humanity is an ocean. If a few drops of the ocean are dirty, the ocean does not become dirty."

Mahatma Gandhi

Email the author at: big.brotherwatching@live.com

This book is a work of love!

Acknowledgement

THANK GOD

ABOUT THE AUTHOR

RENEE PITTMAN is the author of six books in the Mind Control Technology book series:

- Book I – "Remote Brain Targeting"
- Book II – "You Are Not My Big Brother"
- Book III – "Covert Technological Murder"
- Book IV – "Diary of an Angry Targeted Individual"
- Book V – "The Targeting of Myron May, Florida State University Gunman"
- Book VI - Deceived Beyond Belief
- Book VII - The Heart is Another Name for God

She is the divorced mother of three daughters and resides in Southern California.

www.ingramcontent.com/pod-product-compliance
Lightning Source LLC
Chambersburg PA
CBHW071802080526
44589CB00012B/651